LIVING ABROAD IN
AUSTRALIA

JAMES M. LANE

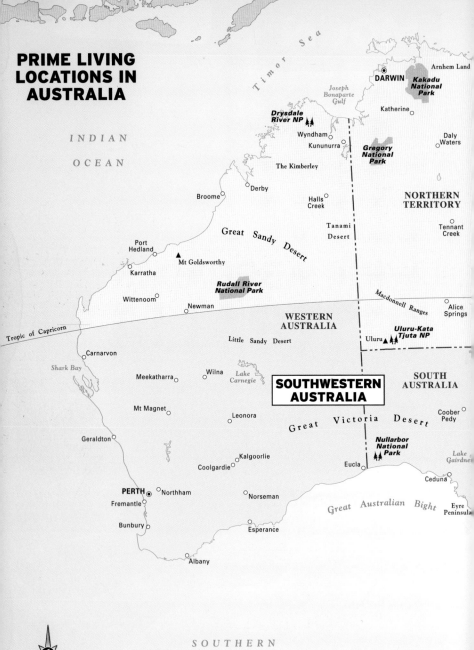

PRIME LIVING LOCATIONS IN AUSTRALIA

INDIAN OCEAN

Timor Sea

Joseph Bonaparte Gulf

DARWIN
Arnhem Land
Kakadu National Park
Katherine

Drysdale River NP
Wyndham
Kununurra
Gregory National Park
Daly Waters

The Kimberley

Derby
Halls Creek

Broome

NORTHERN TERRITORY

Great Sandy Desert

Tanami Desert

Tennant Creek

Port Hedland
▲ Mt Goldsworthy

Karratha

Rudall River National Park

Wittenoom

Newman

WESTERN AUSTRALIA

Macdonnell Ranges
Alice Springs

Tropic of Capricorn

Carnarvon

Little Sandy Desert

Uluru-Kata Tjuta NP
Uluru ▲

Shark Bay

Meekatharra

Wilna

Lake Carnegie

SOUTH AUSTRALIA

SOUTHWESTERN AUSTRALIA

Mt Magnet

Leonora

Great Victoria Desert

Coober Pedy

Geraldton

Kalgoorlie

Nullarbor National Park

Lake Gairdner

Coolgardie

Eucla

Ceduna

PERTH
Northham

Fremantle

Norseman

Great Australian Bight

Eyre Peninsula

Bunbury

Esperance

Albany

SOUTHERN

OCEAN

0   300 mi

0   300 km

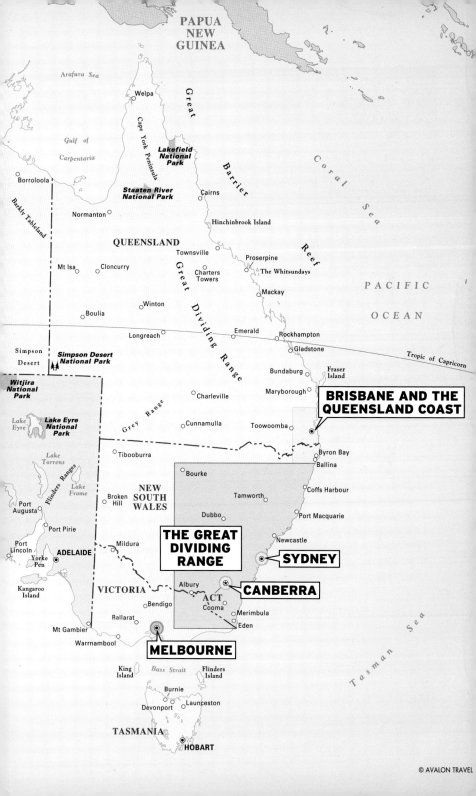

Contents

At Home in Australia

"A y, where ya goin', mate?" The bus driver asked me with a soaring Aussie accent and a look of concern. We had reached the end of his line, and as he turned to me, the only passenger remaining, I felt as if we had reached some dark corner of an unknown world from which there was no return. It was all I could do to hold back the tears and keep myself from wetting my new school uniform trousers. I was 10 years of age, three days in Sydney, alone, and lost.

As a relocation guy, I have asked this question many, many times. But on that day, in the middle of my own first relocation, I didn't have a clue.

We did it all wrong, my family. My relocation preparation consisted of a metric converter given to me by my fifth-grade teacher in the United States and a record album of traditional Australian songs from an English family who lived down the road.

We had a Murphy's beginning: Everything that could go wrong, did. We hadn't understood the cost of living, schools, taxes, phones, transport, or directions. Moving to Australia in February, we were halfway through the U.S. school year but at the beginning of the Aussie school calendar. Should my sister and I jump ahead to the next grade or repeat half a year?

We didn't know that, in Australia, there are no yellow school buses that leave from one marshaling location. Students routinely take commuter buses, ferries, or trains, and no one had thought to explain that to us, which is how I came to jump on the wrong bus.

But we adapted, made friends, and never lost the feeling that we had arrived at heaven on earth. We heard, tasted, and smelled paradise at every turn: From being woken by cockatoos and galahs at dawn to being lulled to sleep by the hum of the cicadas in the night, there wasn't a day we didn't

agree that Australia was, indeed, "The Lucky Country" and that we were lucky to be there.

Slowly, over time, we became new Australians. "Mom" transformed into "Mum." Cricket replaced baseball and rugby replaced football. We played tennis like everyone — and I mean everyone — else. We spent our time at the beach, or thinking about the beach, or plotting to get down to the beach, like all our mates. To make it better, the lessons we learned were filtered through the unique, rhyming, slangy Aussie dialect that was a complete mystery at first but became second nature in no time at all.

Eventually we gained something more powerful than a new vocabulary. We gained that most precious of Australian gifts, the Australian ethic. We learned about the importance of loyalty in a society where cooperation has always been crucial to survival, though we called it mateship. We learned about giving the underdog a chance, although we called him a "battler" and we gave him "a fair go." We learned about the vital importance of honesty, but we called it the "dinky die." We learned to empathize with others and reassure them when they were down, though we said, "Not to worry, mate, she'll be right."

On the outside, people see the natural beauty, healthy lifestyle, and cultural richness that make Australia such an attractive place to live. But under it all, the values are what make Australia Australia. The country's charisma doesn't show up in a poster or in a tourist commercial. Once it gets inside you, though, it is as permanent, unexpected, and mysteriously pleasing as the spelling of Woolloomooloo.

▶ WHAT I LOVE ABOUT AUSTRALIA

- Hitting a pure six over the wall in backyard cricket.
- Watching *The Castle* on DVD, having a good laugh at its depiction of extreme Australian attitudes, and loving a country that enjoys having a laugh at itself.
- The ever-present smell of eucalyptus in the air.
- Fresh lamingtons.
- Swimming in oceanside saltwater rock pools while the waves are crashing into the pool.
- A flat white (latte) with an egg, bacon, and cheese roll at Curly's in Curl Curl.
- Christmas afternoon at the beach.
- Riding a Sydney ferry from Cremorne Wharf to Circular Quay.
- Rosellas and cockatoos on the balcony every morning.
- Perfect two-meter waves at North Narrabeen on a weekday afternoon when no one is around.
- Singing "C'mon Aussie C'mon" under the lights at Sydney Cricket Ground.
- Guitars and bonfires on the beach at Wamberal.
- Australia coming to a halt every November when the Melbourne Cup is run.
- The taste of apples in Bunbury, Western Australia.
- Hanging out with the wild kangaroos at Pebbly Beach.
- Pavlova, smothered with kiwi fruit and strawberries, served with champagne.
- Thinking that 32°C (90°F) is super hot, and 4°C (40°F) is super cold.
- Someone inevitably saying, when things look hopeless, "She'll be right, mate," and sure enough it is.
- Seeing the endless sea of red terra-cotta tile roofs, after a long flight across the Pacific, and knowing that you are home.

WELCOME TO AUSTRALIA

INTRODUCTION

Moving to Australia can be "hard yakka" (tough work). But it doesn't have to be.

It took Australians 40 years to find a passage out of Sydney across the Blue Mountains to the grazing lands beyond, but today it takes less than a minute to find the route on a National Roads and Motorists' Association (NRMA) map. It's all a matter of realizing that "it's been done before" and that millions of immigrants have blazed the trail in your behalf. Based on their collective experience, a few general observations and cautionary notes should be offered, before we begin.

You should like the ocean. You will see a lot of it. Seaside real estate, however, cannot be counted on.

About the outdoors . . . It is not the case that everything that happens in Australia happens outdoors. It just seems that way. Walks, attending the footy, barbecues, backyard cricket, and festival-going are just a few of the many, many things you will find yourself doing outdoors.

A fondness for barbecue helps. But don't feel as if you have to be a meat-eater to enjoy Australian barbecue. A ridgy-didge Aussie can barbecue almost anything: meat, fish, veggies, shoes, socks, auto parts, documents, you name it.

Laughing is a must. You will hear a lot of it. Occasionally it will be at your expense. Aussies love to tease, but it's all in fun. Take it with a laugh, and tease back. If your mate calls you a "hopeless Yank," refer to him as a "sunboggled Aussie."

Did I mention sports? Is there another country in the world that has declared a sporting event an occasion for a public holiday? Melbourne Cup day, a public holiday in Melbourne, is an international pioneer in odd-but-great reasons for a holiday. The rest of the country effectively shuts down.

It will feel like a new language. Not only does the Australian language evolve its slang vocabulary at light speed, it is already sprawling to begin with. Suffice it to say that speaking Strine (the Australian dialect) takes a minute to begin, a lifetime to master.

Hope you like lots of friends. At the shops, at the office, at the pub, at parties, at events, at other people's homes (OPH), or at your home, friends are everywhere. They will often issue strongly held opinions. No worries, mate, she'll be right; it's just the Aussie way.

You have to like the singer Rolf Harris. I am just "bunging it on" (kidding). You do not have to like the singer Rolf Harris. But he's actually a good bloke from all reports. If you have no idea who Rolf Harris is, you will find out upon migrating to Australia.

Do you like national health insurance? Australia has it; for better or worse it is known as Medicare, and the private supplementary scheme is known as Medibank.

There's traffic. Some people like it. If so, you will love Australia. Otherwise, it's something to overlook.

Brevity is important. Don't say "garbage collector," as in the States; say "garbo." In Strine, less is more.

Australia can't defend itself, militarily. Australia has a notoriously inadequate navy, with 13 frigates to protect more than 16,000 kilometers of coastline. But although preparations for repelling unfriendlies are in doubt, Australia's beachside tourist services are world-class. It's all a matter of perspective.

There's so much sunshine you want to mail it elsewhere. There's plenty of sun, except in Hobart and Melbourne. But the other cities more than make up for it. The country is drowning in sunlight. If you have very fair skin, strong sunblock is the order of the day.

Did I mention sports? No matter what you do, or what you feel about

SOME SPECIFIC CHALLENGES FOR AMERICANS MOVING TO AUSTRALIA

- **Getting to Australia in the first place.** Australia has a restrictive immigration policy based on a points test, which it pays to understand in order to gain enough points to be able to emigrate. (See the *Making the Move* chapter for details on Australia's points system.)

- **Employment.** Like many countries, Australia has the "chicken and egg" syndrome in immigration, where it is hard to get a visa before landing a job, but hard to land a job before getting a visa. Understanding those jobs that match well with American skills and training is critical. An excellent skilled occupation list, covering more than 200 occupations and offering a detailed job description that will allow comparison between required skills in Australia and other countries, is available online at www.accurateimmigration.com/australia/sol.html. Each job is shown with the points it earns towards a skilled migration visa.

- **Schools.** The Australian school year runs on a different calendar, and how this is handled is hugely important for relocating families. Students arriving in May must repeat an entire year of school or miss the initial three months of the next grade. In addition, minimum mathematics requirements are more difficult than those in America. And because attendance of private schools is widespread, parents must study up on the topic of schools much more than is typical in the United States.

- **Getting around and driving.** Aussie cities are built primarily around public transport, with even high-priced Sydney barristers commuting to the CBD (central business district) on public buses, trains, and ferries. Plus, how easy is it to convert to driving on the left side of the road and shifting gears with your left hand?

Australian sports, affect an interest. If you are truly bored by it all, pick out the most pathetic team that you possibly can (likely a perennial at the bottom of the competition ladder) and announce that you "barrack" (cheer for) them. Out of respect, no one will talk sports with you again. Otherwise, choose your teams and heroes wisely; many countries and peoples are described as sports-crazy, but Aussies top the lot.

"Where you goin' mate?" is a question I ask of many people nowadays, and I hope that the answer for you is "I'm going to Australia, mate." But when you make your decision to move, you won't catch me saying "well done." That's a direction for cooking a steak. Instead, you'll be ready for a full-on, warm-hearted "good on ya," and good indeed it will be for you, for there is no adventure in the world like living in Australia, because no experience stays with you, and changes you, and brings joy, like time down in Oz. Long after you have stopped gawking at kangaroos every time you see them, you will find

- **Legalities.** Australia has no Bill of Rights, and expats in particular have to pay attention to some legal niceties while living in Oz. For example, random breathalyzer testing is legal and common.

- **Metrics.** The metric system is in wide use, and understanding the common conversions for temperature, area, length, and volume are survival "musts."

- **Electrical and communications systems.** Australia is on the PAL color standard, which makes U.S. televisions inoperable. Plus, most U.S. cell phones do not work in Australia, which uses the GSM standard. Finally, all appliances will require an adapter, as Australia uses a 240-volt current. Moving appliances to Australia is essentially a waste of time and money.

- **Pets.** Australia has extremely strict regulations regarding the importation of pets, owing to the absence of resistance to rabies.

- **Language.** Understanding the Australian idiom is without question the subject that American expats wished they had studied more prior to arrival. While standard English is completely understood by Australians and they follow 98 percent of American idioms (because of television), Americans struggle mightily following everyday Australian conversation, which is filled with Australian idiomatic dialect.

- **Cultural values and differences.** Australians like Americans, but aren't much like them. Values such as "fair go," "mateship," "battlers," and "cutting the tall poppies" have little or no meaning in the United States, yet are all-important in Australia. Woe betide the U.S. executive who does not study these, or Australian attitudes to entertaining colleagues, vacation, overtime, rules, tolerance, confrontation, and authority.

yourself amazed and surprised by the warmth of the people and the appeal of Australia's unique and magical culture.

The Lay of the Land

Australia is an island continent, far, far away from just about anywhere. From Sydney, the nearest country is New Zealand, some four hours away, and besides the small island nations of the South Pacific, it is nearly 8 hours flying time to Southeast Asia and nearly 13 hours to the United States.

The splendid isolation has given Australia a unique flora and fauna, culture, outlook, and economy. In a famous essay on Australia's early history, Geoffrey Blainey referred to the isolation from the West as "the tyranny of distance," but Donald Horne called it, even more memorably and optimistically, "The Lucky Country."

CHRISTMAS IN SUMMER

If you have ever been on George Street in the Sydney CBD in early December, when the temperature can range as high as 100°F (38°C), and hear the strains of "Jingle Bells" playing at one of the local department stores, you know you are in a very different country.

Christmas is not only celebrated, but enthusiastically so in Australia, but Oz has its own traditions. First of all, very few Aussies are devout Christians and so the churches are not exactly overflowing on Christmas Eve. The beaches, however, absolutely are completely stuffed with people, so get out early if you can.

Christmas and Boxing Day (the day after Christmas) are national holidays. Australians typically spend Christmas Day with their families, and although the family may opt for cold chicken and salads at the beach for Christmas dinner, they generally will be together throughout the day. Popular activities on Christmas are gift-giving, swimming, beachgoing, and, for some more traditional families, a Christmas dinner with many of the traditional trimmings. Some attempts have been made to popularize Australian alternatives to northern Christmas traditions and stories (such as substituting kangaroos for Santa's reindeer), but it hasn't come across well.

Australians typically spend Boxing Day watching sports, with Melbourne traditionally transfixed by the beginning of an international cricket "test" match between Australia and England or one of the other test-playing nations. In Sydney, the beginning of the Sydney-to-Hobart yacht race brings tens of thousands to private house parties along the harbor, with occasional glances at the race breaking up the general flow of beer, wine, and good times.

New Year's Eve is celebrated in Sydney like almost nowhere else, giving even New York City a good run for its money. The annual New Year's Eve festival brings out one million people to watch some of the most spectacular fireworks in the world. Since the 2000 Olympic Games, the Harbour Bridge has been the focus of the Harbour Bridge Effect, a "can you top it" annual spectacular where fireworks are fired from more than 20 stations along the bridge.

In addition to its isolation, Australia is totally dry except for a Mediterranean climate around its extensive coastline, and 75 percent of the population lives within 80 kilometers of the Pacific or Indian Ocean. The interior is dry, yet loaded with mineral wealth and a growing agriculture based on irrigation, primarily wheat, sheep, and cattle.

Overwhelmingly, the most important coastline is the southeast, which was the first to be settled and remains the financial and population hub of the country. The coastline from Brisbane in the northeast to Adelaide in the south-central is well-populated, but easily the most important centers are Sydney, Melbourne, and the federal capital city of Canberra.

The country as a whole is roughly the size of the United States, excluding

the Three Sisters, a Blue Mountains landmark, with surrounding bushland

Alaska, and consists of plateaus in the west tapering off into the Indian Ocean, a series of massive interior deserts second only to the Sahara in size, and on the east coast a fringe of mountains, called the Great Dividing Range, which shelters the humid, subtropical coast from the desert winds. Amid the Great Dividing Range are pockets of temperate rainforest, which contain the most extensive collection of unique Australian birds and plants. But Australia's famed and unique animals, especially the kangaroos, are found throughout the country in areas away from population centers.

COUNTRY DIVISIONS

Australia is divided into six states, plus the Australian Capital Territory surrounding Canberra and the Northern Territory in the north-central sector of the continent. Each state revenue-shares with the federal government and provides basic and vital services such as health care, police, most social services, employment, and transportation. Each state, in turn, is divided into counties, but the county system has never gained much importance as an administrative unit, and power flows generally from the states to municipalities and shires. Shires are generally larger than municipalities, typically are in more rural areas, and handle typical local services including emergency response, waste treatment, water, and power.

In Australia, the central cities are quite small, limited to their historical boundaries of a few square kilometers typically known as the central business district or CBD, although it's known in some locales as "Civic" or "the

City." The CBDs are generally important as the symbolic centers of each metropolitan area, and in Australia the largest city is invariably the seat of state government, which makes the CBDs sometimes more influential over state than municipal matters.

POPULATION DENSITY

Australia is one of the least populated countries, with only remote areas such as Mongolia giving it a run for "most underpopulated place on earth." The lack of water is the primary reason for the small population, although Australia has gone through periods where it has carefully restricted immigration, which has also held back the numbers. As a result, Australia's incredible array of natural resources such as minerals and oil is especially impressive given the small population that benefits from it. This makes Australia one of the most affluent nations in the world, despite an international reputation for high wages, long vacations, and a laid-back attitude toward hard work.

AUSTRALIA AND THE UNITED STATES, BY THE NUMBERS

	Australia	United States
Population in 2006	20,434,176	301,139,947
Olympic medals in 2004	49	103
Medals per capita (per million)	2.398	0.342
Area (square miles)	2,967,909	3,718,712
Population density (per square mile)	7	85
Arable land	6 percent	18 percent
GDP in 2006	US$655 billion	US$13.1 trillion
GDP growth in 2006	2.7 percent	3.2 percent
Per capita GDP in 2006	US$32,300	US$44,000
Inflation in 2006	3.54 percent	3.23 percent
TV sets (per 1,000 people)	716	844
Radios (per 1,000 people)	1,391	2,116
Life expectancy (male)	77.8	75.2
Life expectancy (female)	83.6	81.0
Literacy	99 percent	99 percent

Source: 2008 World Almanac

WEATHER

Did I mention that Australia is dry? It is, on the whole, parched, with some Australian towns receiving rainfall as infrequently as once every several years. But around the coast the situation is much better, although frequently there are severe restrictions on watering and home use of water during the extended droughts that strike the regions. In general, Melbourne, Adelaide, and Tasmania enjoy a temperate climate, with more rain and cold the farther south one goes. Canberra and the Great Dividing Range enjoy warm summers and cool winters but are notably drier than other temperate cities; in the higher elevations of the mountains, winter snow is common. Sydney and Perth enjoy a Mediterranean climate with warm summers with some humidity, and mild winters that are dry with no freeze days except in outlying areas. Both Sydney and Perth have occasional buildups of summer humidity, broken by fierce offshore winds that can drop the temperature 20 degrees in a single hour. Brisbane and the Gold Coast enjoy a humid subtropical climate featuring sultry summers and mild winters.

FLORA

Australia is home to thousands of unique plant species, but overwhelmingly people notice the eucalyptus trees, known as gum trees locally, which are found in all nondesert areas and give the entire country the faint smell of Halls "Mentholyptus" lozenges, because of the prevalence of eucalyptus oil in the air. In the world-famous song "Waltzing Matilda," when the jolly swagman is camped "under the shade of a coolibah tree," that is a type of gum tree found in Queensland in the north. But despite the prevalence of eucalyptus, Australia is home to more than 30,000 species including wattles, tea trees, and brilliant flowers of the Grevillia family, including bottlebrush, waratahs, and banksias. In sheltered areas of the Great Dividing Range are rainforest ecosystems with unique ferns, and Australia is home to extensive pine

typical southeastern Australian foliage, including bougainvillea and palm

© JAMES M. LANE

© FLAVIA MARPLES

the mysterious echidna, a marsupial counterpart to the porcupine

forests on outlying islands, palm groves near the northern and central coasts, and oaks and fig groves in the vicinity of Sydney.

FAUNA

There is perhaps no single country more identified with unique fauna than Australia, rivaled only by the continent of Africa for exotic quality. Australia is home to a unique form of mammal, known as the marsupial, which tends to raise its young in pouches, where highly immature babies suckle and shelter while acquiring sufficient size and skills for survival. The best-known and least-seen of these by new immigrants are kangaroos, which avoid urbanized areas but are easily spotted in the countryside. Kangaroos and their closely related cousins, the wallabies, range from half a meter in height to more than two meters; they are found in all states. Perhaps equally famous are the koalas, teddy bear–like tree dwellers that are found primarily in Queensland. Koalas are highly shy and nocturnal, and are rarely seen in nature. Most Aussies see

© JAMES M. LANE

Wild cockatoos grace a suburban balcony.

koalas (which, despite their nickname, "koala bear," are not related to bears) in urban zoos. Other well-known species are the burrowing, nocturnal wombat; the beautiful wild dogs known as dingos; the duck-billed platypus; and the porcupine-like echidna. The latter two are monotremes that lay eggs but suckle their young. Tasmania is home to the skunklike, carnivorous Tasmanian devil, and possibly to the elegant predator the Tasmanian wolf.

Australia is also home to an astonishing range of birdlife, including the majestic cockatoos, the laughing kookaburra, the flightless ostrichlike emu, and a vast array of brilliantly colored parrots, including tiny budgies and larger rosellas. City dwellers in low-density areas with lots of trees will enjoy many of these in their own backyards, and rare is the bird enthusiast who cannot coax a few rosellas to perch and enjoy some bird food.

Social Climate

Australia is a laid-back, well-educated, affluent country that is highly accustomed to visitors because of the extensive number of tourists, and the inner city dwellers are highly cosmopolitan and worldly. However, there's a continuing tension between "country" and "city," with the country-dwellers representing a more insular, traditional culture where women's rights should not be taken for granted, immigrants may face some lack of acceptance, and generally more conservative values are in place.

However, Australia as a nation places a high value on consensus, and though

© MITCHELL CHESHER

Australia's lovable patriotism is often on evidence in flag displays and city festivals.

the newspapers are quite racy with their coverage of scandal and controversy, and parliamentary politics are highly adversarial, Aussies place great emphasis on consensus and cooperation. Aussies are also usually quite polite, although seldom reserved. Reconciliation of disparate elements is a consistent feature of national governments, especially the less conservative ones, and Australia played a key role in the end of apartheid in South Africa and has been working hard to resolve differences between Aussies of European and Asian descent as well as with the Indigenous Australians.

As a general rule, Aussies dislike self-aggrandizing individuals and place a very high value on fairness and transparency. Being "real" is important to Australians, and a "real" conflict sometimes emerges between different sections of the population. But although there are sharp class divisions and ethnic divides, each year they become of less importance as Australia continues to develop its national culture and wean itself from its British colonial cultural roots.

AUSTRALIA AND FOREIGNERS

For a long, long, time Australia was generally hostile to immigrants that did not come from white, English-speaking countries, and even immigrants from the United States and England have found that during periods when British or American foreign policy is unpopular, times can get tougher for immigrants. For years, Australia pursued a White Australia policy that restricted immigration to white people. Since World War II, Australia has made a strong attempt to broaden the ethnic base of its population, and at one point Melbourne was home to the largest Greek-speaking population outside of Athens. Starting in the 1970s, immigration from Asian countries was liberalized. Today, the children of immigrant parents who were ridiculed as "wogs" a generation ago are filling important positions in every sector of Aussie society, and in the inner cities and upscale suburbs there is an active interest in foreigners. This is generally less so in poorer neighborhoods, where some racial tensions and anti-immigrant attitudes remain in pockets.

HISTORY, GOVERNMENT, AND ECONOMY

Australia is the world's oldest continent and the last to be settled; it is famed for its geographic isolation and low population density, and yet its European settlers were utterly dependent on cooperation for survival; it is called "The Lucky Country" even though it is the world's driest; the breadbasket of Asia even though its soil is the poorest. The most conservative political party is called the Liberal Party. The National Party is a regional party. It is a modern industrial democracy more economically dependent on its primary resources than the most rudimentary empire from the Middle Ages. Australia is defined by its splendid contradictions, not at all surprising for a land called "Down Under." The familiar lives alongside the baffling with apparent ease.

Australia was settled by Europeans as the result of an enthusiastic report on Australia's wonders by the 1770 Captain Cook expedition, but more pressingly because the end of the American Revolution left merry old England with no

© MITCHELL CHESHER

Australia's beginnings as a convict colony are still celebrated with facsimiles of convict and Royal Navy ships.

place to dump its unwanted convicts. Accordingly, "Botany Bay" became a byword for a terrifying journey to the unknown and unwanted, not entirely dissimilar from "Devil's Island" in more recent times, but today Botany Bay is the location of Sydney's Mascot airport, which welcomes a continuous flow of immigrants who consistently rate Australia as one of the most desirable destinations in the world.

It took just over 200 years for Australia to progress from "perdition to paradise," and the Aussies did it with a curious combination of taking the best from the old and combining it with the best of the new. It makes Australia not only the best place in the world, but also unique.

History

BEFORE EUROPEAN CONTACT

The story of people in Australia goes back to a period approximately 50,000 years ago when the first immigrants arrived. They themselves call their distant past Atjeringa (Europeans have translated it as "the Dreamtime" or "the Everywhen"), a period of "time before time" when the world was created by "sky heroes" and to which state the Indigenous Australians believe we return every time we dream.

Today, Australians call the ancient past "yonks ago" and the arrival from across the seas is called "arriving from O.S." In the modern Aussie age, things are described with a matter-of-fact brevity that is universally appealing, but the Indigenous Australians have preserved more than a trace of wonder in their own memories of arrival.

The intrepid settlers crossed the Java Sea in boats and via a land bridge from New Guinea to the Top End (northern Australia), and found there a land that had broken off from remnants of the supercontinent Gondwanaland more than 50 million years before; this splendid isolation is the cause of the unique plant and animal life that greeted the first human settlers and continues to delight us today. They hunted three-meter-tall kangaroos, marsupial lions, tigers, and the hippopotamus-sized diprotodon.

These settlers continued to arrive for around 45,000 years when the end of the Ice Age caused the flooding of the northern lowlands and created what is now known as the Torres Strait between New Guinea and Australia. Their descendants are today known as the Indigenous Australians, formerly known as the Aboriginal Australians, from the Latin *ab* (from) and *origen* (beginning).

The settlers were among the most creative talkers in history, spawning a prodigious total of between 350 and 750 distinct languages at the time of European contact; however, they didn't choose to develop a writing system, and so we don't have any written account of their arrival or lifestyle, except as recorded after contact (and primarily by the Europeans who ultimately displaced them from the rich coastal areas they primarily inhabited).

Anthropologists who have searched around their settlements tell us that, except in the Torres Strait Islands where agriculture developed, the first Australians arrived as hunter-gatherers and remained steadfastly so right up to first contact. Their concept of property was in line with all hunter-gathering cultures—that is to say, they believed in reserved tribal hunting grounds but had no fixed system of land ownership. They had a regular cycle of movement between their favored hunting grounds and a complex civilization and mythology.

Among their innumerable contributions to modern Australian life were their names for animals, plants, and places, which are in wide use today, and their unique hunting and musical tools, such as the boomerang and the didgeridoo.

EUROPEAN CONTACT AND
FIRST SETTLEMENTS (1788-1850)

Dutch sailors gone "troppo" (off course; gone tropical and perhaps a bit mad) on voyages from Cape Town to Indonesia first began to make contact with the west coast of Australia in the early 1600s; Abel Tasman discovered Van Diemen's Land (Tasmania) in 1642 and charted the western Australian coast, which he named New Holland. But Aussies generally date the European contact to April 29, 1770, when Captain James Cook, commanding the HMS *Endeavour* on a mission of exploration, landed at Botany Bay, adjacent to modern Sydney. Even today Aussies, using rhyming slang, use the phrase "have a Captain Cook" when they mean "have a look."

Cook's meticulous charts of the eastern Australian coast were highly valued by the Royal Navy and the government, but it was the 800 specimens of Australian flora collected by Sir Joseph Banks, the ship's botanist, and tales of the fantastic Australian animals that caused a sensation in London. The local flower genus Banksia, the Canberra suburb of Banks, and the Sydney suburb of Bankstown are named in his honor. Banks himself became a leading proponent of colonization, and as president of the Royal Society from 1782 to 1820, he was the most prominent supporter of the fledgling colony of New South Wales.

Prior to 1776, transportation of convicts to America for 7-year, 14-year, or life terms had been a popular expedient for relieving overcrowded prisons and providing low-cost labor to American enterprise. With the outbreak of the American Revolutionary War in 1776, English prisoners sentenced to "transportation" had nowhere to go, and were held in rotting hulks off English harbors in bad conditions. With the granting of American independence in 1783, the problem had become permanent in nature and by 1786 reached crisis proportions. William Pitt's government in England ordered a fleet of ship-borne convicts off to Botany Bay under the command of Captain Arthur Phillip.

The convict fleet arrived January 26, 1788, in Botany Bay, a date celebrated as Australia Day, although the colony was to be called New South Wales and the continent itself was not named Australia until 1824.

After realizing that Botany Bay did not offer sufficiently good land for farming and lacked fresh water, Captain Phillip removed northward to what is now known as Port Jackson or Sydney Harbour, still recognized as one of the great harbors of the world, and thus counting as the finest day of work Captain Phillip ever did.

He landed at Sydney Cove, today known as Circular Quay, where the

Sydney ferries still transit from the central business district (CBD) to the harbor suburbs. Captain Phillip named the settlement for England's Home Secretary, Lord Sydney.

Convict transportation continued until 1850, peaking after 1800 when a second penal colony was established at Hobart in Van Diemen's Land in 1803. Subsequently, the cities of Melbourne, Brisbane, Adelaide, and Perth were settled. The colony of New South Wales passed from the command of Captain Phillip to (briefly) Captain Bligh of *Mutiny on the Bounty* fame, who found himself the object of a coup d'etat staged by disgruntled army officers. A governor named Lachlan Macquarie was sent to straighten out the situation, and so he did, cleaning up the administration, bringing the military in line, improving agriculture, and sponsoring exploration. "Macquarie" continues to be a by-word for "quality" in Australian life, so institutions, streets, towns and enterprises routinely have taken the Macquarie name as a branding strategy.

Conversely, the term POHM ("Prisoners of His Majesty") has transformed into "pom," "pommy," or "pommy bastard," and is widely used as a derogative description of the British. A "pommy shower," for example, is a slang term referring to someone who uses a deodorant as a substitute for a bath. The rivalry between Australia and England is out of all proportion to the numbers of English in Australia and the extent of modern trade relations today. It is mostly played out on the cricket oval, where a victory over the English is valued above all others; the roots of this rivalry go back to the convict period.

The cities themselves continued to be named for British officials and

© JAMES M. LANE

Australia continues to bustle right where it was settled: Circular Quay in Sydney.

members of the Royal family—after Sir Thomas Brisbane (Colonial Secretary), the Duke of Newcastle (Prime Minister), Lord Melbourne (Prime Minister), and Queen Adelaide. The colonies of Queensland and Victoria acquired their names during the long reign of Queen Victoria. A good working knowledge of British cabinet and royal history is invaluable in calculating a rough sense of the age of a given neighborhood or street in Australia.

The period of convict history was marked by a considerable social divide between the descendants of the convicts (many of them stayed on following completion of their sentences and were granted lands, married, and had children) and the military and gentry classes.

The distinctions between the classes have ebbed across the generations since the end of transportation in 1850, but there are two distinctive "Australian" accents and dialects to this day, and there continue to be subtle yet broad divisions of Australian society between the gentry and the laboring class. The gentry tends to speak with a light Australian accent using mostly standard English, while the laboring class has traditionally sported a much thicker accent and draws heavily on slang (often rhyming slang) and the dialect known as "Strine," which is how "Australian" is pronounced in Strine.

Today there is considerable mobility between the classes, and considerable numbers of people with plebeian roots sport gentrified accents while many

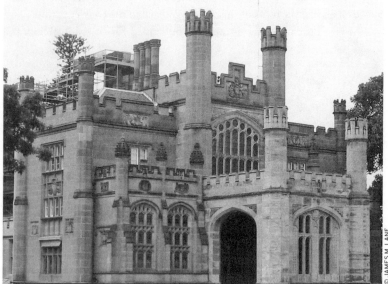

© JAMES M. LANE

The governor of New South Wales resides in a historic colonial mansion dating back to the early 1800s.

members of the gentry mix a considerable amount of slang and dialect in their speech. It reflects the easy truce that emerged between the classes over the years, but firmly fixed in the Australian ethic is a persistent and profound egalitarianism that is both shocking and delightful to new Australians. Almost all Australians are on a first-name basis, and nicknames are prevalent.

For example, few cultures reserve as much suspicion as Australians do for people who try to rise above the crowd. "Knocking" (mocking or belittling) the rich, the well known, or the "strivers" is a well-known feature of Australian life, where "tall poppies" are often gleefully cut down to size in media or in day-to-day conversation. Conversely, Australians have a strong sympathy for the underdog, who they sometimes describe as a "battler."

ESTABLISHING COMMONWEALTH AND CULTURE (1850–1901)

Beginning with the end of transportation, Australians began to lobby London for a stronger role in determining their own affairs. The English, learning from the mistakes of the American Revolution period, wisely devised the Dominions—nations that retained allegiance to the British crown and conducted a common defense and foreign policy, but were internally self-governing. New South Wales, Victoria, Tasmania, Queensland, South Australia, Western Australia, and New Zealand began a decades-long evolution toward self-government at the colonial level and ultimately federated in 1900 with the notable defection of New Zealand. The transition went in stages that have echoes in Australia's current political system: An appointed royal governor with full powers eventually gave way to a strong governor advised by an appointed legislative council; eventually that appointed council became an upper house with the election of a legislative assembly, from which a colonial premier and cabinet were elected; ultimately, the royal governors were limited to a largely ceremonial role.

The period was remarkable also for the commercial development of Australia. Massive gold strikes near Melbourne, at Ballarat, made Melbourne one of the richest and fastest-growing cities in the world in the 1850s. This coincided with the era of the great clipper ships that would ride the hard-blowing westerlies from Cape Town to Melbourne before crossing the Pacific to the United States. During this period Melbourne eclipsed Sydney, and a good-natured rivalry between the two cities has been a center point of Australian life ever since. The presence of large amounts of currency in the colonies resulted in a massive increase in bushranging. The traditional English highway robber transformed into the Australian bushranger with distinct overtones of Robin

Hood, so that several bushrangers such as Ned Kelly and Mad Dog Morgan became folk heroes.

In this period of growing economic importance, the Australian Outback was opened for sheep and cattle on a massive scale, and a mythology grew up around the hard life of the drovers managing the sheep, jackeroos working as cowboys on the gigantic "stations" (ranches) that could be more than 500,000 acres in size, and the wandering shearers who would travel the Outback from station to station and engage in famous shearing contests that were the subject of significant betting at the time.

The great love of Australians for gambling stems largely from this period, although shearing bets were largely replaced with horse racing and by a street game called Two-Up in which two coins are flipped from a paddle with the winnings to the bettor who correctly calls the toss.

ANDREW BARTON "BANJO" PATERSON

It is rare when a poet achieves great popularity in his own lifetime, remains continuously in print for generations, and is more popular in the present. Shakespeare comes to mind, but more recently there could hardly be a better example than Andrew Barton "Banjo" Paterson.

"Banjo" Paterson, circa 1890

NATIONAL LIBRARY OF AUSTRALIA

Today, Banjo's face adorns the $10 Australian note, and just below his picture are a facsimile of lines from his famous poem *The Man from Snowy River*. It is ironic that you can see him on Australia's $10 note because he infamously sold the rights to his poem *Waltzing Matilda* to the publishers Angus & Robertson for what equals $10 in today's currency.

Paterson was born in 1864 near the gold-rush town of Orange, about 160 miles west of Sydney on the western side of the Great Dividing Range. He lived in the bush full-time until he was 10 and during his summers home from school until he became a Sydney solicitor in the mid-1880s.

In the Australian bush of his youth, sheep stations could be thousands of acres in size, and horses were necessary to maintain contact between stations and to bring in the nomadic shearers and jackeroos that would work seasonally on the herds. Accordingly, the loss of a horse − especially a champion − was a blow to the entire community, and riders came together from a wide area to help out when a horse escaped to join the *brumbies* (mustangs) in the wild.

It was such a chase that Paterson immortalized in *The Man from*

Also from this period stems the great Australian love for what is called Outback, the Outback, Back of Beyond, Back o'Bourke, Beyond the Black Stump, or simply the Never Never. Beyond the cities lies the bush, and back beyond the bush is "out back." There is no firm agreement on exactly where the Outback begins, but certainly no farther west than Bourke, which is more than 600 kilometers west of Sydney. The Outback to Australians has a mythological significance best expressed in the bush ballads of Australia's folklore poets Andrew "Banjo" Paterson and Henry Lawson, who traveled the sheep-grazing country of the west and reported it in city magazines like *The Bulletin*. To them we owe the memory of slang terms such as "jumbuck" (lost sheep), "swagman" (wandering day-laborer), "squatter" (the sheep-owning class), and a persistent love of the bush and the characters and "larrikins" (harmless troublemakers) who populated it.

Snowy River, which was published in 1890 in the nationalist magazine *The Bulletin*:

> There was movement at the station, for the word had passed around
> That the colt from old Regret had got away,
> And had joined the wild bush horses – he was worth a thousand pound,
> So all the cracks had gathered to the fray.

Paterson's rhythmic stanzas and bush settings electrified his readership. "The Man" in Peterson's poem title possessed bush-riding skills, imagination, and courage of a high order – skills that Australians rightly suspected were non-existent in the mother country.

His great classic, *Waltzing Matilda*, was first published in 1903. The vocabulary and the culture of the bush came through from the opening stanza:

> Oh there once was a swagman camped in the billabongs,
> Under the shade of a Coolibah tree,
> And he sang as he looked at the old billy boiling,
> "Who'll come a waltzing Matilda with me?"
> Who'll come a waltzing Matilda, my darling,
> Who'll come a waltzing Matilda with me?
> Waltzing Matilda and leading a water-bag,
> Who'll come a waltzing Matilda with me?

Readers responded enthusiastically to the image of an itinerant worker carrying only his clothes and food in a small roll-up called a *swag* and his water in a leather container called a *Matilda*, waltzing with his Matilda by the fireplace as his *billy* (teapot) boiled on a small campfire underneath a type of eucalyptus. His readers discovered in themselves a deep continuing suspicion of authority, and a sympathy for the underdog, that were born during convict days, but which continue within the Australian character even today.

The Australian bushland remains the source of much of the mythology of the Outback.

It is easy but perilous to compare the Australian bush mythology to the American mythology of the "wild, wild west." The old American west was a land of self-sufficiency, competition, and personal opportunity, but in Australia the conditions were too arid and harsh for loners, and a culture of cooperation and fearsome personal loyalty emerged. Australians call it "mateship," and it was forged in the bush, where cooperation was essential to survival. Mateship as a cultural value quickly reached the cities, and it is a sort of informal free-masonry that in many ways binds neighbors, workers, friends, and the country together. Because trust was essential to survival, too, Australians developed the term "dinkum," meaning genuine; it appeared in the 1880s and is part of everyday speech and everyday culture to this day. There are cultures that celebrate wiliness and trickery, but Australia, broadly speaking, is not one of them. It is an important lesson to learn from history.

Also to this period we owe the Australian love for beer. Many historians have traced the love of alcohol to the convict period, when grog (usually rum) was a daily ration for convict and soldier alike, but in truth it is simpler than this: Water in 19th-century rural Australia was always suspect and rarely potable, and beer was the safer choice for traveling drovers. Pubs emerged as way stations in the bush and community meeting points that were segregated until the 1960s between men's and women's areas, and not open on Sunday until the 1970s out of deference to religion.

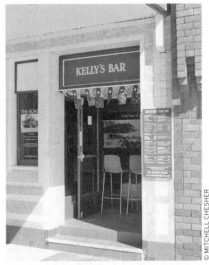

Australia's social history is often recorded on the walls of local pubs.

By the end of the 19th century there was a collapse in worldwide commodity prices that laid low the great Australian economic boom. This led to a rapid expansion of a substantial labor movement that ultimately resulted in the formation of the Australian Labor Party and the Australian Council of Trade Unions (ACTU), which are still massively important organizations in Aussie life. But the resource-dependent economy recovered later in the decade, and Australia pressed on to achieving independence as the Commonwealth of Australia on January 1, 1901.

EARLY 20TH CENTURY (1901-1945)

The great issues of the 1890s had been labor-capital challenges caused by a worldwide commodities price collapse and the fight over the terms of federation into a single commonwealth. New Zealand opted out of the federation, and several of the states and sections of society as a whole had been uneasy about the concept of federation and the constitution that had been hammered out. With the return to prosperity and the debut of the commonwealth, these issues faded to a great extent, and Australia enjoyed a golden period that was rudely shattered with the arrival of World War I.

Although formation of the commonwealth had given Australia control over her own foreign policy, broadly speaking the public and the government were pro-British Empire, and Australia dutifully followed Great Britain into the war in 1914. They were in for a rude shock. Respect for the Australian military was low among the Allied command, and initially Australian units were planned to be used as replacements in existing British divisions. Australia was initially denied any role in the direction of the war in the strategy rooms or on the battlefield. A public uproar led to combined Australian-New Zealand forces, the Australia New Zealand Army Corps (ANZAC), but not to an autonomous command. The initial major force was sent to the Gallipoli peninsula, in modern European Turkey, to fight under British generals in a combined army-naval attack on Constantinople, the capital of the Ottoman Empire.

The invasion of Gallipoli on April 25, 1915, is celebrated today in Australia as Anzac Day, and most Australians believe the nation was born at Gallipoli. But the attack itself was a bloodbath and resulted in defeat, massive casualties, and eventually withdrawal. The defeat profoundly shocked the country. Australians would never again participate in large-scale operations under direct British field command, although they served loyally under overall Allied command.

For most Aussies, the British disregard for essential preparations at Gallipoli was due to a general British disregard for Aussies and Australia, and although

Australia had the second-highest volunteering rate among all nations of the Empire, a split emerged in Australian society over loyalties to Great Britain. The debate rages on today, with a small but highly organized pro-monarchy faction still fighting to keep the British monarch on the Australian throne, while republican forces have been gathering strength since 1915 and in 1999 almost toppled the monarchy in a national referendum.

To World War I, Aussies owe not only a sense of national identity as "Australians," for at Gallipoli they served for the first time not as members of colonies but as a united national army, but also the cultural values of the "fair go"—the idea that people need to be given a fair chance (a fair go was exactly what the slaughtered Anzacs were denied at Gallipoli). It was an idea long in the culture before Gallipoli, but seared into the fabric of the culture thereafter. Even today, governments have gone down to defeat with more than a little credit given to the idea that the other party deserves a "fair go" at running the country. Corporate, academic, and diplomatic culture is suffused with the "fair go" concept, which, blended with the general egalitarianism of Australia, makes the country somewhat suspicious of certain aspects of economic competition and free enterprise.

Following the war, Australia assumed a role in administering a number of former German colonies in the South Pacific and had its first taste of colonial administration. But the postwar period was significant not for international events, but rather for the great rise in the popularity of Australian sports. Rugby, cricket, and Australian Rules football began to be played in large stadiums before massive crowds. The general prosperity of the times sparked an Australian love of sports that was already profound but now reached epic proportions, where it remains today. Emblematic of the rivalry between Sydney and Melbourne, which reached a peak during this period, Sydney embraced rugby and Melbourne embraced Aussie Rules football. In politics, the two cities could not agree on which would serve as the national capital, so the city of Canberra was established in between the two to serve as a neutral location for the government.

The heady prosperity of the 1920s gave way to a devastating Great Depression period, in which the effects of the worldwide slump were magnified greatly by another collapse in worldwide commodities prices. With the slump came searing and widespread poverty, and political radicalism soared. Tensions reached a peak in 1932 when a pro-fascist military officer interrupted the opening of the Sydney Harbour Bridge by riding up on a horse and slashing the bridge-opening ribbon so that the radical New South Wales premier Jack Lang would not have the honor.

Most ordinary Australians were profoundly shocked by radicalism, the massive poverty and economic dislocation that caused it, and by a growing sense that the British Empire would be unable to provide for Australia's defense owing to its own economic woes. But Australia loyally followed England into World War II in 1939.

The war went very badly for the British in the opening 18 months, and there were few resources that could be diverted to the defense of Southeast Asia. Further, the European colonial system had long sunk into a polite form of despotism that led to the Japanese being hailed as deliverers when they successfully invaded Malaysia, the Philippines, Indonesia, and the South Pacific Islands in 1941–1942. Great Britain attempted to mount a defense of Malaysia and Singapore but was rapidly and comprehensively defeated, and in early 1942 the Aussies found themselves on the retreat and in the clear path of the Japanese advance.

The American-British war strategy placed a priority on defeating Germany. Accordingly, Australia, though still a small nation of 10 million in population, played a leading role in the South Pacific War. Supported by the American fleet, the Australians led the counteroffensive in New Guinea that stopped the Japanese advance. The sacrifices were heavy, but after the end of the war Australia had earned the international credibility to play an important role in the formation of the United Nations and organizations such as the Southeast Asia Treaty Organization (SEATO) and the Australia, New Zealand, United States Security Treaty (ANZUS).

Australia, which had faced its darkest hours before and during the war, returned in 1945 to prosperity and had achieved a new level of international prominence and total independence from England. Australians continue to acknowledge a debt of gratitude to Americans for their support in the war (especially the older generations), and Australian-American trade cooperation and investment would rapidly intensify during the postwar period.

MODERN AUSTRALIA (1945-PRESENT)

Since 1945, Australia has, in many ways, brought many of its individual historic threads together into a new, exciting culture and economy that preserves the Australian concepts of mateship, "dinkum," the fair go, and the "tall poppy," along with a new sense of multiculturalism that reflects significant postwar immigration as well as the country's belated but genuine attempts to address the gulf between mainstream Australians and Indigenous Australians.

Although Australia has generally followed the United States' lead in international affairs (supporting the U.S. with troops and logistics in Vietnam and

ADVANCE AUSTRALIA FAIR

The national anthem of Australia, *Advance Australia Fair*, was written in the 19th century but not officially adopted until 1984, which is why most Aussies don't know the words. Many people remember embarrassing gaffes such as the 2000 Olympic Games in Sydney when thousands of Australians attending the opening ceremonies were spotted on television mumbling along incoherently to the second verse.

The phrase "Advance Australia" first appeared in 1821, in a painting representing an Australian coat of arms. The motto in the coat of arms was "Advance Australia"; a shield framed by the Southern Cross represented Australia and was attended by an emu and a kangaroo. "Advance Australia" proved a popular phrase, and by 1844 the *Sydney Morning Herald* referred to it as the national motto.

Why? The belief in an advancing, progressive Australia that leads the world in advanced democratic and government systems is an important cultural value. Aussies take great pride in being a progressive country with advanced ideas, from the early adoption of labor arbitration, the system of voting preferences, and right through to present-day regulations for auto safety.

By 1884, when *The Song of Australia* was published as a potential national anthem, the songsheet cover displayed a version of the 1821 coat of arms, although the scene was now set on a grassy shoreline with three masts of a schooner visible in the background. In 1908, when the official national coat of arms was approved for the first time, a version of this same scene was used. The schooner and shoreline disappeared and the design of the shield was simplified, but the major change was that the kangaroo and the emu were shown holding the Australian shield.

It had occurred to Australians over the years that the emu and the kangaroo were two animals sharing one unique physical characteristic: they are unable to move backwards. It was decided that the symbolism of the Australian shield being advanced forward by two animals who were incapable of carrying it in reverse was perfectly suited to the idea of a new century of progress, and the idealism of the new Commonwealth, which was born on January 1, 1901, the first day of the 20th century.

A 1912 revision of the coat of arms showed a desire by the country to make its image more "genteel" and "established." Australia had struggled for many years to reconcile its essentially brash, optimistic character with the pompous sedateness expected of national symbology. In 1912, Australia experienced a "cultural cringe" at the fair dinkum simplicity of its national coat of arms. The government replaced the naturalistic grassy mound with ornate and unrealistic foliage, and "Advance Australia" was replaced with a more serene "Australia." Curiously, the emu was no longer holding up the shield. Instead he was content to do bugger all while the kangaroo was left to do the actual work.

Iraq), the country has engaged earlier than the United States with China, and in many ways more successfully, and has participated positively in the postcolonial transition of Africa. After a great resource boom in the 1950s and '60s that led writer Donald Horne to dub Australia "The Lucky Country," Australia found itself in tougher economic waters in the 1970s and early 1980s, and has substantially diversified and globalized its economy since that time and generally reduced governmental controls and regulations to enable the free markets to operate with less friction.

The 1940s and '50s were a period of tremendous investment in infrastructure projects, much of it aimed at irrigation projects to expand the range of land under cultivation. Significant diamond, iron, oil, and uranium discoveries in the postwar period have continued to fuel Australia's economic dependence on resource exports.

To provide a labor force for the resources boom, Australia had to alter its traditional emphasis on allowing only "white" immigrants, and the "White Australia" policy was substantially reformed with a resulting huge influx of southern European immigrants. The policy was abolished altogether in the 1970s, resulting in a substantial Asian immigration. The end result is a highly multicultural society with decidedly British roots but an increasingly internationalized urban population.

In cultural terms, Australian literature and cinema went through a renaissance in the 1970s with filmmakers such as Peter Weir *(Gallipoli, Picnic at Hanging Rock, Witness)*, Bruce Beresford *(Breaker Morant, Driving Miss Daisy)*, George Miller *(Mad Max, Babe, Happy Feet)*, and Australian musicians and actors such as the Bee Gees, Mel Gibson, Olivia Newton-John, Keith Urban, Russell Crowe, and Nicole Kidman becoming internationally known in their fields.

In the 1980s, with the ascendancy of the Labor Party after a long period of domination by the center-right Liberal-Country Party coalition, there was a new level of commitment to opening doors for women and Indigenous Australians, culminating in the latter case with National Sorry Day in 1998. On this day the nation observed a day of national apology to the Indigenous Australian people to, in particular, acknowledge that 100,000 Indigenous Australian children were forcibly removed from their homes between 1915 and 1969 and raised in orphanages and camps.

Since a steep recession in the early 1990s, Australia has experienced a near continuous economic expansion. In particular, Sydney has reached a world-class status among global cities, although Melbourne continues to present itself as a compelling alternative to Sydney's brashness. Regional cities such as Brisbane, Perth, and Adelaide have developed highly attractive economies and are fast growing in population. The 2000 Olympic Games gave Sydney in particular and Australia in general a lift in prestige, and Australia's continued remarkable success in Olympic competition gives the nation a quadrennial focal point as well as a surging sense of national pride and confidence.

Yet Australian confidence, tempered by its own "tall poppy" dislike of cockiness, is appealing rather than annoying. Australia has entered the 21st century with some items on its environmental agenda as a leading resources nation, but in all other respects as a remarkably integrated country where the lessons of the past have paid dividends in the present.

Government

FEDERAL GOVERNMENT

The Commonwealth of Australia is of relatively recent vintage, founded in 1901, and the framers of the Australian Constitution had the opportunity to integrate aspects from the American, British and Canadian constitutions that they admired, plus a few inventions of their own. Consequently, the Australian system of government is primarily British in character but has significant features borrowed from the United States. In addition, there are features that are historical remnants of the development of the country from colonial roots.

Australia is a constitutional monarchy, which means that Queen Elizabeth II reigns as Queen of Australia, and Prince Charles is heir apparent to the Australian throne. In the constitution, her royal powers are nearly absolute, but in practice they are "reserve powers" to be exercised only in a national emergency; those powers are vested in a governor general appointed by the queen based on the recommendation of the prime minister. In 1975, Governor General Sir John Kerr sacked the elected Labor government when it could not pass its money supply bills in the Senate; so, it is not without precedent for the governor general to act, but by and large the "G-G" is a ceremonial figure, usually popular and more seen than heard.

The federal government is composed of a Senate and a House of Representatives. An equal number of senators are elected from each of the six states, and House members are elected in proportion to the population: In this way, the Australian legislature is like that of the United States.

Unlike in Britain, it is common to have members of the cabinet from the Senate, although by convention they rarely serve in the most senior posts, and only one senator, John Gorton, has served as prime minister, and in his case he resigned his Senate seat to obtain a House of Representatives seat immediately upon election as prime minister. In addition to the cabinet, the prime minister appoints junior (i.e., non-cabinet) ministers to run minor departments.

Supporting the government is a permanent bureaucracy of departments, each department headed by a "nonpolitical" permanent secretary.

In addition, Australia has a High Court headed by a chief justice—they are life appointees, and the High Court closely resembles the U.S. Supreme Court.

The most famous omission from the Australian Constitution is a Bill of Rights. Australia simply doesn't have one, and many controls over private property and private conduct are just as perfectly constitutional in Australia as they are perfectly unconstitutional in the United States. For example, in Australia it is legal to have randomized breath tests and to use cameras to photograph speeding vehicles, with the result of fewer road casualties.

Australian governments go to the polls at least every four years, in which elections for half the Senate and all the House seats are contested. The government of the day may, by convention, seek an earlier election date but not a later one. Also, under special circumstances the government of the day may be granted a double dissolution, in which all the House and Senate seats are contested: This is intended to be used in cases where the government's program has been defeated in the Senate, but in practical terms it's used to maximize electoral opportunities.

In Australia, voting is compulsory for citizens age 18 and over, with fines levied against those who fail to vote. Australia uses a preferential voting system. In this system, voters rank candidates in order of preference. If one candidate does not receive a majority of the votes, then the lowest vote-getter is eliminated and his or her votes distributed to the voter's second preference. In this way candidates add to their vote tallies until one candidate reaches a majority.

Voters receive one vote in their House race but in the Senate race have as many votes as seats are up for reelection.

The federal government collects all state and national taxes and shares the revenues with the states in a negotiated split. Another difference between the United States and Australia is that sales taxes (the goods and services tax, or GST) are collected federally instead of by the states, and there is a consistent nationwide rate.

The federal government operates a national health scheme, Medibank and Medicare, and also owns several "vital" national industries such as stakes in Qantas (an airline) and Telstra (a phone company). The federal government also oversees the Australian Capital Territory, which is the area surrounding Canberra and a small coastal enclave at Jervis Bay.

STATE GOVERNMENT

The state governments are structured in essentially the same format as the federal government, although the governor general is replaced by a governor, the prime minister by a state premier, and the upper house is known as the Legislative Council. Queensland does not have an upper house.

State governments obtain their funds from the national income tax via revenue sharing. A key role of the state government is responsibility for schools, police, zoning, roads, and the extensive public transportation in each major Aussie city.

MUNICIPAL AND SHIRE GOVERNMENT

Municipal governments obtain funding from local property taxes and other local fees on businesses and residents for services. In some locations, county ("shire") government replaces the municipality as the local government. In Australia, local government provides garbage collection, local police, local development/zoning, child services, elder care services, and beach/sports facilities.

In Australia, the main cities are often exceedingly small geographic areas with limited populations. The lord mayor of Sydney, for example, presides over only the Sydney central business district, which has approximately 100,000 residents.

LEGAL SYSTEM

In Australia, there are four types of federal courts and three types of state courts (although Tasmania has two levels of local courts and Western Australia has four).

The federal courts include: 1. The High Court, which has final right of appeal and hears constitutional cases. 2. The Federal Court oversees most corporate, copyright, industrial, customs, immigration, and bankruptcy aspects of federal law. 3. The Family Court oversees divorce, custody, and child support cases. 4. Federal Magistrates Courts hear less complex cases that otherwise would be heard by the Federal Court or the Family Court.

The state courts include: 1. The State Supreme Court, which oversees appeals, and in the case of Tasmania, oversees the work handled by District Courts elsewhere. 2. The District Court, which oversees most criminal trials and major civil suits. 3. The Magistrates Court, which oversees smaller civil suits and petty matters such as driving offenses.

POLITICAL PARTIES

The major political parties are the Australian Labor Party (ALP), Liberal Party, National Party, the Greens, and the Australian Democrats.

The Australian Labor Party is the oldest party, founded in the 1890s. In addition to representing the interests of organized labor, it represents the center-left of Australian politics. The Labor Party is typically serving in government or leading the opposition. In recent years it has had conspicuous success at the state level, but less so federally, where it has been in opposition more than 65 percent of the period since World War II.

The Liberal Party was founded in the 1940s to replace the United Australia Party as the leader of the center-right. It has formed a coalition with the National Party during its entire existence, including arrangements regarding contesting of seats.

The National Party was founded as the Country Party in the 1910s and has been the junior partner in coalition with the Liberal Party since the 1940s. The National Party represents the interests of rural Australia and is generally more conservative than the Liberal Party.

The Greens are the newest party of significance, gaining Senate seats in the federal legislature in the past 10 years. It represents environmental causes and in general is the most left-wing party.

The Australian Democrats were formed in 1977 to provide a middle road between the Liberal-National coalition and the ALP. The Democrats have held the balance of power in the Senate on many occasions and have used their power as a brake on the most left- or right-wing ambitions of the governments of the day.

Economy

The Australian economy is primary-resource intensive, and goes through boom-and-bust cycles because of this. In recent decades the economy has diversified and the effects of boom-and-bust are less now than in the past, but the economy still booms when its resource prices are high, and since 2000 this has generally been the case. There are more than five sheep for every person in Australia.

Despite a high degree of dependence on primary resources, 75 percent of Australia's workforce is employed in the service sector, roughly equivalent to the United States. Inflation is generally low, less than 3 percent for most of the 2000s.

The gross domestic product in 2006 was US$655 billion, or US$32,000 per capita. This makes Australia one of the 20 largest economies in the world, and its per capita income is in the top 10 worldwide. The Australian dollar is the fifth most widely traded currency in the world, valued for its stability and for the hands-off nature of the Australian government toward currency manipulations. Major trading partners include the United States, China, Japan, Singapore, Germany, South Korea, India, and New Zealand.

Australia is becoming friendlier to entrepreneurs, but it remains a country where big business and multinationals have been the rule rather than the exception, primarily resulting from the capital-intensive nature of Australian industry. Accordingly, relationships are very important to the conduct of business, and the "old school tie" still opens many doors in Sydney and Melbourne. Dominant multigenerational family enterprises run by the Murdochs, Packers, Holmes a Courts, and others are common in Australia. Media ownership, in particular, has been concentrated in the hands of a few families.

Australia is known for high wages and for a strong trade union movement, which is the mainstay of the Australian Labor Party in political terms and, through the Australian Council of Trade Unions, is a powerful negotiator of rights and benefits for workers.

The country has a strong commitment to infrastructure building and maintenance, strong historical support for power, telecommunications, and transport projects. Internet access is widespread. A national highway system has been in place for many years, and the national ring road around Australia is being upgraded to include more divided, limited-access, high-speed corridors.

The country is less regulated than comparable countries in Europe but has a comparatively strong regulatory oversight compared to the United States.

MAJOR INDUSTRIES

The major natural resource industries are uranium, bauxite, iron, diamonds, coal, and oil. Key agricultural industries are wool, beef, and wheat (Australia is a major food exporter and nearly energy self-sufficient). Sydney is home to world-class banking, legal, and finance industries. Sydney and Melbourne are the centers of the communications industries. Melbourne is home to most "old-line" Australian primary industry. The automotive and wine industries are based in Adelaide. Mining is based in Perth and to a lesser extent Brisbane, while Brisbane is home to the tourism industry. Canberra, as the capital, is home to the government organizations.

In terms of pace and reputation, Sydney is often described as the New York or Los Angeles of Australia, while Melbourne is described as more similar to Chicago. Perth is a mining city, Brisbane a tourism and agriculture town, and Adelaide has a heavy industry focus including much defense-related contracting. Two regional industrial cities in New South Wales, Wollongong and Newcastle, focus on heavy industry, including paper, oil, gas, and coal.

PEOPLE AND CULTURE

Winston Churchill once described England and the United States as "two countries divided by a common language," and the sentiment is true for Australia and the United States, only more so. The shared things that unite the United States and Australia are profound: language, British colonial history, sophisticated Western economies, a large pool of immigrants, and a large and important Pacific coastline. But Aussies and Yanks don't always speak the same language or talk about shared values in the same way.

An observer once pointed out that, culturally, Americans and Aussies are divided by a different approach to pioneer survival. In the American west, self-reliance was a primary means of survival and advancement, and Americans have learned as individuals and as a society to "go it alone," and also to enjoy the "wide open spaces" far beyond the city, where they appreciate noninterference, low taxes, and the opportunity to pursue happiness each in their own manner. In Australia, conditions were so harsh beyond the sheltering coastal

ranges that cooperation, not self-reliance, was as essential to survival as self-reliance was in the States.

"Looking out for your mate" is a major Australian cultural value that cannot be underestimated and permeates every aspect of city and country life. Also, Australia's history as a penal colony, during which thousands were brought to Australian shores for 7- or 14-year prison terms handed down for offenses such as stealing bread or vegetables to feed families impoverished by the Industrial Revolution, has made Australia a country that values the "fair go" more than any other on earth. That history has also inbred a general suspicion of sophistication and power.

Finally, Australia is a country of 20 million people who have inherited one of the richest combinations of mining and agricultural assets in the world. Australians enjoy a fabulous lifestyle compared to the teeming and poor millions living in nearby Indonesia, and a sense of guilt and obligation has made Australia far more progressive than many nations in terms of evolving a new means of engagement with minorities. As a wealthy and diverse nation with many immigrant populations, Australia has a tolerant culture that generally embraces diversity and shuns direct confrontation. Australia is also a land born of the 19th century, when "grog" (beer) was the safest drink in a culture beset by cramped city populations in a time before proper treatment of sewage. Australia retains distinct vestiges of its drinking past.

All of these underpin all aspects of Australian culture, and it is essential to understand them, in order to make sense of Australians and Australia.

Ethnicity and Class

Australians are highly diverse ethnically, but their roots are based in the small surviving pool of Indigenous Australians who arrived some 50,000 years ago as well as in a pool of English, Scottish, Welsh, and Irish settlers who emigrated in the 1780–1850 period as convicts, soldiers, and bureaucrats (or land grantees). The gold rush period of the 1850s through the 1870s brought an influx of Asians, Americans, and other Europeans, including the first sizable German immigration, and the railroad-building era brought some Southern Europeans and more Chinese to the country. The major expansion in immigration commenced after World War II, when a wave of emigrants arrived from Southern and Eastern Europe, to help with major projects such as the Snowy River scheme, and for a period Melbourne had the third highest Greek-born population in the world. Asians began arriving in great numbers after the Vietnam War in the 1970s, as well as many Middle Easterners. Today, the vast majority of Australians have at least one ancestor who arrived after 1900, and truly it is a land of new arrivals.

The country and the city produce quite different characters and accents. Australians love their pioneer culture, and the archetypal Australians in famous Australian ballads and stories are bush-based, often from the 19th century, and exhibit a blend of tolerance, a streak of mischief known as *larrikinism,* and a healthy disrespect for authority. Outlaw figures such as bushranger Ned Kelly are openly admired by many, despite their nefarious careers, and sporting figures are widely idolized.

© MITCHELL CHESHER

Australians rambling on a day off

TOLERANCE AND DISCRIMINATION

The practice of judging people (and assigning inferior status) based on how they look, sound, dress, or act is a global phenomenon, but it impacts immigrant-laden countries such as Australia and the United States more than others. In a global context, Australians are remarkably tolerant of different cultures, but the high percentage of immigrants creates more tension than is experienced in countries that have low levels of expatriates and migrants.

As a matter of law, discrimination on the basis of gender, race, age, or religion is forbidden in Australia; as a practical matter, the concentration of immigrants—especially those lacking English-language skills—in "immigrant neighborhoods" shows that Australia still has far to go in blending immigrants rapidly into the general culture.

Tolerance generally is stronger among those who are more affluent and educated, where there is less competition for jobs with immigrants and more exposure to different cultures through work study or travel. Ethnic divisions and clashes have tended to be located in the lower-income, inner-city areas. Ethnic tensions tend to focus on cultures that are considerably different from the Australian mainstream, and especially among those who show a disinclination to rapidly "assimilate" into the Aussie way of life. Native English-speaking immigrants generally face some kidding, and sometimes are invited into arguments over foreign policy, but Americans, Canadians, and the like face very little trouble on a day-to-day level.

Conversely, Australia has gone to considerable lengths to promote tolerance, even establishing a government-funded national television network that broadcasts in foreign languages (SBS) and brings programming from the "old country" to new immigrants.

Australia does face lingering class divisions that go back to convict vs. free settler days. There is a lingering establishment in Australia, primarily composed of white, Anglo-Saxon Protestants, who continue to send large numbers into high-earning or high-visibility professions such as medicine, law, politics, and finance, and who live in highly affluent circumstances and socialize within a tight circle of the "right people." The influence of the establishment dwindles on a daily basis, but it remains a fact of life. Expatriates on senior corporate assignments will often gain temporary admission to these groups; at their best, they offer a terrific network to introduce or circulate new ideas and acquaintances. In recent years, a much wider variety of cultures and ethnicities have been taking a place among Australia's elite, and that's an encouraging trend.

Australia historically has been beset not only by tolerance issues with foreign cultures, but with its own Indigenous Australian population, which has been the subject of rampant discrimination in past generations. The Indigenous Australians, having been nearly wiped out in the 19th century by European disease, have made a modest comeback in numbers, but their lack of access to education, employment opportunities, and medicines has restricted their presence in the cities, except in lower-income areas. The Australian government recently issued an apology to the indigenous peoples for their treatment, and events that recognize white Australian treatment of the indigenous peoples, such as National Sorry Day, have encouraged a growing rapprochement between the cultures. However, this is tough ground for new Australians, and it's best to spend a considerable amount of time in Australia before engaging with these issues in conversation or activity, as non-Indigenous Australians experience embarrassment in discussing the difficulties and opportunities for Indigenous Australians, and may also react with hostility.

Social Values

Australians are famous for being friendly, and not known for their driven work style but rather for their love of family, sport, travel, and time off. While they are often shy around new arrivals, especially those who speak a foreign language (which few native-born Australians do), they are generally happy suburbanites whose great passions in life revolve around sports on Saturday and the Sunday barbecue, with the occasional requirement to show up for work.

Australians exhibit a strong interest in mild forms of socialism, along with a strong interest in social justice and, for such an isolated country, foreign affairs. Aussies are fairly well-read, although academics are respected but rarely beloved. An Australian is three times more likely than an American to belong to a trade union, and the Australian Labor Party (as of 2008) held power at the national level and in each of the six Australian states. Both the major political parties, the left-leaning ALP and the conservative Liberal-National Party coalition, are politically to the left of their counterparts in the United States. There is a strong republican movement in Australia that aims to replace the British monarchy with a ceremonial presidency, but widespread support for a republic collapsed into confusion over the various alternatives, and Australians ended up choosing to stay with the monarchy in a referendum a few years ago.

Australians like to "tweak" authority on occasion but are generally good rule-followers and respectful of conservative social institutions such as monarchy. They are highly secular, with church attendance very low among the general population, and conservative Christian-oriented parties have not gained much traction in national elections. Occasionally, an anti-immigrant, nationalistic politician will attract attention, but generally speaking Australia is highly supportive of immigration and of "new Australians," especially those who exhibit a desire to assimilate quickly into Australian culture.

A FAIR GO

One of the most important social values has been mentioned but bears repeating: the concept of the fair go. The fair go (giving someone a chance, or a "fair crack of the whip") is extremely important in Australian culture, and Australians and immigrants who ignore this do so at their peril, whether it applies to family, friends, colleagues, or public figures. Political corruption is therefore common but extremely disliked, and activities in politics such as "stacking an election" (called *"rorting"*) can be career-enders.

MATESHIP

Mateship is perhaps the most fundamental value in Australian culture. Your friend, or your "mate," is someone you owe the highest degree of loyalty to. Tattling is frowned on for this reason, for "dobbing someone in" is a violation of mateship. Taking sides against your mate in a fierce argument is accepted, even common, but one never takes sides against a mate in a public argument

WELCOME TO AUSTRALIA

BARBECUE

Along with a beer at the pub with mates and backyard cricket, there probably isn't anything as quintessentially Aussie as the backyard barbecue. Invitation to one of these occasions is "acceptance" in Aussie culture. If invited, go by all means and make sure you dress casually, never take anything too seriously, and have some fun.

Beef is the traditional Aussie barbecue – sausages, burgers, or steaks – but chicken, lamb, and fish are just as frequently served in modern times. Barbecues typically take place in the late afternoon on Saturday and Sunday, but can be at almost any time on the weekend after 11 A.M. Also barbecued are veggies, often in kebab style, including tomatoes, onions, and mushrooms. Typically the beer is flowing, and generally, tending the barbecue is a man's job; his mates will keep him well supplied with beer throughout the preparations. Salads are usually succulent and plentiful and frequently prepared by the women.

Humorist Eric Bogle put it best in "Aussie Barbecue":

When the steaks are burning fiercely
When the smoke gets in your eyes
When the snags all taste like fried toothpaste
And your mouth is full of flies
It's a national institution
It's Australian through and through
So come on mate and grab your plate
Let's have a barbecue.

the ubiquitous Australian barbecue

© MITCHELL CHESHER

or "spill." A mate is to be supported in good times and bad, and because of mateship there is a higher amount of time spent by Australians with friends (versus family) than in other cultures.

SOCIAL ATTITUDES

In the cities there are two basic cultural types: those who tend to go down the route of "right school, right car, right house, right suburb, right club" that exhibit a high degree of insularity and social snobbery, and a large section of Australians who have little or no patience for social snobs. The pejorative term "tall poppy syndrome" is an outcome of this, which is the curious spectacle of Australians taking delight in personal or business tragedies suffered by public figures who have become "too full of themselves." Generally speaking, Aussies are pretty proud of their Oscar winners, Olympic champions, rock stars, and billionaires, but secretly take a bit of delight when bad fortune "brings them back to earth."

Gender Roles

In Australia, the legal role of women has been essentially on an equal footing for a long time, but equal rights in practice as well as theory have been a longer time in coming, more especially in the country than in the city. Careers of all types are open to women in Australia, and the current deputy prime minister (Julia Gillard) and the deputy leader of the opposition (Julie Bishop) are both women.

Women lead men in university enrollment in Australia and are fast approaching parity in professions such as law and medicine. Scientific research is still predominantly male, but the gap is closing fast. As a general rule, professions dominated by women are paid less than professions dominated by men, and there is also a gender gap within professions that reflects an old double standard that has not quite gone away. But it improves each year, and generally women have an equal or better status in Australia than in the United States.

In day-to-day life, many old stereotypical roles remain, with women primarily looking after health care, children, education, cooking, and cleaning in most Australian homes. However, progressive homes with better "load sharing" are common in the main cities, particularly among the younger generation.

GAY AND LESBIAN CULTURE

Gay men and lesbian women live in a culture that, in many ways, is similar to that in the United States, where a general tolerance in educated, urban circles is balanced by diminishing but still common cultural hostility in other regions and demographics in the country. Homosexuality is fully legal in all states except Queensland, where limited bans on homosexual activity are not generally enforced. Same-sex marriage is prohibited in Australia at the federal level, but all states and territories recognize same-sex civil unions. Gay and lesbian couples are permitted to adopt children in Western Australia, Tasmania, and the Australian Capital Territory, and allowed to adopt step-children in Victoria. Lesbians may use assistive reproductive technologies, while gay men can utilize "altruistic surrogacy" in New South Wales, Victoria, Western Australia, and the ACT. Gays and lesbians are allowed to serve in the military, and change of gender has been legal throughout Australia since 2006.

While legal discrimination is disappearing, gays and lesbians will face a typical range of social discrimination, but less intensively expressed, from the same sorts of demographics as in the United States, for many of the same reasons. Anti-gay humor is not acceptable in mainstream media but lives on at a conversational level, and Aussie tolerance should not be mistaken for active acceptance. In general, Australia tends to be a far more tolerant culture than the United States, but opposition political parties oppose the expansion of rights for gays and lesbians, and the path to full equality is not yet mapped out.

Australian gay men and lesbians are well organized socially and politically, and especially visible in Sydney and Melbourne. In Sydney, the heart of the gay scene is Darlinghurst on the eastern edge of the CBD, while the "inner west" suburbs of Newtown, Erskineville, and Glebe are also popular. In Melbourne the mainstream gay scene is in South Yarra, while an alternative gay community thrives in Collingwood.

Religion

Australians as a rule are not deeply religious, although strong communities of faith exist in most religions and in most major cities and the bush. Just 16 percent of Australians attend church every week, compared to 44 percent of Americans, and only 20 percent attend monthly. Australians generally feel, when surveyed, that church services are boring and unfulfilling.

The main churches in Australia are the Anglican Church (Episcopalian), the Catholic Church, and the Uniting Church (Presbyterian, Methodist, Congregationalist fusion). There are small Jewish, Islamic, and Buddhist congregations in all cities. Also, a strong Pentecostal movement has grown up with 400,000 members now, the fastest-growing segment in Australian religious life.

Church schools, however, remain highly popular in Australia, with roughly

© TOURISM NEW SOUTH WALES

historic church in Leura, New South Wales, amidst the stunning Blue Mountains

20 percent of schoolchildren attending a private religious school, primarily Catholic. The Presbyterian, Anglican, Lutheran, and Pentecostal churches all operate day schools (and in some cases boarding schools).

The Arts

Australia has made a significant government investment in the arts, recognizing that the small population base makes it difficult for local artists, writers, and performers to compete with their peers in more highly populated counties. All states and the federal government each have an Arts Ministry that provides development programs plus direct financial support of dance, classical music, theater, and the visual arts. The Sydney Opera House is perhaps the most visible symbol in the world of the public support of the arts.

LITERATURE

Australia has lacked a popular national literature, although Patrick White picked up the Nobel Prize in the 1970s. The bush balladeers Henry Lawson and A. B. "Banjo" Paterson penned classic stories and poems in the late 19th and early 20th centuries, including Paterson's "Waltzing Matilda" and "The Man from Snowy River." In recent years, James Clavell found an audience with novels of the British colonial era in *Tai-Pan* and *King Rat,* while Nevil Shute won acclaim for novels such as his cold war thriller *On the Beach.* Thomas Keneally wrote the highly regarded *Chant of Jimmie Blacksmith* and

Schindler's List, while Kate Grenville has been among the most successful female writers.

MUSIC

Australia has produced a large number of popular international recording stars in the past 30 years, including AC/DC ("Akka Dakka"), Olivia Newton-John, Men at Work, Peter Allen, the Bee Gees, Midnight Oil, Kylie Minogue, and Natalie Imbruglia. Many of the local acts have honed their skills appearing in the lively Sydney and Melbourne club scenes, which are well supported by the outgoing city population.

FILM

In film, Australia was "discovered" in the 1970s when influential film directors such as Peter Weir, Bruce Beresford, and George Miller arrived on the scene. Weir's *Picnic at Hanging Rock* (1975) started off an art-house revolution that brought broad attention to the national film industry, which was receiving government support. Bruce Beresford's *Breaker Morant* was the first Australian film to win widespread acclaim, as well as an award at Cannes. The post-apocalyptic *Mad Max* introduced Mel Gibson to international audiences, and *Crocodile Dundee* was an international comic hit for actor Paul Hogan.

Owing to the absence of national support for film, budgets are low and work is scarce, and talented actors and producers generally make the move to the United States. Guy Pearce, Cate Blanchett, Toni Collette, Nicole Kidman, Judy Davis, Geoffrey Rush, Hugh Jackman, and Heath Ledger are among the best known Australians who emigrated to the United States, with Blanchett, Kidman, Gibson, and Rush winning Oscars for their work in various roles. Baz Luhrmann *(Moulin Rouge)* and Gillian Armstrong *(My Brilliant Career)* have had notable success in Hollywood.

Sports and Games

There is hardly anything more important in Australia than sports. Whether it is the Olympics, the "footy," the cricket, the Melbourne Cup, a host of other exciting professional events, or just a game of backyard cricket, nothing unites and rivets Australians like sports.

The biggest crowds come out for football, but Australia plays four codes of football—soccer, Rugby Union, Rugby League, and Australian Rules football—so the focus is divided. The truly unifying national game is cricket, and the 11 members of Australia's national team are household names throughout the country. It doesn't hurt that Australia has been the dominant force in world cricket for more than 10 years, winning three consecutive World Cups in 1999, 2003, and 2007.

Although soccer is played everywhere and even rugby has a following in the United States and is close enough to American football to be easily understood by new arrivals from the United States, Australian Rules is the most

AUSTRALIAN RULES FOOTBALL

Also known as "Aussie Rules" or "footy," Australian Rules football is the most popular form of "footy" played in sports-mad Australia. Rugby Union, Rugby League, and soccer all have a following, but the biggest crowds come for Aussie Rules. Centered in Melbourne, where for years the only major Aussie Rules professional competition was the Victorian Football League (VFL), today the competition features 16 national teams. Even the heart of Australian rugby, Sydney, is devoted to the Sydney Swans. Perth and Adelaide have 2 teams, Brisbane and Sydney 1 each, and the remaining 10 come from the Melbourne area.

Aussie Rules is played on a massive ground, up to 180 meters long and 155 meters wide. The game is played in four quarters of 25 minutes by 18 players on each side. The ball is advanced by running, or kicking, but runners must bounce the ball every 10 meters, and kicking is the preferred medium. A player who cleanly catches the ball is awarded a "mark" and may take a free kick, used to tactically advance the ball up the field. Scores are made by kicking the ball through the goalposts, 6 points for a goal and 1 point for a "behind," a near miss through a secondary goal post on the right or left.

Professional teams often score more than 100 points in a game, and the competition is known for high speed, grueling fitness requirements, and the athletic skill in kicking long distances for goal, or for soaring leaps to grab a clean "mark."

© MITCHELL CHESHER

a suburban "oval," where sports-mad Australians gather to watch their Aussie Rules, rugby, or soccer teams

different and popular. Aussie Rules is most popular in Melbourne, Perth, and Adelaide (although Sydney has a popular team in the national Aussie Rules competition), while rugby is more popular in Sydney and Brisbane. These are the main winter sports.

Cricket is a relation of baseball and is the main summer sport. Innumerable families and kids play "backyard cricket," which supplies a stream of players to local clubs, who in turn supply the state teams and the national team. The national team plays five-day matches, called "tests," against the top nine other cricketing nations, and these events grip the nation, either by television, radio, or at legendary cricket grounds such as the MCG (Melbourne), Sydney Cricket Ground, the Gabba (Brisbane), the Wakka (Perth), and the Adelaide Cricket Ground. Cricket and football memoirs are routine best-sellers in Australia.

In addition to the main spectator sports, golf, tennis, surfing, and the Olympics are highly popular, and Australia wins a completely disproportionate number of medals in comparison to its population. In 2000, Australia won 58 medals at the Summer Games in Sydney, good enough for fourth among all nations and one behind China, which has 60 times Australia's population. Australia has racked up large numbers of medals in almost every Olympics in men's and women's swimming. In 2004 in Athens, Australia again finished fourth. There is a National Sports Academy, and promising young athletes are whisked away at an early age indeed. In golf, legends such as Greg Norman, Stuart Appleby, Ian Baker-Finch, and Steve Elkington have been noted winners of major championships, while numerous Australians have achieved tennis fame at Wimbledon and other grand slam events, including John Newcombe, Margaret Court, Evonne Goolagong, Pat Cash, Patrick Rafter, and Lleyton Hewitt.

In Melbourne, the Melbourne Cup horse race is a public holiday, and for years the country has shut down for a few minutes during the running of the race.

To many Australians, it is the personal sports that are of far more importance—surfing, skiing, running, windsurfing, sailing, climbing, tennis, golf, and backyard cricket. There is hardly an Aussie who is not involved in some sort of sporting experience at least in younger days, and sport is a regular outdoor feature of Australian school life. Most private boys' schools (and some girls' schools) make two sports compulsory through year 10 or 11, and Australians are generally relentlessly fit and eager to participate in a wide variety of sporting activities. It is often the glue that holds families and neighborhoods together.

PLANNING YOUR FACT-FINDING TRIP

Exploring Australia cannot only be highly rewarding in making a transition to living in Oz, it can be a totally "bonza" (great) experience. In this chapter, we'll explore a few strategies for making sure you accomplish both.

Virtually all trips to Australia will start in Sydney, although a few flights overfly Australia's capital of flash and land in Melbourne, and there are an increasing number of direct flights to Brisbane. Plus, immigrants from Europe to Perth come in directly to the west. But 90 percent or more start in Sydney, and that's good because the majority of them stay right there. Getting to know Sydney is a lot of fun, and is an excellent introduction to the country no matter where you end up. In most cases, a fact-finding trip should include a stop in Sydney for acclimation purposes and then a continuation on to a second city if that is your ultimate destination. For a few lucky folks, such as

prospective retirees or business investors, a full-on Aussie fact-finding trip is in order, and a full month will be needed to take in all the potential delights of the cities and countryside of Oz.

Preparing to Leave

WHAT TO BRING

Australia is a country so like the United States that first-time arrivals have to take some special care with respect to understanding the differences between the two countries.

Electric Converters

Australia is a 240-volt country, which is to say that appliances made in 110-volt countries such as the United States will possibly short out when plugged into Australian electrical outlets. Plus, the shape of the standard prongs is different. Accordingly, devices that can handle a variable voltage will need a simple plug adapter, which you can buy at most airports or stores such as Brookstone, in the travel section. Typically, this is what you will need to charge your laptop, iPod, or cell phone. But check the instructions or with the help desk at the manufacturer; they may advise you to get a small transformer that steps the voltage down to 110.

Clothing

Outside of hotels and major businesses, Australian buildings have fairly rudimentary heating and cooling systems owing to the mild climate, and at extremes of winter and summer there can be episodes of humid heat or cold that can be a bit of a shock for those accustomed to modulated temperatures. If you are planning a visit to Australia July–August or January–February, plan to dress in layers to maintain the coolness or warmth you need. Heavy jackets or parkas are not necessary unless you are planning to visit Tasmania or the elevated mountain areas, but leather jackets and cardigan sweaters do come in handy.

Generally, Australia is a highly informal and tolerant country when it comes to clothing, so light and casual tourist attire is always acceptable as day wear. For restaurants, smart casual is typical. Suits are commonly worn in business settings, although jackets are optional during summer months.

If you are attending formal events (such as theater opening nights) or dining at a very upscale restaurant, suits and cocktail dresses are more typical than anything else, but casual dress is the norm for most nightlife that caters to tourists.

Sun Protection

When traveling in Australia, be highly conscious of the sun. There is less ozone in the southern hemisphere, and you will burn far faster in the Aussie sunshine. There's tons more sunshine in Oz than in most places that immigrants come from. So be on guard. When out for a day where you will be exposed to the midday sun for more than 30 minutes, apply sunscreen, and step up the screening factor a notch above what you are used to. If you typically wear SPF15, wear SPF30 in Oz, for example. Also, a good pair of "sunnies" (sunglasses) is a must, and a good hat is highly recommended. If you are feeling like assimilating into the Australian "look," buy and wear an Aussie Akubra hat, the iconic slouch hat available at www.akubra.com.

Money

The good news for travelers in Australia is that the country is highly adapted to electronic payment systems—more so than just about any country on earth—and establishments of almost any size or distinction will accept credit cards such as Visa and Mastercard. ATMs are available in every city suburb within a two-block radius of the main train or bus stop, and most shops that cater to tourists accept debit cards.

However, it's always a good idea to carry Australian currency, and you would be well advised to invest in a money holder, because Australian coins are large and heavy compared to those of most countries. Because there are no $1 or $2 notes, only coins, there can be a lot of change in your pocket. Plus, Australian

© MITCHELL CHESHER

ATMs are called auto tellers at some locations, as seen here at the Bendigo Bank.

notes are different sizes depending on the denomination, and the $100 note is significantly larger than the $5 note; it will not fit into a standard wallet because it is too wide top to bottom, so it sticks out. If you don't mind a bit of heavy jingle in your pocket, a standard money clip will do just fine.

WHEN TO GO

There are about 300 good days to visit Australia; the only times to avoid are generally holiday periods. They include the period between December 25 and around January 20, because this is the heavy summer holiday season: Airfares are high and seats hard to find. The same goes for the Easter holiday, from the Wednesday before Easter to the Tuesday after. The end of January is no picnic for airfare bargain-hunting (in fact, forget about finding a truly low-cost fare), but the excitement of Sydney in late January, when the monthlong Festival of Sydney culminates in the Australia Day weekend around January 26, tempts a lot of travelers.

For pure enjoyment of great weather and low crowds, try the period immediately after the Easter holiday or any time in October or November; both are just magnificent. The Anzac Day national holiday on April 25 inspires a lot of people to hit the road, so tickets are expensive around then as well. School holiday schedules are different for public and private schools, and this tends to spread the load of holiday travel demand in school holiday months such as May and September.

Arriving in Australia

VISAS AND PASSPORTS

From a tourist perspective, obtaining an Australian entry visa is really not much trouble, but you do have to remember to obtain a visitor's visa. This will permit you to stay up to three months in Australia at a time, although you will not be able to work.

Travelers from most countries can obtain an electronic travel authority, called an ETA, which takes about five minutes to get online and costs $20, payable by credit card only (Visa, Mastercard, or Amex).

An ETA is equivalent to a visa, only there's no stamp on your passport. Airline personnel (and immigration officials in Australia) will be able to access your record at check-in time. You can apply at www.eta.immi.gov.au if you live in the United States, Canada, or most major Western European countries. A full list of countries is found at www.eta.immi.gov.au/ETAAus1En.html.

An ETA is equivalent to a visa, but there is no stamp or label in your passport and there is no need for you to visit an Australian diplomatic office to submit an application. Applications for ETAs can be submitted through travel agents or airlines, and all you need is your passport and credit card information. The ETA is valid for 12 months and for stays of up to three months per visit. If you are planning to combine some business meetings with your fact-finding trip, make sure you apply for the short-validity business ETA, which has the same time frames.

If you do not live in an ETA-eligible country, you can find the right office to contact at www.immi.gov.au/contacts/overseas/index.htm, and you will make a traditional visa application through a visa office or an authorized third party. Allow up to one month to process a visa application via the traditional channels.

TRANSPORTATION
Taxis
Most first-time visitors arrive in Sydney or Melbourne and take a taxi to their first-night hotel. Taxis are widely available, especially at airports. The cost will be about double what you are used to if you are living in a U.S. city outside of New York, but the trip is short from Sydney's Mascot airport to most hotels either in the CBD (central business district) or airport area. In general, taxis are an acceptable and common option to/from the airport, but less reliable for getting around the city and not cost effective. It's better to simply get used to public transportation if you are not renting a car.

Driving and Renting a Car
Car rentals are usually arranged via the airport, as with all major cities. It's best to book the rental through your travel agent, although major global brands such as Avis and Hertz are in most locations. Cars, by the way, tend to be much smaller in countries outside the United States. You do not need a special driver's license to drive while you are in Australia. However, you should familiarize yourself with a few basics for the road.

First of all, in Australia, driving is on the left, and the driver is on the right-hand side of the car, so you will shift with your left hand. It takes a little getting used to, but it sounds harder than it is. The pedals are configured the same for manuals, but the gearbox is typically backwards, so you will shift differently when putting the car into reverse in a manual. Save yourself some trouble by getting an automatic transmission so that all you have to focus on is driving on the left. You will find that it is quite easy to follow the flow of traffic while driving, or even changing lanes. The biggest thing to guard

© MITCHELL CHESHER

In Australia, driving is on the left.

against is in turning, when you may habitually drift toward the right side of the road, which will put you up against oncoming traffic. It's easy to learn; just make sure you concentrate fully on your turns (instead of thinking about directions, kids in the back seat, etc.).

Australia is freeway-challenged, and you will find yourself more often than not on crowded urban arterials. It's not too tough—just allow for extra time for urban transit.

The other complication is that, in Oz, speed limits and distances are expressed in kilometers per hour (kph) and kilometers. Generally speaking, you will be at 50–60 kph on city roads, 80 kph on highways, and up to 130 kph on freeways. For an exact conversion, divide miles by five and multiply by eight to get kilometers or kilometers per hour (do the reverse to determine miles from kilometers—divide the kilometers by eight and multiply by five). Or for a quick calculation, halve the miles and multiply by three.

Private Transportation

Private car transport is widely available, especially to/from airports, but it is an expensive and unusual way for egalitarian Aussies to get around, and use of private cars is not highly recommended. If you are traveling in conjunction with a corporate relocation, you may wish to use a private car in lieu of a taxi if you are headed for an outlying suburban corporate headquarters. Stretch limos are very rare; private cars tend to be less conspicuous sedans.

© MITCHELL CHESHER

an older suburban bus

Public Transportation

Aussies use public transport more than people in most countries, especially those that have a highly decentralized population. Typical options in most cities are bus and light rail, although the coastal cities have ferry systems, and Sydney's is a very important part of getting around the inner harbor area. In each city, there are multiday transit passes available from ticket offices (e.g., at rail stations), and these cannot be highly enough recommended for reducing the cost and aggravation of public transport. Major rail stations and ferry and bus hubs have route, schedule, and fare information available, but the best way to get information is via each state's transport authority page, as transit is controlled at the state rather than metro level, which makes everything much easier.

CUSTOMS

When entering Australia, the old sayings "know before you go" and "if in doubt, throw it out" apply. Don't bring any food, pet products, or furs, hazardous materials, cash over $10,000, farm products, or pharmaceuticals you do not have a prescription for or are clearly over-the-counter. Since Oz has not been exposed to many common Western viruses and pox, the country is extremely vigilant about this subject, and taking it seriously is advised. A full list of no-nos is at www.customs.gov.au.

Your duty-free concession is $900 worth of goods ($450 for people under

18), excluding alcohol and tobacco products; 2.25 liters of alcoholic beverages; and up to 250 cigarettes or 250 grams of other tobacco products, per traveler 18 or older.

Sample Itineraries

Most travelers to Australia arrive there from Los Angeles and head to Sydney as their ultimate destination. The best way to explore Australia is to base out of one city and explore outlying areas as day trips whenever possible, unless you have a two-week or one-month exploration period, in which case we have prepared multicity sample itineraries for you. We have chosen Sidney for the base city, but you can substitute the other cities fairly easily in the one-week and two-week itineraries. In the one-month itinerary, we have worked out a complete "all-Australia" schedule that will give you some unforgettable tourist delights as well as the opportunity to see all the prime living locations in some depth.

Getting There

The flight to Australia is a long one, and your first day will consist simply of getting there, particularly if you are arriving from Western Europe or the east coast of the United States. Typical itineraries involve a connection in Los Angeles. Qantas is a good airline to fly on this trip, but Air New Zealand (ANZ), Air Tahiti Nui, and United also fly this route (ANZ connects in Auckland, while Air Tahiti Nui will connect in Papeete). Qantas connects with American Airlines from many major cities nonstop from LAX, so you may not have to face a "double connection." Plus, Qantas is the best way to start acclimatizing yourself to Australian accents, vocabulary, and etiquette. Not to mention that it has incredible service from great staff and well-kept planes that never have had a fatal accident in the airline's 80-year history.

If you can fly business or first class (it's a good time to use those frequent flyer miles), you can use the Admirals Club Lounge in LAX to freshen up, get Internet access, or even take a shower or get a meal.

ONE WEEK
Days 1-2

On the day of travel, try to rise early and not nap until the Sydney leg, so that you maximize your chances of getting some sleep. The leg is 13 hours, and make sure you walk up and down the aisles at least once during the flight to keep the impact on your body to a minimum. Fill out your landing cards early in the flight and have them ready with your passport and hotel accommodations printout, so you will have less hassle on arrival.

While traveling to Australia, you cross the international date line, so you will arrive on a Wednesday morning if you leave the United States on a Monday night; it's not a typo when we skip directly to day 3. Generally speaking, a passenger flying out of New York should expect to be on an afternoon "day" flight to Los Angeles and arrive in Sydney the morning after next!

Day 3

Typical flights arrive in the morning, first thing, and you have to fight the temptation to sleep upon arrival. You will feel tired after a long flight, but the best way to fight jet lag is to stay up until evening and get a full night's sleep. Westbound jet lag is not as bad as eastbound, so you should find this not too tough. But definitely take it easy today. You won't remember much if you are completely jet-lagged and nodding off throughout the week. The perfect itinerary would have you booked in a small boutique hotel in Manly, where you will see a much more typical Aussie lifestyle than if staying in the central business district (CBD)—plus you will save on cost. You head out to Manly by JetCat, which involves a taxi ride of about 15–20 minutes from the airport to Circular Quay, and then a 15-minute JetCat ride across Sydney Harbour. JetCat service typically runs three times an hour on weekdays and hourly on weekends. Taxi service costs around $30, and the JetCat is $67 per person for a 10-trip pass, which will be enough for the week. Many hotels are within walking distance from the Manly ferry, or you can arrange a pickup by the hotel or a $10 taxi from the ferry wharf.

Today, you should expect to clear customs and be in your hotel by around midday. Spend the afternoon near the beach. Walk the Corso down to Manly Wharf and back again to Manly Beach, then hang around beachside getting a feel for the climate. If it's between November and April, by all means have a swim or a surf; from May to October go into the water if the weather is nice, but it will be a bit bracing, and in July and August the water is downright super-frosty and a wetsuit is recommended. The pleasant kiddie beach and surf is at the south end at Shelly Beach, and the more adventurous surf is north at North Steyne. Watch the beach flags posted by the Surf Lifesaving Clubs, and swim between the flags or you will get a visit from rescuers if not something more dire. Rips are super serious on Aussie beaches, so keep very much on top of your surroundings so you do not find yourself pulled out to sea unawares.

Your strolling will bring you by a large assortment of cafés and pubs. If you are feeling "quiet" head for the café. If you are ready to experience a bit more

© MITCHELL CHESHER

Manly is a good place to base yourself for exploring Sydney.

of Australian life, by all means head for the pub for a fine Australian beer and a light meal. Afterward, you might stroll the beachside streets and pick up real estate booklets or explore listings via your laptop from your room.

Day 4

Today is your main opportunity to explore the Sydney CBD for some familiarization and a touristic "high" point. Head back to Manly Wharf and take the JetCat into the CBD. You arrive in Circular Quay, which is a short 10-minute stroll from the Sydney Opera House, where you can take fantastic pictures of the harbor. Heading back to "the Quay" (pronounced "key"), take the city loop train from the Circular Quay Station to Town Hall Station. From there, you can walk across the Sydney CBD to the Museum Station through Hyde Park and take in the sights in that part of town in less than an hour. If you are feeling chipper, walk down Pitt Street toward Circular Quay through the main business and shopping districts. Back at the Quay, head west to the Sydney Harbour Bridge and take the 3.5-hour Bridge Climb (www.bridgeclimb .com for rates and bookings), which will take you over the top of the bridge for a bird's-eye view of your potential new home.

Once over the bridge and returned safely to your start point, backtrack to the Quay, JetCat back to Manly, and enjoy another evening at a beachside café.

Day 5

Today is your main day to get to know a bit more of the outlying areas of Sydney, in this case the eastern suburbs and the inner harbor. Taking the JetCat into Circular Quay after a morning beach stroll, try a midmorning harbor cruise. These are available for a variety of budgets right at the Quay. The harbor cruise will give you an invaluable look at Sydney's harbor suburbs, as well as an opportunity to ask any questions you like from the staff of guides, who will be delighted by your interest in their city and your trust in their knowledge! Once back into Circular Quay, head to the railway station and arrange for a trip on the eastern suburbs line to Bondi Junction, where you can see typical "fun" suburban life, some great shopping, and explore potential real estate agents who will have listings "to let" or "for sale" in their windows. If you are interested in a Sydney-based academic assignment, by all means vary one of your trips to include a quick bus trip out to the campus location of your choice.

Day 6

This is your "out of Sydney" exploration day. It's up to you to decide if you would like to rent a car or take a train, but there are three basic directions. North, you'll find the beaches of New South Wales's central coast an hour north of the city by car. Gosford is the gateway to famed beaches like Terrigal. To the south, you can reach Kiama and get back in a day. Westward, you'll head into the Blue Mountains by driving across the western suburbs of Sydney and reach Katoomba, where you might visit the Three Sisters monuments and see a typical mountain town. In the late afternoon, retrace your steps to Sydney. Throughout your expedition day, be sure to keep the car filled with petrol (gas), as there sometimes can be long gaps between stations in the bush areas, and take lots of water and sun protection.

Day 7

Your journey is done, and you've seen beach, city, bush, and harbor. Job well done! It's back to Sydney's Mascot airport for the flight back home. Keep in mind that heading west–east you pick up a day crossing the international date line, so typically you will arrive in the States "before" you leave Australia, as the calendar records it! Flights generally leave Sydney in the late afternoon or early evening, so you will fly through a shortened night and land the afternoon that you left. Eastbound jet lag is always worse, so make sure you are prepared for "light duty" for a few days upon your return, as you will feel a little disoriented at night when it's time to sleep. Or, that may simply be the memories of a great trip.

TWO WEEKS

In this two-week itinerary, we'll keep the first five days the same, and only on day 6 will we leave Sydney behind and do some exploring of Canberra and Melbourne, by car, before heading back up the coast to Sydney. An alternative two-week itinerary would be to take a week in Sydney, followed by a few days on the Gold Coast, if you are considering that as a possible living location.

Day 6

Having spent the first five days duplicating the one-week itinerary by exploring Sydney, on day 6 we will head by car or train down to Canberra. It's a solid half-day drive, directly southwest of the city. A good idea is to pick out a town like Yass along the way to have a typical Aussie lunch or snack. Travel down the "high street" (main street) of any small Aussie town and look for a pub with a back garden, or a café. The outlying towns are also surprisingly well-populated with fairly good Chinese restaurants, if that's your lunchtime fancy. For a typical Aussie lunch, try a meat pie with tomato sauce, or a sausage roll, with "chips" (french fries) if you like them.

You should arrive in Canberra in the late afternoon, and there is a wide selection of good hotels in the Civic area. You might try a steakhouse if you are

Take a day for tourism: Parliament House and Lake Burley Griffin, as seen from Red Hill.

so inclined, as Canberra is a country town and the beef is quite good in that part of the country. A quick drive around Lake Burley Griffin will complete your initial familiarization.

Day 7

Today is a good day for some basic tourism, as we could use a day away from the car after your drive down to the ACT. You'll move around the city by car, but you can take in the Australian Parliament and the Australian War Museum or the National Gallery, the highlights in town. One in the morning and one in the afternoon will provide you with an excellent introduction to Australian culture and history.

Day 8

The final day in Canberra should include an exploratory drive around Yarralumla and the diplomatic row. Your concierge will have a map of the major missions, many of which are quite attractive and all worth seeing. While in the mission search, keep an eye out for real estate offices, and do some browsing if you like. After lunch, head south for Melbourne, either by rail or car, stopping in the Snowy Mountains town of Jindabyne along the way, at the Lake Jindabyne Hotel (www.lakejindabynehotel.com.au), or check www.tripadvisor .com for a low-cost hotel of your choice if you're traveling on a tight budget.

Day 9

Today, you'll explore the Snowy Mountains by car, with a side trip to Perisher or Thredbo highly recommended if weather permits, or just enjoy Lake Jindabyne and a little of Aussie alpine life. Then, around lunchtime head for Melbourne. A stay in the Victoria Harbour area is recommended as a starting point for fantastic city views and a situation right in the heart of "fun" Melbourne.

Day 10

This morning is for exploring Melbourne's CBD. Starting from your base in the Docklands you'll take a tram into the CBD. The Queen Victoria Market is a first stop, which can be experienced via a two-hour tour or just wandering from stall to stall. The National Gallery of Victoria is one of the best museums in all of Australia, and worth a visit. Finally, for a wide-view vista experience comparable to climbing the Sydney Harbour Bridge, take the "lift" (elevator) to the top of the Eureka Tower. The observation deck is at the 88th floor, and the views are unparalleled in Melbourne.

© FLAVIA MARPLES

the author with several of his readers at Pebbly Beach in New South Wales

Day 11

Melbourne is the home of Aussie sport, and a visit is not complete without a pilgrimage to see sports-mad Aussies in their element. Depending on the season, you could take in VFL Park (for Aussie Rules football), the Melbourne Cricket Ground (cricket, naturally), the Flemington Racecourse (the iconic Melbourne Cup horse race, or other daily events), or Melbourne Park (Australian Open tennis).

Day 12

It's back toward Sydney on this driving day, and you'll head up Princes Highway along the coast toward New South Wales, stopping anywhere you like for typical Aussie lunch fare, but aiming to reach Mollymook by the late afternoon. A stop at Pebbly Beach will give you a chance to stand on a deserted, gorgeous beach with wild but friendly kangaroos all around you. It's best not to feed them. In Mollymook, you have a number of small inns and hotels to choose from, such as the Mollymook Beach House (www.southcoast.com .au/beachhouse). This classic, low-key Aussie beach retreat is much loved by landlocked residents in Canberra just two hours away.

Day 13

We are back to Sydney, with driving in the morning, arrival in midafternoon, and perhaps a chance (if time permits) to head to the harborside in the CBD to a restaurant that specializes in fresh Australian fish. Your concierge can suggest a myriad of choices.

Day 14

Back to Sydney's Mascot Airport for some last-minute duty-free shopping and the long flight home. You've seen four of the six regions in this book in just two weeks. Good on ya!

ONE MONTH

In this itinerary option, add on two extra weeks to the 14-day trip, but keep the first 13 days exactly the same. Starting at day 14, you will be accessing the rest of Australia by plane, as we have distance issues to overcome, while taking in not only the great living locations of the north and west, but a little extra tourism to take us to the center of Australia at Alice Springs, where lies the mysterious monolith Uluru.

Day 14

Instead of heading back home, in this itinerary we will head to the domestic terminal at Mascot for the flight on Qantas to Brisbane. It's a fairly short and scenic flight, and try to get a window seat on the port side of the aircraft (left side) on the way north, as the views are generally better because you look out toward the land. On arrival in Brisbane, a taxi into the city is expensive; instead rent a car to use to head down to the Gold Coast. The evening of your arrival would be well spent strolling along the Brisbane River, taking in the sights.

Day 15

This is your Brisbane exploration day, so your car will be in heavy use. Start by heading northeast toward the airport and then up the Bruce Highway toward the Sunshine Coast, stopping in Maroochy for shopping. Then swing to the southwest and take in the classic northern suburbs. After lunch, head back briefly into the city to take in the Brisbane Markets, and then out toward the Gold Coast along the Pacific Motorway, an hour south of the city, just in time for the evening meal.

Days 16-17

Two days at the Gold Coast are a must, for you'll need some pure relaxation after all your running around, and the Gold Coast is the place to do it. There are nearly 70 kilometers of exquisite beaches, with golf and casinos that add to the excitement. But sitting under an umbrella, taking in the sun and dipping occasionally into the ocean, might be just what the doctor ordered. Meanwhile, in your daily walk or ride to the beach, you can pick up some real estate brochures to study between waves.

Days 18-19

On this day, fly to Cairns via Qantas and, picking out an overnight trip from a service such as http://reeftrip.com, take in the Great Barrier Reef with some classic snorkeling and diving options. The best way to see the reef is to stay overnight on a catamaran, but if you are on a budget then by all means stay at a local hotel and take a day trip out to the reef. In the evening, fly back to Brisbane.

Day 20

Today is essentially a travel day, as we will be flying all the way to Australia's southwest coast, and the five-hour flight will take up most of the day even though you pick up two hours by flying west. The best bet is to head to the beach section in Perth, with Cottlesloe Beach fairly unbeatable unless you are looking for big waves, in which case you have the wrong ocean. Check in and spend the evening relaxing, as you've had hard "yakka" (work) the past few days.

Days 21-22

Your two days in Perth include a day by car exploring the environs of the city, particularly the north side of the Swan River and heading out west from the CBD toward the beach suburbs. If you have some academic or corporate visiting needs, feel free to curtail your beach excursion on these days to accommodate. The second day, try a Swan River wine cruise (particularly if you are a wine lover), which will stop in at a few wineries and is a lot of fun. Check out www .captaincookcruises.com.au to arrange the cruise into the Swan Valley.

Days 23-24

In the early morning, it's over to the airport to catch the first flight into Adelaide. You'll spend two days here, with one day spent exploring the suburbs, especially the western suburbs in the beach areas, and one day to explore the Adelaide Parklands, which form one of the most extensive urban park systems in the world. It's a good place to pick up some more exposure to sport, either with Aussie Rules or cricket at the Adelaide Cricket Oval, depending on the season.

Days 25-26

The morning of day 25, head out to the Adelaide airport and catch the first flight to Alice Springs. From there visit Alice Springs and Uluru. The Ayers Rock Resort has seven different hotel options for varying budgets. Uluru is a one-hour climb of moderate difficulty if you are in decent shape, but it can be windy at the top; a chain-hold makes it a snap, really. Some areas are off-limits, and some photography is limited owing to special tribal taboos. On day 26, if you are feeling ambitious, take a bus trip to the Olgas rock formations, which are eerie and magnificent.

Day 27

Today, we fly Qantas back to Sydney, and with an afternoon arrival, you can choose whether you want to head out to the beach, shopping, or to the Sydney Cricket Ground or Sydney Sports Ground to watch sport. On this day, a good idea is to pick out a hotel fairly close to the airport and taxi to the location of your choice, or take public transit such as the express train to the CBD from Mascot. You'll be the one to choose between a quiet meal near the hotel or something more adventurous by the water. If the weather is cooperative, try to make sunset at the Sydney Opera House a last "thing to do," as the sight of the sun going down behind the Harbour Bridge will be just the image you want to keep in your head when you are back at home, going through the hassle of moving.

Day 28

Return to the home country, as detailed in the one-week and two-week itineraries.

Practicalities

ACCOMMODATIONS AND FOOD
Sydney

For a great stay, try the **Sebel Manly Beach Hotel** (8–13 South Steyne, Manly, tel. 02/9977-8866, www.mirvachotels.com/sebel-manly-beach) for around $180 per night plus taxes. For a lower-priced option, a good place to start is the **Manly Guest House** (6 Steinton St., Manly, tel. 02/9977-0884, www.manlyguesthouse.com.au), from around $50 per night.

Whitewater (35 South Steyne, tel. 02/9977-0322) is an excellent, high-quality dining experience in Manly. **The Old Manly Boat Shed** (40 The Corso, Manly, tel. 02/9977-4443) offers something a little more laid-back. The classic Sydney restaurant is **Doyle's on the Beach** in Watson's Bay (11 Marine Parade, Watson's Bay, tel. 02/9337-2007), but it is pricey and hard to get a table. On more of a budget, try the **Australian Hotel** (100 Cumberland St., The Rocks, tel. 02/9247-2229), which has all sorts of only-in-Australia

MEALTIME

All Aussies recognize breakfast and lunch, and eat them at the same time as Americans, although the portions are usually smaller. Aussies tend to eat more but smaller meals, although work life imposes a three-meal regimen on an increasing percentage of the population.

The morning break is not universally observed, but is fairly close. Traditionally, in tradesmen settings it was called "smoko," but that word has all but died out. "Morning tea" or simply "tea" is served in offices and homes, and consists of tea, coffee, and sometimes small cookies (called "biscuits"). At primary schools it is often called "play lunch," and cakes such as lamingtons are typically served, along with juice. On weekends, morning tea is often called "elevenses" and can include alcoholic beverages.

Afternoon tea is served in the "arvo" (afternoon; pronounced "ahhh-vo") and is less common nowadays except for hungry school-age kids, who will consume snack foods, dried fruit, and perhaps a "Milo" (mixed chocolate milk).

"Tea time" in Australia is not a time for tea at all; it is time for the evening meal, or dinner as it is called in the United States and also by an increasing number of Aussies. It is very similar to the U.S. evening meal except that Aussies eat more meat than Americans, so it is easier on the pastas and breads as a general rule. Some Aussies also cling to the tradition of a late supper, which can mean milk and biscuits, or other light fare, usually taken just before bedtime or later in the evening.

cuisine such as emu and crocodile steaks, as well as more traditional fare, and it's not pricey at all.

Melbourne

The main city area for hotels is east of Elizabeth Street between Lonsdale and Collins. Top of the line would be the **Westin Melbourne** (205 Collins St., tel. 03/9635-2333, www.westin.com.au) from $340 per night, with the **Hotel Grand Chancellor** (131 Lonsdale St., tel. 03/9656-4000, www.ghihotels.com) a little more on the affordable side, starting at $169 per night.

For meals at the high end, **Oyster Little Bourke** (35 Little Bourke St., tel. 03/9650-0988) is great for intimate dining and a menu far beyond oysters. **Bluestone Restaurant Bar** (349–351 Flinders Ln., tel. 03/9620-4060) gets rave reviews. Both are pricey. For those on a tighter budget, the lines outside the **Supper Inn Chinese Restaurant** (15 Celestial Ave., tel. 03/9663-4753) convince most that it's the best Chinese food in town. It's been around for more than 20 years, which makes it a Chinatown landmark.

Brisbane and the Queensland Coast

At the high end in Brisbane is the **Conrad** (130 William St., tel. 07/3306-8888, www.conradtreasury.com.au), which includes a great casino, from $275 per night. In the same area along the Brisbane River but more affordable is the **Marque** (103 George St., tel. 07/3221-6044, www.marquehotels.com/brisbane), from $189 per night.

In dining, the most lauded and recognized restaurant in Brisbane is **E'cco Bistro** (100 Boundary St., tel. 07/3831-8344). In Fortitude Valley, for incredible Thai that's very easy on the budget try **Thai Wi Rat** (Shop 48, 20 Duncan St., Fortitude Valley, tel. 07/3257-0884).

Canberra

The five-star Canberra hotel is the **Hyatt in Yarralumla** (Commonwealth Ave., Yarralumla, tel. 02/6270-1234, http://canberra.park.hyatt.com) in the diplomatic district. It's an art deco–era classic, averaging $330. The **Hotel Kurrajong** (8 National Circuit, Barton, tel. 02/6234-4466, www.hotelkurrajong-canberra.com) is near Parliament and is very nice and more affordable, averaging around $185.

For dining, **Anise** (in the Melbourne Building, tel. 02/6257-0700) is high-end and very authentic Australian cuisine, while **The Habit Café** (1 McPherson St., O'Connor, tel. 02/6162-0033) is the best of the cheap eats.

The Great Dividing Range

This region is very widespread, so we've focused in on the **Echoes Boutique Hotel & Restaurant** in Katoomba (3 Lilianfels Ave., tel. 02/4782-1966, www.echoeshotel.com.au) for fantastic views and a great introduction to country life by being in a smaller hotel setting.

For food, **Mes Amis** (56–64 Waratah St., Katoomba, tel. 02/4782-1558) doesn't have a liquor license but you can bring your own, and it delivers on every other level.

Southwestern Australia

The **Hilton Adelaide** (233 Victoria Square, tel. 08/8217-2000, www.hilton.com) is the top five-star in South Australia. **The Manse** (142 Tynte St., North Adelaide, tel. 08/8267-4636) is the place to head for food in Adelaide at the high end. Aim for the CBD and the cluster of restaurants on **Gouger Street** for cheap eats and excellent value.

In Perth, the **Sheraton Perth** (207 Adelaide Terrace, tel. 08/9224-7777) has a good location and is pricey, but many feel this is the best in the CBD. It has been recently refurbished. In dining, at the high end, **Opus Restaurant at the Richardson** (32 Richardson St., West Perth, tel. 08/9217-8880) will not disappoint. On the budget side, the **Red Tea Pot** (413 William St., Perth, tel. 08/9228-1981) is everything you need: super-affordable, deliciously fresh, fast, and authentic Asian cuisine.

COMMUNICATIONS

In a good fact-finding trip, the first thing upon landing is to obtain a good communications setup, which is important for keeping in contact with friends and family, and also for communicating while you are on the go in Oz. And you will be on the go!

For phone access and good rates, we recommend Skype (www.skype.com), which works off your Internet-enabled PC or Mac and offers free calling to other Skype accounts, plus a penny or two per minute for calling landlines from your PC. The connection is good, and you can receive calls into your PC as well, plus sign up for a voicemail account if you like to catch important calls.

For mobile access, if you have a 900/1800 compatible GSM phone, you will likely have roaming service while in Australia. If you have an older, non-GSM phone, you are not likely to have access to voice service, so you will need to rent a phone or a chip (if you would like to bring your handset). A good service is Telestial (www.telestial.com), which offers a great $49 package, including $20 in starter airtime credit, free incoming calls, outbound calls at $0.39 per minute, 94 percent coverage, text messages, voicemail, and no contract.

DAILY LIFE

MAKING THE MOVE

The most difficult part of moving to Australia is not the packing, the good-byes, the arrival, or the settling in: It is getting permission to come to Australia in the first place. As a dry, water-challenged continent that has found prosperity by carefully balancing population growth needs against resource allocations, Australia thinks a whole lot more about who moves to Australia than countries like the United States, which fights over its leaky borders more than over the regulations and quotas for legal immigration.

Visas and Immigration

Permanent residency is a special, highly-prized form of visa that allows longer term stays and access to social services. There are 12 basic types of immigrants to Australia, who follow different paths toward obtaining a visa:

Workers. People who want to migrate permanently to Australia and who have the required skills and qualifications.

© JAMES M. LANE

© MITCHELL CHESHER

The emergency services sector in Australia, and health as a whole, are fast-growing areas of employment.

Businesspeople. People who come to Australia to establish, manage, or develop a new or existing business, or to invest in Australia. In cases of investment, there are reduced net worth requirements and age restrictions if you apply through a state program; states require that sponsored visa applicants be under 55 years of age. Typically, business owner visas are restricted to persons under 45 years of age, and there are restrictions based on net assets and business experience. There must be a sponsoring business in most cases.

Family members. Fiancé(e)s, spouses, partners, siblings, children, parents, and other family members of Australian citizens, Australian permanent residents, or eligible New Zealand citizens.

Refugee or humanitarian entrants. People seeking assistance under the refugee and humanitarian program. More than 600,000 people have entered Australia under this program. Application is made in person, and either a temporary protection or permanent protection visa would be granted.

Returning residents. Former citizens or permanent residents seeking to relocate back to Australia.

Student guardians. Parents or relatives who stay in Australia as the guardians of a student who is studying in Australia.

Sponsored training. People who want to come to Australia through a professional development program or to undertake workplace-based training.

Employer-sponsored workers. People with recognized skills seeking to work in Australia after being sponsored by an Australian or overseas employer.

Professionals and other skilled migrants. People who are not sponsored by an employer but who have skills in particular occupations required in Australia.

Doctors and nurses. Doctors and nurses who want to work in Australia. Nurses are in particular demand, and if they have good health and the requisite education and experience background to be approved by the Nursing & Midwifery Council, this is one of the easiest ways to get into Australia.

Regional employment. Skilled migrants or temporary entrants who live and work in areas outside of Australia's major cities. Typically, applicants are under 45, have English-language skills, and have passed the health exam.

Working holiday participants. People aged 18–30 from countries with a reciprocal arrangement to have an extended holiday supplemented by short-term employment.

MIGRATION ADVISER

In Australia, there are registered migration advisers, and they are extremely helpful in providing assistance to businesses, individuals, and families. They help you to explore business opportunities and make quality referrals for jobs, homes, visas, and Migration Review Tribunal Appeals.

The managing director of AusArrivals Immigration Agency, Dr. Vicki Clayton (reg. no. 0531177), holds a BA (Honours) and a PhD degree from the University of Melbourne, as well as a certificate in legal processes and procedure, making her one of the most qualified in the field. When employed as migration adviser at the Inner Western Region Migrant Resource Centre, the Springvale Community Aid and Advice Bureau, and the Australian Multicultural Education Service, Dr. Clayton provided advice to recently arrived migrants and refugees from all over the world, including Africa, Asia, and the Middle East, as well as European and U.S. locations.

"I love asking people about where they come from, their stories and experiences," says Vicki. "It sounds a bit corny, but the best thing about my job as a migration adviser is meeting fascinating people from all walks of life."

While moving to Australia is definitely something that can be accomplished on your own, you'll take less time and experience less aggravation working with a registered migration adviser, and I recommend it!

AusArrivals Immigration Agency
tel. 03/9391-1243
cell 04/3159-1842
vicki@ausarrivals.com.au

DAILY LIFE

SUPPORT ORGANIZATIONS
FOR HOMESICK YANKEES

There are a number of organizations where Australians and Americans meet up, and it's just about the best move you can make, upon arrival, to join one. The associations organize celebrations on U.S. holidays, education support for expat children (including courses on U.S. history and geography that expat kids will miss out on), and discounted tickets for "home leave" travel. Plus, sometimes a friendly person who has "been through it" is just the friend you need, whether it's finding ingredients, meeting business contacts, or just coping with the wonders of life in a strange land.

In most cities, the American Chamber of Commerce in Australia maintains an office and provides a valuable source of business contacts as well as opportunities for civic activities. The Australian-American Association is in most cities, although in Sydney the American Society has traditionally been just as lively. In Sydney, the American Club on Macquarie Street counts mostly Australians among its members, but it has incredible views, great dining, and board room facilities. Each Thanksgiving, they serve a traditional turkey dinner – they provide the food, and you provide your Yankee, Yozzie, or Yank-curious Australian friends and family, and carve a turkey they prepare. It's a lot of fun.

See the *Resources* chapter for contact information in each prime living location.

A full list of visa types, restrictions, fees, and forms is available at the Australian Immigration Service website, at www.immi.gov.au/e_visa/index.htm.

REQUIREMENTS FOR VISAS
Values Statement

All applicants aged 18 years and over sign a values statement when applying for selected visas. Applicants must confirm that they will respect the Australian way of life and obey the laws of Australia before being granted a visa. All provisional and permanent visa applicants are required to have read the *Life in Australia* book before signing the values statement. The book covers Australian history, culture, society, and values. Humanitarian visa applicants are the exception, because of the unusual circumstances they are facing. They have the values statement read to them or explained upon entry into Australia. New Zealand citizens entering Australian on a special category visa do not have to review the book.

To download a free PDF version of the *Life in Australia* book, visit: www.immi.gov.au/living-in-australia/values/book/index.htm.

APPLYING FOR A PERMANENT RESIDENCE VISA

In Australia, there are temporary visas (for both work and tourism), and permanent residence visas. One way to obtain a permanent residence visa is to apply through the skilled migrant stream (another is to marry an Australian).

Using a points table, applicants score marks based on work and language skills, age, and other criteria. Currently the passing score is 120 for independent applicants, while 110 is a passing grade for applicants with family sponsors. The Australian Government Department of Immigration and Citizenship website is an excellent resource for learning about Australia's immigration points system (www.immi.gov.au).

The criteria and points for a passing score are as follows:

Age:

- Over the age of 44, you cannot obtain a skilled migration visa, and points are awarded on a sliding scale.
- 18-29 Years (30 points)
- 30-34 Years (25 points)
- 35-39 Years (20 points)
- 40-44 Years (15 points)

English Language Skills:

- Proficient English (25 points): At least 7.0 in each of the four test components of the International English Language Testing System (IELTS) Test (speak, read, write, listen).
- Competent English (15 points): At least 6.0 in each of the four IELTS test components.
- Passport holders from the United Kingdom, United States, Canada, Ireland, or New Zealand are automatically considered to have "competent English."
- Vocational English (15 points): At least 5.0 in each of the four IELTS test components.
- Concessional Competent English (15 points): An average band score of at least 5.5 in each of the four IELTS test components.

Specific Work Experience:

- Worked in a 60-point occupation or a closely related field for three out of the last four years (10 points).
- Applicant has worked in a 60-, 50-, or 40-points occupation on the Skilled Occupation List (SOL) (http://www.accurateimmigration.com/australia/sol.html) for three out of the last four years.

Australian Work Experience:

- Employed in Australia in the nominated occupation or a closely related field for at least one of the last four years (10 points).
- Completed a "professional year" in the nominated occupation or closely related field for at least one of the last four years (10 points).

Migration Occupations in Demand List (MODL):

- Occupation is on the MODL and applicant has a job offer from an Australian employer with 10+ employees the past two years (20 points).
- Occupation is on the MODL but applicant has no job offer (15 points).

Academic Qualifications:

- Completed a PhD after two years of full-time study in Australia (25 points).
- Completed a Masters or Honors degree after two years of full-time study in Australia, and completed a bachelor's degree after one year of study in Australia (15 points).
- Completed a degree, diploma, or trade qualification after two years of full-time study in Australia (5 points).

Regional Study:

- Completed two years full-time study in a regional area or a low population growth metropolitan area (5 points).

Designated Language:

- Holds a university degree in a designated language (5 points).
- Qualifies as a Level 3 interpreter from the National Accreditation Authority for Translators and Interpreters (www.naati.com.au) in a community language (5 points).

Skilled Spouse/Partner:

- Applicant's spouse or partner also meets the age, English, work qualification, occupation and work experience requirements (5 points).

State/Territory Nomination:

- A migrant can be invited, or nominated, by a state or territory government if applying for a regional sponsored visa. This will generally require employment in the designated state or territory (10 points).

Designated Area Sponsorship:

- A migrant can be sponsored by an eligible relative who resides in a designated area in Australia (25 points).

DAILY LIFE

Health Requirements

You must meet Aussie health requirements before a visa can be granted. This means in most case a health examination, which you will pay for, and passing the exam is no guarantee of a visa.

You will need to undertake a health examination if you are likely to enter a hospital, a classroom environment, have a medical condition, are aged 70 or older, or if otherwise requested. All members of your immediate family must meet the health requirement.

After you file your application, you will be advised by the Immigration Department if and when to attend a health examination. You have to go to an approved panel doctor, nominated by the Immigration Department.

Visa Fees

Fees range from a nominal $200 or so for a returning Australian permanent resident to more than $8,000 for a worst-case scenario. Students pay $500 for an application and visa. Visas are typically paid in installments, with a nonrefundable application fee of $60–500 and up to two progress payments. Higher payments are required for business visas, and for visas of individuals with English-language challenges, or for retirees. Workers who aim to hold jobs in remote areas are given more than half off the visa costs.

A complete set of visa types and rates is online at www.immi.gov.au/allforms/990i/visa-charges.htm.

Character Requirements

Everyone who wishes to enter Australia must pass a character test, which may mean providing police certificates for every country lived in for more than 12 months in the past 10 years. The Australian Immigration Department determines when the police certificates are required. A police certificate is obtained by contacting a local court or police authority and having them provide a criminal background check report.

TAX CONSIDERATIONS

The United States has a tax treaty with Australia that allows U.S. citizens to be taxed at a lower rate on income they receive from foreign sources; this takes into account that the taxpayer is already paying tax in Australia. Essentially, the tax treaty eliminates double taxation. Paragraph 1 provides that the United States shall give a foreign tax credit for income taxes paid to Australia, subject to the limitations provided in U.S. law. The credit is allowed for taxes paid directly by or on behalf of the U.S. resident or citizen.

The full scoop on the tax treaty can be found at www.irs.gov/pub/irs-trty/austtech.pdf.

Moving with Children

SCHOOLS AND SCHOOL CALENDAR

Not everyone moving to Australia has a lot of control over the timing; visa approval factors or job requirements often dictate the pace, but if possible it is ideal to move to Australia during the summer school holidays, so that the child can acclimatize before entering school.

Regardless of the timing, the student will either repeat some of the year already passed, or skip ahead. For example, a student moving in February will have completed more than half a year of the current grade, and would either have to spring forward to a new grade or fall back to do a half-year's work over again. As a rule of thumb, moving backwards is better not only for acclimation reasons but to keep the child from being the youngest, smallest kid, and also in recognition that Aussie subject matter will be different, particularly in the social sciences. If the child is clearly bored after starting in the backward grade, by all means consider moving up, but do it quickly.

The best way to contact the school is to do so immediately after selecting a neighborhood, by checking online or with neighbors about the public school district.

The school will be able to provide an online or printed calendar, and resources for joining the local P&C (parents and citizens organization—equivalent to a parent-teacher association or organization), obtaining books, uniforms, and obtaining transportation information and free transit passes for the children.

PREPARATIONS AT HOME

The most important things in preparing a relocating child for the move are:

Cultivating activities that can be carried forward in Oz. There's no point in pursuing a lot of ski trips, but it's a good time to learn to surf.

School uniforms. What they consist of, and why they are not the end of the world.

Social networking. Kids will miss their friends. Encourage them to establish a Facebook page or equivalent, if you permit this online activity, as a way of keeping in touch with old friends and making new ones.

Australia awareness. It's difficult to get kids to read dry recitations of

Australian history or customs, but try to find television shows and movies featuring Australian actors or themes. Try to find Aussie sports in your cable package and invest in watching them (possibly with a rule book or guide in hand!). The more your child knows about Aussie culture and history on arrival, the better. Show your child the currency, and maybe try a few classic Aussie foods.

Metrics awareness. It will be helpful to have awareness of the metric weights and measures system—just the basics. Length, area, and volume are fine.

Moving with Pets

Generally, dogs and cats can be brought to Australia. Hamsters, gerbils, and the like cannot. Australia has extremely strict regulations regarding the importation of pets, owing to the absence of resistance to rabies.

REQUIRED QUARANTINE

Cats and dogs entering Australia must meet import conditions prior to moving. This is to ensure no exotic diseases are introduced into Australia. You apply for an Australian Quarantine and Inspection Service (AQIS) permit via the Live Animal Imports Program. AQIS officers will assess the application and grant a permit. This gives you the right to book your pet into a quarantine hospital for 30–65 days. Pets are quarantined in Sydney, Melbourne, or Perth. AQIS is typically quite overloaded in handling quarantine, so apply as early as possible for a slot. You have to have the import permit to make the booking, and you must have a booking to have your pet in quarantine. The alternative is waiting until a slot is available and bringing your pet later.

Different import conditions apply for the importation of disability assistance dogs. Check with the Australian Customs Service on timeline and tasks, to ensure that your dog or cat can travel as comfortably as possible. Details can be downloaded online (www.daffa.gov.au/aqis/cat-dogs/countries/cat4).

Your pet will also need to have a microchip inserted in its skin prior to importation. Dogs and cats must be identified by a microchip that can be read by an Avid, Trovan, Destron, or other ISO compatible reader. The microchip must be implanted before any blood testing or vaccination takes place.

Applying for a Permit to Import

Dogs and cats must be vaccinated against rabies and must have a certificate of vaccination. The certificate is a form called the Rabies Neutralizing Antibody Titre Test (RNATT) Declaration, and a form is available online (www.daff .gov.au/_data/assets/pdf_file/0005/112856/rnatt_declaration.pdf). The form must be completed and signed by an Official Government Veterinarian from the exporting country. The veterinarian must use a generally accepted and approved "inactivated rabies virus vaccine." Questions regarding vaccines can be directed to a U.S. Department of Agriculture Animal and Plant Health Inspection Service (APHIS) area office, which can be located at www.aphis .usda.gov/animal_health/area_offices.

Official Government Veterinarian

According to the Australian Government an Official Government Veterinarian is a government officer usually employed by the government veterinarian administration in the exporting country. Official Government Veterinarians generally do not work in private practice. These veterinarians are able to sign certificates on behalf of the government's veterinary administration, endorse Veterinary Certificate A, and complete Veterinary Certificate B that is provided with your AQIS import permit. The Official Government Veterinarian may assist you with locating a "government approved veterinarian" and a "government approved laboratory."

You should contact the government veterinary administration in your country to determine which veterinarians you can use to prepare your pet for export. This government approved veterinarian will prepare your pet for export to Australia and fill in the details of this preparation on Veterinary Certificate A provided with your AQIS import permit.

Government Approved Laboratories are approved by the veterinary service in the country of export for testing samples from animals destined for export. AQIS accepts the use of laboratories approved by the veterinary service within the country of export for testing for export purposes provided that the testing laboratory is in an AQIS approved country.

To locate appropriate veterinarians and laboratories, contact the United States Department of Agriculture Animal and Plant Health Inspection Service (APHIS) (www.aphis.usda.gov) or an equivalent government department in another country.

DAILY LIFE

MOVING TO AUSTRALIA, 1860s-STYLE

The document you see here is an arrival record from Sydney in May 1860 of the *Royal Saxon,* arriving from Puget Sound after a three-month voyage. That's my own third great-grandfather, Henry Ward Collier, the chief officer, and traveling with him was 12-year-old William Hoyle Collier, later a Pacific captain himself, serving as cabin boy.

It goes to show how things have tightened up in Australia over the years. For some reason, the immigration officers put Henry's home as Halifax (he was born in Hartford), and young William (who was born in Savannah) was listed as hailing from Van Diemen's Land (modern-day Tasmania).

Although Henry was killed on the docks of Shanghai in 1865, young William worked for the *Sydney Morning Herald* and *The Bulletin,* although he took off two years to serve in the Confederate Secret Service during the Civil War.

Like many families, ours has kept moving back and forth between Australia and the United States, with six generations living at least part of their lives in both Oz and America, and 2010 represents the 150th anniversary of our family's first arrival − not exactly as momentous as arriving with the First Fleet, but something we think about when the Manly JetCat brings us into Circular Quay, where the *Royal Saxon* landed so long ago.

Henry's three fourth great-grandsons all live in Sydney, just a few miles from their ancestor's arrival. It just goes to show that a move to Australia can have momentous consequences, even though the paperwork is just a little tougher these days.

1860 Australian immigration document, marking the arrival of the Royal Saxon from Puget Sound, USA

What to Bring

In general, the best approach in moving to Oz is to leave everything behind that you can. Whether because of shipping costs, driving incompatibility, or electric power incompatibility, your major home possessions (such as furniture, car, and household appliances) are just not compatible with your new Aussie life. So save up, and buy when you get there, to the extent that you can. Homes, while roomy by European or Japanese standards, are somewhat smaller than typical modern American homes, and some shrinkage of your list of possessions is mandatory in most cases. Laptop computers are an exception to the rule, because many are built to be compatible with 240 volts, the price of computers is high in Australia, and the shipping charge is negligible.

SHIPPING OPTIONS
Required Customs Documents
Shippers (unless you are an Australian or New Zealand citizen) are required to have a B534 Unaccompanied Effects Form. Download this form at www.customs.gov.au/travel/unaccomp.htm. Customs will not accept faxed or photocopied forms. Customs will also ask for a photocopy of each page of your passport and a list of contents of the packages.

Household goods and personal effects are allowed into Australia duty free, provided that they have been owned more than one year.

Prohibited Items
There are several items that are restricted upon entering Australia.
- Fresh fruits and vegetables
- Grains
- Meat and dairy products
- Plants, soil, seeds
- Most animals including wildlife
- Nonprescription medications and narcotic drugs
- Firearms, ammunition, explosives
- Radio transmitters, citizen band radios, cordless telephones

DAILY LIFE

DAILY LIFE

MOVING TO AUSTRALIA CHECKLIST

Six Weeks Before the Move

- Review your relocation package if you have one, and determine expenses that will be paid by your company.
- Start a log of moving expense receipts (some may be tax deductible).
- Get written estimates from moving companies, including their written commitment of pickup and delivery dates. Get references. Check the limits of insurance they offer, and if it covers replacement cost.
- Purchase additional insurance if necessary.
- Arrange for a storage facility if you plan to store any contents. Again, check insurance.
- Arrange transport service for pets or automobiles if needed.
- Contact your bank and arrange transfer of your accounts; order checks with your new address; clean out your safety deposit box.
- Submit change-of-address forms to the post office; mail postcards to friends and creditors.
- Give day care center proper notice of withdrawal.
- Contact schools and arrange for transfer of student records.
- Contact your doctors for medical records.
- Change your insurance policies on property, auto, and medical.
- Organize all important documents in a fire-safe box. Some things you want to include are school records, home purchase/sale papers, will, marriage/divorce papers, pet documents, financial records, stock certificates, social security cards, birth certificates, and passports.
- Give notice of resignation to any clubs, organizations, or volunteer activities you belong to.
- Cancel newspaper subscriptions.
- Arrange for hotels, rental cars, or temporary housing as needed.

Four Weeks Before the Move

- Take a ruthless walk-through to determine what you really want to take.
- Tag the rest of it and hold a garage sale, or call a charity for pickup.
- Clean out club, gym, and school lockers; pick up all dry cleaning.
- Arrange for the disconnection or changeover of utilities.
- Have measurements taken of the rooms in your new residence and use floorplans to determine where everything will go.
- Begin packing less-used items. Number and label each box, and keep an inventory.
- Retrieve and return all borrowed items from neighbors and friends; return library books.
- Clean out the cupboards and plan remaining meals so you can pack what you don't need, and don't buy any more perishables than you have to.

One Week Before the Move

* Make an inventory list of all items going with you personally. Keep valuable and irreplaceable items such as jewelry and heirlooms with you, not movers.
* Confirm arrangements and dates with moving and storage companies.
* Confirm arrangements with auto and pet transportation companies.
* Confirm hotel, rental car, or temporary housing accommodations.
* Clean out and defrost the deep freezer.
* Disassemble furniture or other items.
* Be sure to check yard and sheds for all items to pack.
* Inform all friends and relatives of your forwarding address.
* Take pictures of furniture or get fabric samples for anything you will want to reference for color or decorating before your goods are delivered to your new home.
* Set aside a box of cleaning supplies and the vacuum cleaner.

One to Two Days Before the Move

* Clean and defrost refrigerator and freezer.
* Withdraw cash needed for move, and convert currency.
* Reconcile and close bank accounts, unless you will be using another branch of the same bank.
* Conclude financial matters relating to the sale or lease of your home.
* Movers or your family should complete packing of all household goods for the move. Make sure all boxes are clearly marked.

Moving Day

* Confirm delivery address, directions, and delivery date with the movers.
* Carefully supervise the move. Make sure boxes are clearly marked and your instructions are understood.
* Clean the home and check entire grounds before leaving.
* Check thermostat and make sure temperature is set appropriately. Make sure all windows and doors are closed and locked, and all appliances are turned off. Leave forwarding address, garage door openers and any keys, if agreed to, for the new owners or renters.
* If your home is going to be vacant when you leave, make sure a relative, neighbor, or real estate agent has the keys and how to contact you. Also, notify your insurance agent and police department that the home will be empty.

Arrival Day

* Check to make sure all utilities are on and working properly.
* Let family members or friends know you have arrived safely. Check in with your employer and real estate agent to confirm itineraries.
* Supervise moving crew on location of furniture and boxes. Begin unpacking necessary basics first – basic kitchen utensils, bath toiletries, etc.
* Go over the Bill of Lading from the moving company very carefully before signing; check for damaged items first, as this is usually binding once signed.

HOUSING CONSIDERATIONS

Home ownership is a cornerstone of the life that Aussies dream of for themselves, bringing visions of backyard cricket, barbecues, and bustling preparation for expeditions to the beach or bush. The strong tradition of typical Aussie life is the house in the suburbs, and most people keep to this tradition if they can afford it.

But an increasing number are choosing the rental path, primarily in recognition of the high cost of Australian housing, the traffic congestion in the outer suburbs, and a growing enjoyment of inner-city dwelling among young professionals. For expats, as well, there is the risk of getting caught in the wrong segment of the real estate cycle, and "buy high, sell low" is an unappetizing formula that drives many short-term immigrants to the rental market.

The best way to "find" a dream home is to work at it a bit, and as a general rule, allow for six months to find your home from time of arrival if buying,

© MITCHELL CHESHER

and allow 3–4 weeks if renting. That time will be used to measure a few key items—primarily commuting time and accessibility to work and shopping, not to mention a little due diligence on schools and local services—before taking the plunge into a lease or contract.

Housing Options

APARTMENTS

Apartments are known as "flats" in Australia, and a "flat" is advertised "to let" when it is available for rent. For some reason, generations of Aussie school-children find great delight in inserting an "i" in between "to" and "let" on signs that are posted on building doors and in windows; if you see a sign saying "toilet" where there shouldn't be one, have a second look, as your dream home may in fact await you within.

As a general rule, flats in Australia are always advertised in weekly rental prices, so don't get too excited when you see a "killer" rate. Flats are generally in low-rise blocks and as a standard rule have no air-conditioning or built-in heating, but have nice, sunny balconies. There is an increasing number of towers with large numbers of flats, especially in more modern sections of the inner city and along the Gold Coast of Queensland, but six stories or fewer is usually the limit for buildings.

COMMON AUSTRALIAN HOUSING TERMS

In housing, Australia sometimes shows its British heritage, and some terms may be unfamiliar to immigrants from the U.S. and other non-U.K. regions. Here's a glossary of typical terminology:

- **agent:** realtor
- **building society:** savings and loan bank
- **conveyance:** due diligence or inspection period
- **flat:** an apartment
- **exchange contracts:** following agreement on price, the term for making a real estate contract

- **garden flat:** ground-floor apartment with a courtyard area
- **ground floor:** In Australia, the ground floor is considered a distinct floor, so that a high-rise block of flats will have a ground floor and a first floor.
- **let:** rent ("flats to let" is the same as "apartments to rent")
- **settlement:** real estate closing
- **solicitor:** commercial lawyer
- **strata unit:** condominium
- **unit:** apartment

Typical flats have small, fairly rudimentary kitchens—basic appliances such as a stove and refrigerator are included, but microwaves are something you will buy and bring. Bathrooms are small and will generally not have stand-alone showers, but will have either a built in shower/tub (newer) or a freestanding tub with jury-rigged shower appliances. Sinks generally do not have built-in disposals and are known to clog easily. Most windows are of the single-pane type, so they can blow in during extreme weather and allow a lot of cold to seep in during the winters. Heating will be provided by freestanding space heaters except in very high-end or newer buildings, and dressing warmly in winter is standard Aussie fare. Closets are generally tiny, and in many older flats you will need to buy a freestanding wardrobe to hold your clothes. Washers are usually shared within a building, or launderettes are used, while dryers are rare and line drying is the most common (again, except for very new or very high-end accommodations). Elevators, known as "lifts," are rare, and almost never seen except in buildings six stories or higher.

As in most countries, the higher the floor the bigger the floor space, the better the view, and the higher the price. Penthouses are generally on the top floor and may include rooftop garden areas, although many of these are open to all residents by custom or rule. Most apartments have a courtyard area used for barbecuing and drying the laundry, but only new or high-end building

© MITCHELL CHESHER

With the major Australian cities all situated by major rivers and the ocean, extensive numbers of people live within steps of the waterfront.

have amenities such as fitness rooms and swimming pools. For most renters, it's "head for the beach." Parking is in short supply, and for smaller buildings and older ones, street parking may be required. Pets are generally not OK, but older buildings tend to be more pet-friendly, and small dogs and cats are sometimes just fine. For pet lovers in a "no pet zone," by all means put bird feeders on your balcony; depending on your location, you will have an amazing assortment of Aussie birdlife eating out of your hand, from brilliant rosellas and lorikeets to elegant cockatoos and galahs.

Crime is an increasing if not pressing problem in Australian cities, and care should be taken with lower-floor flats that windows and doors are locked, particularly in areas near portable electronics such as iPods and laptops. "Smash and grab" is not common, but it does occur, and this is a factor to consider when looking at less expensive inventory on lower floors, in marginal neighborhoods, or in older buildings.

One more thing. The number-one thing people forget to check is the water pressure; yet, who isn't annoyed by the lack of it? Many homes in Australia—especially those with newer plumbing—have technologies in place to reduce water consumption. Toilets have a two-button flush system, and not everyone is a fan of the systems as multiple flushes are often required in older units. Also, showers can have restricted water pressure, so make sure you like what you have.

Short-Term Apartments

Hotel apartments are a growing trend in Oz. They are used generally for stays of less than six months and offer a hotel-like range of amenities, including access to swimming pools and fitness centers, plus inner-city locations convenient to offices for commuters. In some cases they offer maid service, which is pricey but enjoyable for those who can afford it. Expect to pay roughly 60–100 percent more for a hotel apartment than a comparatively sized traditional apartment in the same neighborhood.

SINGLE-FAMILY HOMES

One really good thing about housing in Oz is that, while prices will vary a great deal from market to market, the look and type of single-family housing is generally the same across all sectors, except for the absence of a true Victorian-style historic district in Canberra.

In all cities, there are the inner-city suburbs that feature smaller homes, often of the narrow Victorian row house type. If "gentrified" neighborhoods are to your liking for their Victorian row architecture and access to services and nightlife, Sydney and Melbourne are full of options.

Farther out are the suburbs from the early to mid-20th century, typically featuring small single-story houses on small lots, with terra-cotta tile roofing. These houses sometimes needing a remodel to get contemporary closet space installed or bedrooms and bathrooms expanded to modern size.

For this reason, additions are relatively common in this band of the city. In the farthest commuter suburbs, some very large and modern homes are intermixed with many smaller "starter" home developments, generally better planned for access to main highways and shopping areas. Finally, in each city there are magnificent waterfront homes—especially the majestic harborside homes of Sydney—that combine extensive gardens with spacious and gracious living.

One thing you won't notice is a lot of HVAC; forced air heating and cooling is becoming more popular and is very common in offices, but open doors, fans, and space heaters are the order of the day in many Aussie homes, especially the older type.

STUDENT ACCOMMODATIONS

Student accommodations are rare in Australian university settings; typically, students live at home or in shared flats or houses near the universities. Some limited dormitory-type accommodation is available, but institutions such as fraternities and sororities do not exist. For younger students on exchange programs, typically accommodation is provided via a guest stay in an Australian home. Boarding school is also an option for schoolchildren between 6 and 17, although the institution is waning in popularity and expensive. Typically, boarding is for students whose families live in remote parts of the bush. Most boarding schools are single-gender, private schools that offer dormitory-style accommodations in houses that include a range of ages, so that a student lives in the same house during his or her entire tenure at the school.

ROOMMATES

Sharing a flat is hugely common in Australia, particularly for twentysomethings. Typically these are collections of friends or referrals-from-friends, or family members, but occasionally a vacancy occurs and the word goes around via bulletin boards (electronic and physical) or occasionally newspaper ads. Men and women sharing apartments is fairly common, and "flatmates" set their own rules as far as payments, use of facilities, etc. Smoking is not common in Oz any more, and smokers should expect a smaller range of options and to smoke outside.

Renting

In Australia, no flat is going to be ideal in location, price, and amenities. Australian real estate can be expensive in good areas, compared to cities in other parts of the world, and so compromises on quality may be required depending on your budget. The important thing is to focus on those aspects that are important to you and "don't sweat the small stuff." Once you see the flat or house you like, by all means go for it—never wait for the market to change. A good flat doesn't stay on the market very long, and price changes happen far too gradually to make up for feeling like a gypsy when you are looking for your home. Negotiation is frowned on in Australia, unlike in other countries, so keep that in mind when you are asking for extra considerations or a lower

DAILY LIFE

GREEN LIVING AND ENERGY EFFICIENCY

Australia is an eco-friendly country with a strong emphasis on recycling, preservation, and environmental protection. Here are some typical tactics.

Solarize. Install a solar hot-water system, and a solar heating system if you want heat. Although solar power usually cannot generate enough heat to take care of an American home during winter cold, it does well for Australia.

Awnings. Put broad awnings on your home to shade the fierce Aussie summer sun, providing some relief from harsh sunlight as well as cooling the house.

Window placement. Large vertical windows facing northward (compared to southward, as in the United States) will maximize warmth in the winter when the sun is low and be shielded from the light when the sun is high in the summer.

Light bulbs. Compact fluorescent light bulbs last as long as five years.

Electronics. Turn off computers and other "stand-by" electronics while at work. Most people keep their home computers on during the day, while they are at work. This adds to the electric load, and during peak capacity times during the day, your power company may have to use greenhouse gas-emitting coal-fired electricity to keep the power on. You can reduce this by turning off stand-by electronics such as chargers, computers, and iPods.

Recycle. Every major city has a recycling program; get involved in it. Plus, create a compost heap in your backyard using vegetable matter, grass clippings, leaves and so on. Rather than burning or tossing, you can renew your soil with the compost after a few months using an inexpensive composter.

price. It's not unknown to negotiate, but generally it is fairly easy to offend someone if you are not well versed in the culture enough to know when you have really found the "final price."

Especially in the inner city, not only look at the home, but also listen to the noise (especially imagine what commuter noise is like), and ask about water restrictions and test the showers and toilets. Make sure you know as much as possible about how it will feel to live in the apartment.

Other questions to ask:

What rules and restrictions are in place? Ask for a copy of the bylaws or house rules to determine if you can live within them. No point in paying extra for a flat with a swimming pool if your kids can't swim in it.

Are there many move-ins and move-outs per year? First, they are disruptive. Second, lots of movement could be a sign of trouble.

Is there enough closet space and storage space? Will you have to buy wardrobes and lockers?

Is there enough outdoor space? Is it safe for your family? Are there enough barbecue spaces, or chairs at the tables, or laundry lines for the wash?

How good is security? Are there locks on the main doors, and a squawk box to let guests in via the push of a button? Guards are very rare except at the largest or most high-end buildings.

What are the maintenance arrangements? Is there a handyman associated or employed with the property who can handle small jobs?

What will the commute be like? How far is it to public transport? How long is the commute to the city? Are there dedicated school buses, or will the kids walk to school or have to use public transport (or worse, get rides). Generally speaking, the farther from the city, the better rail transit becomes over buses.

REAL ESTATE AGENTS AND LEASING

Generally speaking, renters list with agents, and local agencies represent the landlord and post opportunities in their windows and (increasingly) online. The best way to work this is to travel to the suburbs, park in the main shopping area, and cruise the main shopping streets, where you will see a number of real estate offices with rentals posted on the windows. It's an old-fashioned technique but it still pays dividends, as good places don't last long and sometimes don't make it online.

For students, universities maintain departments that specialize in student accommodations, and they maintain list of inventory available with registered landlords. That's a good basic technique for weeding out any nasty landlords, as the uni will take landlords off the list if there are excessive complaints.

FINDING A PLACE ON YOUR OWN

Most people work through friends if they are hunting on their own. Online can be a good place to start, but keep in mind that flats and homes are listed by suburb instead of by city. "Sydney apartments" is not a good search term in Oz; use "flat to let in Manly," "Neutral Bay flat," "Glebe roommate," etc., instead.

MOVING IN

Before move-in, test absolutely everything: every outlet, switch, appliance, light, shower head, toilet, and door. Make a list before physical move-in and get repairs done right away while the landlord is available and motivated. There are rental companies such as U-Haul for a truck, but use a friend if you can because rental vehicles can be daunting and you have to watch extremely carefully the height of bridges and overpasses. Australian coastal areas, especially around Sydney, are full of short, sharp hills, and many of the old overpasses are lower than U-Haul rooflines, so it can be a recipe for delay or disaster.

Buying

If you have enough time in Australia to consider buying a home (typically a minimum of three years) and the real estate prices are within your means, definitely buy a house if you can. There's no better way to enjoy the full-on Aussie experience than in your own home, with your own backyard (the "true home of Aussie cricket").

PRICES

The Australian dollar is worth nearly twice what it was 10 years ago, compared to the U.S. dollar, and this means that large-scale asset purchases such as real estate are expensive, because current assets in the United States may not translate well into Australian dollars. Real estate will generally cost five to seven times the median annual income, with Melbourne the highest on this scale at seven times. In the United States, by comparison, the average is around three times. The most expensive cities are Sydney and Perth. The average home in Sydney sold in 2007 for $553,000, while Melbourne was third at $463,000.

DAILY LIFE

© MITCHELL CHESHER

Many Aussies combine waterfront residence and boat ownership; the country has one of the highest incidences of boat ownership in the world.

REAL ESTATE AGENTS AND CONTRACTS

Real estate is generally sold in the same manner as in the United States, with agents working on 6 percent commissions and generally representing the seller, and splitting the commission with the buyer's agent if there is one. The major real estate agencies are LJ Hooker (www.ljhooker.com.au), Real Estate Australia (www.realestate.com.au), Coldwell Banker (www.coldwellbanker.com.au), and Century 21 (www.century21.com.au), and they are also the best means of obtaining a recommendation for a real estate solicitor (attorney) who has experience in the local area. There are no restrictions on buying property in Australia as a permanent resident. Temporary residents can buy new houses, such as ones in the preconstruction phase.

The process works just a little different in Australia than elsewhere, and a real estate attorney is usually involved. The first step is to agree on the price, and then you "exchange contracts," which is the actual contract of sale and establishes not only the price but the move-in date and special conditions. You then have a "cooling off period," which varies from state to state (except in Western Australia, where there isn't one), followed by the "conveyancing," which is the equivalent of due diligence or the inspection period in other countries. Following conveyancing and financing, you proceed to "settlement," which is the same as a "closing" in the United States.

In Australia, land is freehold just as in the United States, with the exception of land in the Australian Capital Territory, which is held under 99-year

Crown leases, which would be extended after expiration upon payment of an administrative fee.

COMMUTING

Imagine a circle around your place of work that is drawn not in miles, but in minutes. This circle represents the travel time from work to home, and studies have shown that long-term happiness in a new home is dependent on having a commute of less than 30 minutes for each adult. The best way to understand the commute is to try it—so, if possible, drive from your intended residence to work (or return) during commuting hours. If it takes more than 30 minutes, think again. After an 8–9-hour workday, long commutes create problems, not only at work but at home. Also, consider that the average homeowner stays seven years in the new home but only five years at the job—so consider to the best of your ability whether the next job is likely to be in a favorable commuting pattern as well.

NEIGHBORS

No one tells you about nasty neighbors—for one thing, what is nasty to you may not bother someone else. Short of running background checks on the neighbors, there are some telltale signs of unhappiness, and the best sign to look for is a high turnover rate on houses (look at the number of "for sale"

DAILY LIFE

WATER EFFICIENCY

Australia is dry, dry, dry, and water restrictions are cruel and may become crueler. Here are some things you might install or see already in your home.

Use less water by installing a water-saving showerhead – these restrict water usage to nine liters per minute, or about two gallons. Another water-saving device is a two-button flush toilet, with the second button for the less-intensive flush needs.

Use gray water, which is waste water from a washing machine, shower, bath, or sink – everything except the kitchen and toilet. You can put in a gray-water treatment system that allows you to collect, treat, and store gray water. There are no restrictions on the use of gray water during water restrictions, so you can use this to save a cherished garden or lawn when everyone else's is browning into dust. You can't pipe gray water directly into the garden – you need a treatment or irrigation system. If you don't treat the water, you have to use it right away.

signs in the neighborhood if this is a resale); a large number of new neighbors increases the risk of a bad dog, bad teenager, or bad adult moving in nearby. A second tactic is to drive through the neighborhood at 10 P.M. on a Friday or Saturday night (or walk through the apartment building). The noise and activity level will tell you "volumes." Nasty, noisy, or nosy neighbors are a major source of unhappiness for new residents.

SCHOOLS

If you have children or are planning to (and keep in mind that the average new homeowner stays for seven years), schools are a huge issue. There is no substitute for test scores, and your school will be able to provide them, or ask your relocation consultant or real estate agent if you have one. If you have high-school-age children, look not only at test scores but at graduation or "matriculation" rates. With younger children, look at teacher/student ratios (ideally 20:1 or better in grade, or "primary," school). Finally, for all ages but especially for older children, look for a lively activities program with plenty of participation from the kids—idle hands do the devil's work.

INSPECTIONS

Make sure you have the house inspected, but even in the case of an apartment check the place out, including: 1. Water pressure. 2. Adequate electrical outlets. 3. Reputable cable TV provider. 4. Quality Internet access (if it is DSL, make sure you are close to a local office, as your speed will depend on the distance). 5. Air-conditioning unit noise, and location of vents. 6. Privacy from noisy, nosy, or nasty neighbors. 6. If you are in a resident's association, you are likely to meet board members in an interview; be sure to ask them about the reserve funds—there's no better way to gauge a well-run association than by seeing if the future is well-provided for.

NEW VERSUS RESALE

In Australia, generally one looks at resale. New housing is only for those willing to live a great distance from the city. It is prohibitively far away for almost everyone except for those whose employer is based in a remote area, away from the CBD. If this applies to you, by all means try for a new home: Construction prices are high, and you will pay 10–30 percent more for a new home than for a comparative resale, but you will have the opportunity to build the house according to modern needs, instead of adapting to life as it was lived in the 1920s, or 1950s, or what have you.

If you are looking for something closer to the CBD but the inventory doesn't precisely match your need, there is always the option of remodeling. Some quick rules on Aussie remodels:

1. Get three written estimates.

2. Get references and call them, for sure. Ask about timeliness—contractors everywhere are chronically overbooked and Australia is no exception.

3. State the job as accurately as possible on the contract, and provide drawings, pictures, or schematics where possible. Make sure that the contract states exactly what is to be done and how change orders will be handled. In a dispute, your extra efforts will pay off; otherwise, you may be labeled a "pushy foreigner," and it's tough to win sympathy from judges or arbitrators if that handle is successfully put around your neck.

4. Never pay more than half up front, and try to pay just the raw cost of the materials.

5. Check your contractors' licensure, and get every permit without exception. As a foreigner, you can't fight City Hall.

6. In your contract, state the penalties for late completion clearly, and enforce them.

FINDING THE RIGHT HOME

As a new arrival, you'll need all the help you can get, so by all means get a real estate agent. However, there are a few rules of the road to observe before you select your realtor, because they specialize in very small geographies. You have to do the work of culling down a wide range of opportunities into one that is sized to an agent's expertise.

Drive neighborhoods. If you are not driving right away because you are nervous about driving on the left, by all means use public transport, and time it! Walk the main areas and see if you like them, but more importantly make sure you will be able to get to them quickly enough to enjoy them.

List your family activities, and match them with the places you visit. Especially if you are religious, look hard, because Australia is famously "at the beach" on Sundays and "can't be bothered" with church, so make sure the churches are to your liking. If you want to visit the beach or waterfront a lot, how will you get there—how will your kids get there?

Look at the schools. If you plan on private schools for your kids, just test out the commute. It's not much fun for your 13-year-old to start the daily commute at 6 A.M.! If you are going public, look at the local primary and high schools. The older buildings can be daunting learning environments. Information on school performance is available from the state department of education, so check that as well as activity programs for school, holidays, and after school.

Kids will often measure home by the proximity to good friends, and parents often measure a good home by the proximity to happy children.

Safety. Ask friends, and look online. Look beyond raw numbers to the type of activity—burglaries, robberies, violent crimes.

See for yourself. Once you've narrowed your focus to two or three neighborhoods, go there and walk around. Are homes tidy and well maintained? Are streets quiet? Pick a warm day if you can and chat with people working or playing outside. Are they friendly? Are there children to play with your family?

In general, we recommend that you give yourself six months to buy a home, consisting of 60 days for closing, 30 days to find the ideal place, and 90 days for general familiarization.

FINANCING AND MORTGAGE ISSUES

The first thing to do is to determine your borrowing power. Generally, this is around three times your salary. Use a mortgage calculator such as those at http://mortgagecalculator.com to look at your payment options based on current rates.

Mortgages are generally available at 5 to 30-year terms, and as elsewhere are available at fixed or adjustable rates (ARM). There are real estate–oriented banks called "building societies" that tend to have a good range of products; St. George Bank is probably the best known of this type. If you are looking at a stay in Australia of less than five years, the adjustable rate is probably a

Building societies are the Aussie equivalent of a savings and loan bank; the largest is St. George Bank.

good option for you if the rate is lower, as often you have a five-year lock-in period before the rate "floats." Loans are in Australian dollars, so keep this in mind if for some reason your company pays you in U.S. dollars. Typically, credit conditions are comparable to those of the United States, but as a rule real estate prices are higher relative to the average household income, so you may find yourself borrowing more than you are accustomed to.

SELLING

Generally, when it's time to leave the country, you will be in a moderate rush to get the house sold, and your period of notice from your new job back in the "old country" may not permit you to get everything accomplished as quickly as you need to. The good news is that closing is often done "remotely" now, and you can sign papers wherever you happen to be.

But here are a few things that will help speed up the sale.

Smart pricing. Ask your agent for a range of fair market values, and set your starting price at the lower end, and then try to hang on tight in negotiations.

Make your home ready for showing a week before you show it. Get an inspector from the pest company to come by and treat the house, and have your own inspector come in and do a presale inspection so you can handle small repairs while you are still around, to make sure the work is done right and at a fair price.

Be the most flexible person you can be about showings. This means clearing out of the house on a moment's notice. Never be around when buyers are—it distracts them.

Be ready in your mind with how you will deal with a low offer. Never refuse to negotiate.

Be ready. Know the name and contact info for your real estate attorney, appraiser, home inspector, mortgage loan officer, title company, insurance consultant, and moving company

Know the comparables in your area. If possible, go ahead with an appraisal, which will cost you less than $500 but will give you a strong negotiating tool to improve your price or speed up the negotiation.

Household Expenses

Generally speaking, if you're renting a place you are responsible for all your utilities unless they are advertised as included, which is rare except in roommate situations or renting a room in a house. Expect to pay a deposit, and keep in mind that Australia is 240-volt country, so U.S. appliances usually won't work (although many laptops do), so there are some upfront expenses involved. Some utilities will allow you to fund a deposit over 2–3 months. You don't need to register for mail service (unless you are forwarding mail).

If you haven't switched yet to electronic bill paying, consider doing so now. With the move, it is necessary to contact many new and current service providers, and you will make this move easier (and the next move a snap!) by switching to electronic bill paying. But you will also want to visit your post office to file a change of mailing address.

Some questions to ask yourself before move-in:

1. Are there jacks for cable TV and broadband Internet, and where?

2. Are there enough phone jacks?

3. Does the home or flat have ADSL already wired in from a company such as Big Pond? Does it have a local area network for linking computers?

Electricity, water, and gas are paid quarterly, and utilities for a two-bedroom apartment in Sydney will cost $400–600 per quarter. In addition to electricity, there are council rates, which will run about $300–400 per month for a standard two-bedroom apartment in a good suburb of Sydney (they are related to land value). Strata rates run $300–1,000 per quarter and cover garbage collection and property maintenance.

Electricity and gas have been deregulated in Australia (except in Western Australia), and you may choose the old monopoly, Energy Australia, or a competitor such as Jackgreen, Origin Energy, or AGL. AGL (www.agl.com .au) is the largest, with more than six million customers for gas and electric services. Water service is supplied by the state governments, and accounts are set up and managed online through each state water board.

LANGUAGE AND EDUCATION

Understanding the Australian idiom is without question the subject that American expats wish they had studied more prior to arrival. Americans can run into severe problems with slang, when acceptable terms in the States become vulgarities in Australia and vice-versa. While standard English is completely understood by Australians and they follow 98 percent of American idioms (because of television), Americans struggle mightily following everyday Australian conversation, which is filled with Australian idiomatic dialect. The subject of language is an important one for Australia. Although it is an English speaking country and Australians understand standard American English and even slang and idiomatic speech very well, Americans have a hard time with Australian idiomatic speech.

© ISTOCKPHOTO.COM / CLINT SCHOLZ

Learning the Language

Everyone knows the lilting, drawling Aussie accent; it is world famous from movies, commercials, and television, and it is popular. Even more delightful to hear are the strange words used in Australia. Living in splendid isolation—like the kangaroos and emus that are national symbols of the country—Aussies have developed not only an accent, but an entire idiomatic vocabulary that can be wonderful to appreciate, frustrating at times to deal with.

Aside from the accent itself, which can vary between city and country, and by social class, Australia has three types of differentiation in language: there are slang expressions that are common to nearly all Australians; there is rhyming slang, which crosses some social and geographic boundaries and is nearly universally understood if not used; and there is Strine, the "ocker" accent and vocabulary that at times feels like a whole new dialect, so replete it is with unique expressions and words.

SLANG

All Australians use Aussie slang extensively, right from the first "g'day" to the last "righto." Like all slang, phrases common in one generation do not always cross over to the next. Aussies don't really call each other "cobber" except on rare and often ironic occasions, despite the universal presence of the word in dictionaries of common Aussie slang terms. "Righto" is itself fading out, although it's been popular for several generations. Words like "swagman" and "billabong" that feature in popular songs like "Waltzing Matilda" are no longer in common usage.

But mastering slang is essential to following even average-length conversations of moderate complexity.

The first thing is to get a decent online or printed dictionary of slang and read it through once in its entirety, just to familiarize yourself with the sound of the phrases and words. A good example is at www.koalanet.com .au/australian-slang.html.

Next, keep an ear out for unusual words from Aussies you know, write them down if you like, and look them up. You'll find, for example, that some examples of slang are impossible to figure out logically. Aussies say "stoush" where you say "fight" or "brouhaha." Some slang expressions, on the other hand, make perfect sense; for example, Aussies express some diminutives in "o" rather than "y," so that the friendly garbage collector is a "garbo" and afternoon is "arvo," but football is "footy."

In general, the use of Australian slang words by new arrivals is a no-no;

it's just too difficult to understand the nuances, and a well-meant phrase can give offense. Generally speaking, the use of diminutives and basic words like "g'day" are safe to use when around "yer mates."

Certain words that are common elsewhere should not be used in Australia: fanny, root (as in "root for Yale"), and bung or boong (as in "I bunged my car right into the wall"). They have bad or vulgar meanings in the Australian idiom. "Bastard" can be a term of affection in Australia, but avoid trying to use it.

Rhyming Slang

Then there is the prevalent rhyming slang of Australia, which needs to be explained so that Americans understand that "have a Captain Cook" is rhyming slang for "have a look." Rhyming slang is often combined with the diminutive: Yank rhymes with septic tank, which becomes "seppo," a derisive slang term for Americans. Trouble becomes "rubble," then "Barney Rubble," which becomes "barney," so that a friend in barney needs your help. Plates of meat are "feet," and so on. It's colorful and is learned example by example.

Strine

Beyond Australian slang, which is common to most Australians, there is an extensive vocabulary and a strongly drawled accent known as Strine. Someone who speaks Strine is an "ocker" (pronounced "OCK-ah"). In phonic circles, Strine is known as the Broad Australian English and generally reflects the working class. The classic ocker says "youse" for the plural of "you," "good on ya" for "well done," and uses "me" instead of "my" as in "tie me kangaroo down, sport."

LANGUAGE SCHOOLS

Standard English is universally understood in Australian life. While some care must be taken to learn the considerable vocabulary of Australian idiomatic speech and Strine, language classes for newcomers focus almost entirely on serving the population coming from non-English-speaking countries.

Education

The Australian school year is different, and how this is handled is hugely important for relocating families, as students arriving in May face repeating an entire year of school or having to miss the initial three months of the next grade. Americans will also find the minimum standard for mathematics much more difficult, and the widespread attendance of private schools requires parents to study up on the topic of schools much more than is typical in the United States.

COLLEGES AND UNIVERSITIES

In Australia, the basic structure of tertiary education includes graduate education, professional education, and undergraduate education known as "uni," and also the Technical and Further Education (TAFE) system, or "tech." Tech draws students aiming for trades and in some cases professionals, especially those looking for specialized courses, or for teaching certificates or continuing education credits.

University in Australia is generally three years for an undergraduate degree in arts or sciences, with an additional year required for an "honors" degree. Professional degrees such as law and medicine are also three-year programs. Most major universities offer an option for students to take a combined undergraduate and professional degree program simultaneously, and students who select, say, arts/law, for example, graduate in five years with two degrees, a BA and an LLB. Professional degree are usually accompanied by additional postgraduate study via internships or six-month law training at the College of Law before professional certification is issued.

Admissions are handled centrally for Australian students, through a University Admissions Center. The UAC processes all high school test scores against program quotas established by the universities, and then checks the personal preferences of the students before determining where they will study. Foreign students can apply directly to a school, which gives them more freedom to follow their hearts.

Student Housing

Student housing on campus is rare in Australia. The Australian National University (ANU) is an exception, and it guarantees a place in one of the university's student residential halls. For the most part, students live at home or get private accommodation near the campus. Universities all offer roommate-finding help as well as bulletin boards, which support "flat wanted" and "flat to let" notices. Financial assistance for housing is sometimes available in the form of work-study programs or "in need" grants. Additionally, large-scale apartment complexes catering to students are typically run independently of the university but closely align themselves in terms of making information available on the university website.

ANU in Canberra is a significant exception and offers a number of residence halls; it is highly welcoming of international students.

Financing

Australian students are subsidized heavily by the government. The commonwealth subsidizes tertiary education by offering a number of Commonwealth Supported Places (CSP) to each university or TAFE. The numbers and subsidies differ from university to university, but there are three "bands" of support plus a "national priority" band, which offers the highest subsidy.

Student contribution ranges from $0 to around $8,000 depending on the band, and this can be covered by an interest-free Higher Education Loan Program (HELP) loan, in which deferred repayment commences after graduation. Students are eligible for CSP places for up to seven years. Thereafter, they can continue their studies on a full-fee basis of as much as $20,000–30,000 per year, depending on the course of study, but they can continue to receive scholarships or HELP loans. HELP loans are capped at $80,000 for most courses, or $100,000 for medicine, dentistry, and veterinary sciences. Once CSP is exhausted and HELP limits have been reached, students can continue to take courses on a full-fee basis.

CSP and HELP are available to all Australian citizens and to permanent residents in many cases.

INTERNATIONAL UNIVERSITY STUDENTS

The typical application process for foreign students includes completing an application and shipping the transcript and recommendation letters. Application deadlines are typically by the end of October for undergraduate study; graduate student applications are continuously reviewed.

Australian universities offer all programs to international students. In Australian university, basic university degrees are three-year programs with a degree in arts, science, health, education, social studies, or business. A fourth year may be taken as an honors year. Typically, students take several subject concentrations in year one and become focused on a single subject by the third and final year. Undergraduate degrees may be combined with professional degree studies, so that double degrees such as a BA/LLB may be earned over five years by applying law courses as electives courses within the arts degree program. Similarly, medicine and veterinary studies can be taken directly out of high school.

Transferring Credits

Australian universities are internationally accredited, and credits are generally transferable. There are sometimes credit-hour adjustments made with respect to converting Australian semester credits to quarterly credits at other

DAILY LIFE

institutions, and individual institutions will make determinations on how Australian classes apply toward specialized requirements such as required courses in a major concentration.

Tuition
International students are not subsidized by the federal government and will pay as much as $20,000 per year for a degree program. Scholarships are offered by each university, as well as operating a jobs bank. A university will operate a jobs bank, in which local employers, including the university itself, government and private enterprise will list available jobs for students and graduates. These job banks are typically online, or published on a physical bulletin board, often by a university department and/or at a student union building. International students are not eligible for the Commonwealth Supported Places (CSP) subsidy program or for Higher Education Loan Program (HELP) loans, but they can receive grants and scholarships as financial aid.

STUDY ABROAD
Many Australian universities offer a study abroad year or semester. These are full-fee opportunities, typically taken after a year of university, and require the maintenance of passing grades, plus proficiency in English. Specialized course loads offer opportunities to study Australian history, culture, business, health, or education subjects, and internships are sometimes made available to extend the experience.

PRIMARY AND SECONDARY SCHOOLS
Primary school in Australia is typically kindergarten through year 6, with "kindy" through year 2 students supervised through a specialized "infants" department. Australian secondary schools, or high schools, vary somewhat from state to state, but the basic national standard is six years of secondary school, years 7–12.

States have recently completed a switch from a three-term to a four-term system. Typically, students will have two weeks off in April, July, late September and followed by 6–8 weeks in the summer (January–February).

For many years, Aussie students were allowed to leave school after year 10, typical for the trades and factories. As global competitiveness increases, educators have required students to complete year 12.

For expats, one of the potential areas for trouble is having children complete high school in Australia and then apply to universities in the United States and elsewhere without the benefit of a traditional high school grade point average. Since Australia does not issue traditional grades, but rather bases university entrance on scores achieved in comprehensive examinations taken at the end of year 12, the incompatibility of systems can create confusion. However, the SAT exam is offered in each major city, and non-Australian universities are becoming more adept at evaluating international student applications.

Public vs. Private School

About one-third of Australian students in secondary school attend a private school. Most of these are attending Catholic schools, and about one-quarter attend mainstream Protestant denomination schools. The remainder attend independent private schools. For many years, the Australian government has subsidized private school education, so fees have historically been well below what they are at comparable private schools in the United States, although the plummeting U.S. dollar has made Aussie private schools more expensive

THE OLD SCHOOL TIE

Throughout the pages of this book, we have talked about the egalitarian nature of Australian society. So why are so many children – up to 40 percent in some cities – sent to private schools?

Primarily, the decision to send children to private school is for religious reasons (the majority go to private Catholic schools), or for the superior education that many parents presume is available at expensive institutions with smaller class sizes and more freedom on curriculum, and committed students backed by committed parents.

But secondarily, elite Australian private schools offer some professional and social advantages that are declining in value but undeniable. A school's membership in an elite association, such as Sydney's Great Public Schools, is a "brand" with some value in terms of making connections, and students who attend these institutions will find some level of access in career-building, as well as social engagements, that is certainly not impossible for public school students, just more difficult. It is often said that great students will succeed in any school, but it is the middling students who benefit from the associations formed on school sport grounds or in school clubs or activities.

In the end, we live in a globalized world, and the marginal advantage of "the old school tie" is increasingly debatable. The author of this book is yet to meet a fellow alumnus of his private school in more than 20 years abroad, or gain an advantage in business or life by a connection through school. However, he cheerfully admits that the happiest aspect of growing up in "The Lucky Country" was his six years at Sydney Grammar.

than ever. Annual tuition ranges $5,000–25,000, and boarding school fees can push this to more than $30,000. Boarding is less popular at the present time, except for students from remote country areas. Typically, private schools have slightly longer holiday periods, have stronger academic results, have smaller class sizes, and offer more depth in religious education. Private schools continue to offer some limited benefits in social status, although the gap is closing as the country continues to become more egalitarian. Many employers offer subsidies, and the schools themselves offer numerous scholarships based on merit or need.

The majority of Australian schools are coeducational, but most private secondary schools and some "selective" or "magnet" public secondary schools are restricted to either boys or girls. Typically, primary school is coeducational, and all universities are.

Study Requirements

In Australia, secondary school students have core requirements in mathematics and, not surprisingly, Australian history and literature that are more rigorous than studies in these areas in other countries. Plus, Australian students receive less education in foreign literature and history than they would in, for example, the United States. Expat parents often supplement secondary school with special lessons in language or history, typically offered by a private tutor or through a local expat association such as the Australian-American Association.

Uniforms

Uniforms are less prevalent now in Australia than in the past, but virtually all schools have a dress code, and more than half of schools have formal uniforms at the primary and secondary school level. These tend to be more formal at private schools (which often have fairly ornate dress uniforms, sport uniforms, and winter and summer uniforms as well). Winter uniforms typically add cardigan pull-overs, scarves, jackets, and ties to the summer uniform. Each school has its own uniform policy and typically has made arrangements with local retailers to supply uniforms, and a lively second-hand market exists at most schools.

HOME SCHOOLING

Home schooling is growing in popularity in Australia, but the numbers are still only in the thousands, or less than 2 percent of school-age children The majority of home-schooled children come from active Christian families at this time. Home schooling is regulated at the state level, and states require registration and a description of a program of studies. There are local service providers who assist with program development. Students can pursue university studies after home schooling through the Open Training and Education Network (OTEN) program offered through TAFE colleges, essentially the same as correspondence or online students. Also, in Australia, students past the age of 25 can apply as "mature age" students, in which case an interview is typically substituted for scores in standard exams.

The Home Education Association (Australia) is the major association promoting home schooling and offering information about options and requirements (www.hea.asn.au).

DAILY LIFE

HEALTH

For more than a generation, Australia has had a national health scheme, called Medicare, which can be called a success in terms of ensuring affordable care for all. The knock on Medicare is that the lines to see a physician and the wait times for elective surgery can be cruelly long, and many people choose to have elective surgery either on a cash basis or overseas.

For most Australians, health care means "think national, act local," which is to say that the national health scheme is run at the federal level, but hospitals, clinics, and the actual daily practice of health care are regulated and supervised at the state level. This means that there are variances between health care quality and availability from state to state, although these are essentially minor in character. There are significant differences in health care availability, if not quality, in the country, where the population is so diffuse that individuals can be hundreds of kilometers from urgent or elective care. But generally, Australians are far healthier, weigh less, smoke less, and live longer than Americans, despite spending less per capita on health.

© MITCHELL CHESHER

Medicare can be supplemented by private health insurance, through Medibank or other health insurance providers. It also has a Pharmaceutical Benefits Scheme (PBS) covering prescription medicines. Overseas students are not covered by Medicare. Medicare does not cover certain items such as ambulance transport, dental care, optical care, or physiotherapy, or offer much control over choice of physician or hospital.

Types of Insurance

PUBLIC VS. PRIVATE CARE

For many Australians, health care means registering for public health care, called Medicare (www.medicareaustralia.gov.au), and then making appointments at public clinics, dental offices, and hospitals as needed. For those who desire "gap" insurance and can afford it, the primary providers are Medibank and HCF. There are a number of other private health care providers, which most Australians learn about through their employer, who may offer supplemental insurance on a subsidized basis or provide access to group rates.

Medicare

The basic national health scheme is known as Medicare, and it is free, national, universal health care. Or, rather, it is paid for via a 1.5 percent income tax surcharge and other commonwealth revenues, plus an additional 1 percent levy on those with incomes over $50,000. Medicare is open to Australian citizens and permanent residents, from birth, and requires only registration and proof of identity. Medicare allows individuals to access primary health care at clinics, screenings, and both inpatient and outpatient care at public hospitals for both urgent and elective procedures. Patients can expect long wait times—excruciatingly long wait times for appointments and for elective surgery—and woe betide if you miss an appointment. Hospital care is ward-style or in semiprivate rooms. In short, it's a fairly basic but comprehensive system of health care, and Australian doctors, although busy, are well trained and internationally respected.

Medicare does not cover dental care except in limited circumstances, such as jaw reconstruction following an accident. Australians receive a Medicare card, which entitles patients to subsidized care at private hospitals and clinics. At these institutions, Medicare will cover between 75 and 85 percent of the basic health care cost, and private insurance picks up the rest.

To enroll in Medicare after receiving your permanent residence visa, you can visit a Medicare office with your passport and immigration papers. You will receive your Medicare ID card and immediate access to services. You may then register for online services and process updated address information, replace lost cards, and so on, via the web.

Medibank

Australians who choose to supplement their Medicare with additional coverage may do so through Medibank (http://medibank.com.au), or through another private health care provider. Medibank was originally a private health care insurer owned by the federal government, but it has been slated for privatization. About 30 percent of all private health insurance is through Medibank, which offers supplements to cover the gap between Medicare coverage and cost, including the additional coverage at private hospitals and with private practitioners, and covers higher charges that are imposed (over the Medicare cap) by certain private practitioners for their services. Medibank is also an insurer who can offer coverage for those not covered by Medicare, such as temporary residents and students.

Several other major private insurers, such as HCF (http://HCF.com.au), offer comparable services.

HOSPITALS AND CLINICS

Each Australian state has a Department of Health, which supervises the operations of public hospitals and clinics and regulates private hospitals and clinics. Typically, the cities have a number of both public and private hospitals, and clinics are located throughout the city. All the major universities associate with a major hospital as a teaching hospital, and these are quite accessible from the campus.

In the country, hospitals are regional in character, and there may be a drive of a few hundred kilometers to reach one, although urgent care is provided at local clinics, which are found in most towns with at least 10,000 in population. In truly remote Outback areas, services are provided by the Royal Flying Doctor Service, which brings doctors by plane to provide on-site care.

INTERNATIONAL COVERAGE

Several countries have signed reciprocal health-care agreements with Australia, which cover visitors and other temporary residents from Ireland, New Zealand, United Kingdom, Sweden, Finland, Norway, the Netherlands, Malta, and Italy. Coverage differs based on the reciprocal agreement, but generally visitors are covered for at least six months. Students are required to take out

AUSTRALIAN MEDICAL TERMS

"Two cultures divided by a common language" is something you may hear from an Aussie, referring to Australia and the U.K., or Oz and America. It comes to mind when thinking about medical treatment. Here are a few tips and translations:

- In Australia, a nurse is often called a sister.
- A doctor's office is called a "surgery."
- A Band-Aid is called a "sticking plaster."
- When you feel sick, people will say you "feel crook."
- You don't say fanny, you say "bum." Fanny is something else, very vulgar.
- A tampon is a "sanitary napkin," which may be why many Aussies say "serviette" instead of napkin.
- Alternative medicine is called "herbal medicine."
- A car accident is called (by some) a "bingle."
- A pharmacist is called a "chemist."

A good place to check out regional variations is the ABC Australian Word Map, at www.abc.net.au/wordmap.

Overseas Student Health Cover (OSHC) when visiting on a student visa, and are thereby covered through Medicare.

Pharmacies and Preventative Medicine

PHARMACEUTICAL BENEFITS SCHEME (PBS)

The PBS gives you access to subsidized pharmaceutical products upon prescription. Participation is automatic if you qualify for Medicare or come from a country with a reciprocal health agreement. Typically, your copay is around $30 for prescriptions, but pensioners, veterans, and seniors get a special concession card that entitles them to a $5 copay.

MEDICAL RECORDS

Medical records are maintained via a national electronic scheme called Health-Connect, which is intended to facilitate the flow of information without compromising your health record privacy. Instances of privacy being compromised are relatively rare.

In Australia, a pharmacy is known as a chemist.

VACCINATIONS

The Australian Childhood Immunization Register, at www1.hic.gov.au/general/acircirgacir, is the most important tool for tracking vaccination projects for young people. Children are registered at birth or upon arrival when they register for Medicare. The following vaccination schedule is provided by the Australian government: Birth: Hepatitis B; 2 months: Diphtheria, Tetanus, Pertussis, Polio, Hib, Hepatitis B, Pneumococcal, Rotavirus; 6 months: Diphtheria, Tetanus, Pertussis, Polio, Hib, Hepatitis B, Pneumococcal, Rotavirus; 12 months: Measles, Mumps, Rubella, Hib, Meningococcal C; 18 months: Varicella; 4 years: Diphtheria, Tetanus, Pertussis, Polio, Measles, Mumps, Rubella. Vaccinations are not required for adults.

ALTERNATIVE THERAPIES

Herbal medicine (known elsewhere as holistic treatment, naturotherapy, or alternative treatment) is widely popular, with more than 50 percent of Australians having sought or obtained herbal medicines or treatment. About two-thirds of these have taken herbal supplements or medicines. A good overview of the herbal medicine industry is found at www.intstudy.com/articles/twealtmd.htm. Generally, some herbal medicines and alternative treatments are covered by private insurance. To find an accredited herbalist, a good resource is at www.nhaa.org.au.

HERBAL MEDICINE

Australia is perhaps the western country that has accepted and embraced herbal medicine and traditional medicine more than any other. Massage therapists, herbalists, acupuncturists, homeopaths, naturopaths, and nutritionists have a strong following in The Lucky Country.

According to research, more than 50 percent of Aussies consult an herbalist or use alternative therapy treatments, so there's a good chance you will encounter an herbalist in your time in Australia. They are widely well regarded.

A number of institutions license and train in these studies, including the Australian Institute of Holistic Medicine, Melbourne College of Natural Medicine, Newcastle College of Herbal Medicine, NSW College of Natural Therapies, Perth Academy of Natural Therapies, Queensland Institute of Natural Sciences, the South Australian College of Natural Therapies, and the Sydney College of TCM.

According to the National Herbalists Association of Australia, "A medical herbalist: is highly trained in the philosophies, principles, and practice of western herbal medicine and medical science; takes a holistic view toward health and illness; will assess you as a person and not a disease; prescribes and dispenses plant medicines in a safe and effective manner; seeks to treat the underlying cause of disease; acknowledges the body's innate ability to heal itself; aims to prevent disease and restore health; provides dietary and lifestyle advice; maintains high standards of professional practice; and is an authoritative source of information about natural medicine."

Environmental Factors

AIR QUALITY AND SUN INTENSITY

Australia has a large ozone depletion associated with the ozone hole over the Antarctic, and the sun is quite intense as a result. Not to mention that Australia is a highly sunny country with low moisture and a culture that celebrates being outdoors as much as possible. Bottom line: Australia has the highest skin cancer rate in the world, and more than 80 percent of all diagnosed cancers are skin cancers. Govern yourself accordingly, by applying lots of sunscreen, or zinc cream if you have very light skin. Keep sun exposure to a minimum by wearing headgear if outside for more than 30 minutes. A classic Aussie Akubra hat (www.akubra.com) will be stylish, authentically Australian, and highly protective.

In terms of overall air quality, the cities are affected by smog and temperature inversions in wintertime that trap particulates near the ground instead of letting them escape into the upper atmosphere. This, combined with the low

© MITCHELL CHESHER

Outdoor play for youngsters is hugely encouraged throughout the country, and local suburbs are typically replete with options.

amount of rainfall, means Australia has a lot of soot in the air. The country areas, by contrast, are quite clear, and by no means is Australia beset by pollution problems comparable to those in China or the United States.

WATER QUALITY AND CONSERVATION

"Water, water everywhere, and not a drop to drink" is a phrase that easily comes to mind in Australia, which has some of the largest desert areas in the world and extremely low rainfall rates as a continental average. Australia is the driest inhabited continent, second only to Antarctica. Aussies conserve water far more diligently than most cultures, and water restrictions preventing lawn watering are near universal and permanent in many areas. Garden watering is highly restricted, and many cities have serious water restrictions in place, limiting family water usage for home use. New Australian homes have a two-button flush system for toilets (which sometimes backfires, by requiring two flushes), and many homes are being converted to low-intensity washers and two-button toilets to save water.

In rural areas, agricultural use of water in irrigation has nearly emptied Australia's longest river, the Murray, which is down to a muddy trickle for much of its course. Restrictions on usage for commercial and industrial plants are very severe, and residents also feel the pinch through every-other-day watering restrictions at a minimum, total daylight watering bans, and sometimes total watering bans.

SMOKING

Smoking is very much on the decline in Australia, dropping from a 75 percent smoking rate among men in 1945 to 25 percent today. Smoking rates among women have dropped from 33 percent in 1976 to 21 percent today. Smoking is generally banned in all public, enclosed spaces (including workplaces) in all states, except that some hotels and pubs are permitted to have designated smoking areas. Smoking is banned in all federal buildings, on public transport, in airports, and on flights.

SANITATION

The Green Party in Australia is a major force in politics, with several seats in the federal Senate as well as seats in many local councils and state legislatures, which reflects the emphasis Australians place on a clean and green Australia. About half of Australia's litter consists of cigarette butts, and generally speaking Aussies are high on clean water and streets. Renewable sources of energy such as hydro power, along with some wind and solar, are popular. However, due to water shortages, there is a concern over water quality, particularly salinity, and many programs are in place to improve water quality. Drinking water from taps (faucets) is perfectly safe, however, and it is better for the environment than drinking from nonbiodegradable plastic water bottles.

Disabled Access and Safety

ACCESS FOR PEOPLE WITH DISABILITIES

The landmark Disability Discrimination Act of 1992 makes discrimination against disabled persons illegal and established the Human Rights and Equal Opportunity Commission as the ruling authority in discrimination cases. The DDA protects disabilities of a physical, sensory, neurological, or psychiatric nature, among other categories.

The best site for information, products, and services for persons with disabilities is www.accessibility.com.au.

The DDA provides an assurance of nondiscrimination against disabled persons in terms of access to premises, employment, health care access, information and communications technology, access to art and culture, access to electronic financial services, accessible consumer electronics and appliances, and access to public transport. It is one of the most comprehensive protections in the world for those with disabilities.

POLICE

Australian police protection is provided at the state level, plus there is a police jurisdiction for the Northern Territory and the Australian Capital Territory. There is also a federal police service (Australian Federal Police, or AFP). There are more than 2,000 local police stations around Australia, 500 in New South Wales alone. In Australia, there is no Bill of Rights, and police have a broader range of powers for crime prevention. For example, in Australia there are strict drinking and driving laws that allow police to randomly breath test and to establish roadblocks to enforce the 0.05 percent alcohol limit for drivers on a national basis; there is zero tolerance for learners and provisional drivers in most states.

CRIME

Australia has a reputation for being a laid-back country, but 30 percent of Australians have been victims of violent crime, the highest rate in the world. It is second in the world in auto theft and has the highest burglary rate, according to the International Crime Victims Survey conducted by Leiden University in Holland. Suburbs are generally much safer in terms of violent crime, although they are subject to burglary and theft.

In Australia, property crimes tend to be much more common than crimes of violence. Locks are recommended, and the use of a security alarm system will bring greater peace of mind. In inner city areas at night, travel with a companion and avoid unlit areas.

FIRE AND EMERGENCY

In Australia, fire and paramedic services are combined into statewide emergency response systems. Fire is taken very seriously in Australia, with total fire bans in place throughout the summer except for small barbecues. Emergency response includes volunteer rescue associations, which conduct search and rescue on land. The ambulance services are also organized on a state basis. The national number for emergencies is 000 for landlines, 112 for mobile phones, and 106 for text phones; 000 can be called from a mobile phone even if it lacks a SIM card or is locked, and any available network will be used to complete the toll-free call. The international standard number for mobile phone emergency calls is 112, but 000 can also be used within Australia.

SURF AND SAIL RESCUE

Australia is home to a large collection of nasty sea creatures and rip tides, and the life-saving clubs are kept busy. The Surf Life Savers are generally

© MITCHELL CHESHER

DAILY LIFE

Surf Life Savers guard the Sydney beaches.

volunteers, organized in 305 clubs with more than 100,000 members around the country. They have made more than 500,000 rescues since 1907. There are also harbor rescue services provided on a professional level, which include shark patrols. Most urban beaches, particularly the notorious waters of Sydney Harbour, are patrolled for sharks, and many beaches have shark nets to provide safe swimming conditions. The Surf Life Savers also provide emergency response for stings and cuts, which can come from shellfish, shark bites, or stings from sea wasps, sea snakes, blue bottles, and jellyfish. Australia has several species of sea snakes and sea wasps, which have fatal stings if untreated, but antivenins are available.

POISON CONTROL, BITES, AND STINGS

In addition to nasty sea creatures, Australia has a daunting collection of snakes, poisonous toads, and spiders. Primarily, the deadly creatures are found in remote areas of the north, but several spiders and tick species are found in highly populated suburbs. The deadliest spider, the funnel web, is indigenous to Sydney. They often fall into local swimming pools, causing some consternation for new residents unused to fishing them out. The redback spider and the funnel web are the most dangerous of species found in city areas, but some snake species sneak into the suburbs. Poison control is nationally accessed by dialing 131-126, 24 hours a day, and connects to an emergency response desk.

EMPLOYMENT

Many people say that they first began to dream of life in Australia when they met Australians traveling abroad on holiday, and heard about the wonderful life "back in Oz." Aussies abroad are some of the most relaxed, cheerful, funny, and interesting people on earth.

But holiday is holiday, and work is work. Work life, in Australia, is far, far different from holiday life. Australia, far from being a country of irrepressible individualists, is one of the most highly conformist countries when it comes to the office.

It's actually good news for the immigrant, because it's far easier to pick up the work ethic and work style in Sydney or Melbourne than in most world cities, because while there is variation between various industries, in general Australians behave very much alike when it comes to the office, and it's easier to pick up the nuances.

The key to finding work as a new arrival, particularly as an American, will be to quickly study and understand the Australian stereotypical behaviors,

© MITCHELL CHESHER

understand which rules can be bent, be broken, or must be observed. In turn, to find your dream job, you will need to overcome in most cases some prejudices that Aussies have about foreigners, especially Americans.

Once you have studied and assimilated the basic Australian work ethic and overcome a few stereotypical behaviors that helped you in the old country but will hurt you in Oz, you'll find that the really good news that work in Australia is basically structured very much like in the United States, with some strong European influences, and that your credentials will be readily understood and appreciated by potential employers.

The Job Hunt

The basic resources for job-hunting, such as the Internet or newspaper ads in the major papers, are much the same in Australia as in the United States, except that newspapers run the most job ads on Saturday instead of Sunday.

However, as with most cultures, the best way to get a job is through a personal connection, and in this day and age, it is easier to make that happen than in the past.

As soon as you know that you are ready to move to Australia—if you don't already have a job or aren't brimming with contacts—get yourself a free account on a social network like LinkedIn (www.linkedin.com), and build a profile expressing your interest in Australia so that recruiters doing keyword searches can find you. Join the LinkedIn Open Networkers (LIONs) at the Lions Lair (www.themetanetwork.com), and this will begin the process of hooking you up to hundreds of Aussie recruiters that use the service. LinkedIn Open Networkers, as a rule of membership, accept invitations from anyone, even if you do not have a prior relationship established.

Within a few weeks of joining, you should have 50–100 direct contacts in Sydney and Melbourne, and up to 20,000 indirect contacts. Use that as a base to get your résumé out and begin discussions. I can't think of an industry that isn't represented, and LinkedIn users are generally very helpful as long as you are friendly in your approach and offer the possibility of returning the favor at a later date.

In addition to your social networking activities on LinkedIn or the network of your choice, by all means contact recruiters. At the executive level, companies like Boyden are excellent (www.boyden.com) in Australia, while PeopleBank (www.peoplebank.com.au) is strong in the middle management ranks, and companies like Finite IT (www.finite.com.au) and HealthStaff Recruitment (www.healthstaffrecruitment.com.au) specialize in IT and medical careers, respectively. The main job site of the Fairfax newspapers (http://mycareer. com.au) is good for the more mass-market type of job.

RÉSUMÉ

Although the term "résumé" is generally understood, your résumé is called a "CV" (curriculum vitae) in Australia, and it is generally longer and more important than a résumé is in a U.S. job search. Given that Australia is a smaller country, the avalanche of 1,000 résumés landing on a manager's desk for an opening is unheard of, so there will generally be more attention paid to each individual response.

Cover letters are still valued and read; do not assume in a blind job application that sending a generic résumé will do. Your résumé can follow standard U.S. formats, but keep an eye on superlatives where you are praising yourself, as this is frowned on in Australian culture. Instead of emphasizing individual achievements, focus more attention on the achievements of the group or brand, and by all means highlight if you have worked on a top brand or for a top company in your field. But try to let the names of your companies and your positions tell the story of your personal excellence, and keep the descriptions in your job summaries factual as to your duties rather than achievements. Pictures are not necessary, nor are high-end graphics, although excellent paper and envelopes still are impressive if you are sending hard copy. Your academic achievements will be important to your prospective employer, so don't skimp.

Having rewritten your résumé for the Australian market, the most important task is to put it in the hands of headhunters and friends who can distribute it. The really good jobs will be advertised on "the bush telegraph" (word of mouth) either formally or informally before they are posted on company websites or with third-party services. With Aussies, always ask permission nicely; never just spam-deliver your résumé to a lot of people.

INTERVIEWS

Firms rarely hire based on overseas interviews except for specialized industries with shortages, such as hotels, cruise ships, nursing, and IT, where a local human resources firm will handle interviews. For most assignments, the interviews will take place in Australia.

Punctuality is highly prized, as is efficiency in providing extra hard copies of your CV. Formal business attire, generally conservative, is appropriate for interviewing, although offices tend to be "smart casual" in daily attire. Generally, Australians prefer a low-key approach to speaking about past accomplishments; any hint of bragging or an air of superiority is generally an interview killer.

Employers generally expect candidates to be friendly, cheerful, and demure in interviews. Australian employers consider a good fit with the existing staff to be a very important consideration, and interviews are generally more successful when the candidate lets the employer lead with the questioning. Except for very small firms, questions about benefits should be reserved for an interview with HR.

WHAT EMPLOYERS WANT

Foreign employees are especially valuable in the medical professions, where foreign workers help fill general shortages and add expertise in specialized areas, often through exchange programs; large-scale project management, where specialized experience in "big projects" will give foreigners an edge over locals; university posts, where specialization in subjects not widely taught in Australia leads to invitations for visiting fellowships; primary and secondary education, although often this involves work in the Outback, where many Australians choose not to work; and IT, where there is a chronic shortage of workers.

There is a special category of visa, the 457, which expedites the granting of visas for skilled foreign workers. The government maintains a Migration Occupations in Demand List (MODL) at www.immi.gov.au, which typically contains 50–100 professions and trades where shortages exist.

In the part-time or seasonal markets, foreign workers are popular candidates for work in summer beach resorts and for winter skiing jobs. Luxury hotels and cruise lines also experience chronic shortages of trained staff and welcome foreigners, although the pay can be low.

Seasonal workers should keep in mind that Australia has a much lower standard rate for tipping; 10 percent is considered a very adequate tip in most circumstances, and tips for housekeeping services are not common.

WORK CULTURE

It is not uncommon to hear an American describe the United States as the greatest nation on earth, the hope of mankind, or something along these lines. You'll never hear that in Australia, although it's not because Aussies are not patriotic. In fact, their quiet pride in Australia runs deep and strong.

Accordingly, Aussies absolutely adore foreigners who approach Australia with great affection, some degree of admiration, and a desire to assimilate. These new arrivals are considered some of Australia's greatest assets. Those

BUSINESS LUNCH

In a business setting, there's nothing more awkward than a business lunch in a country where the customs and the food are foreign. Here's a guide to what the locals say and eat, after they say g'day:

- **arvo:** afternoon
- **barbie:** barbecue
- **courgette:** zucchini
- **fine, thanks:** good
- **John Dory:** local white fish
- **mince:** ground beef
- **prawn:** shrimp
- **rissole:** sausage-filled pastry
- **schooner:** a 21-ounce beer; the standard Aussie size
- **seppo:** Yank; American
- **serviette:** napkin
- **snags:** barbecued sausages
- **ta:** thank you
- **tea:** dinner
- **Tresca:** Sprite
- **tucker:** food
- **yobbo:** lout; rude person

Tipping 10 percent is considered just fine, thanks.

Wine is still quite acceptable at Aussie business lunches, if no one is driving; the safe practice is to drink water.

Bringing a customer home for dinner is rare these days, but bringing home a colleague is less so. Nowadays, people meet at restaurants for dinner, but entertaining colleagues at a Sunday barbecue at the boss's place is still quite common and, though casual, is rarely optional.

who come to the country seeking to impose their culture on Australians are going to have a very tough go of it. That goes for companies too: a key to finding, winning, and holding a job in Australia is studying the corporate culture of the company you wish to join, assimilating it, and reflecting quiet pride in one's company without becoming a braggart or boastful.

In short: What you wear, how you act toward others, the hours you keep, and the way that you approach your work are very important in every aspect of finding and holding a good job.

Dress

In general, Aussies dress casually, and attire is generally light because of the warm weather and the spotty availability record of air-conditioning in years gone by. However, it is "smart casual" in the office as a general rule, and most importantly this will differ from industry to industry. An almost British formalism still permeates the banking business, for example, and barristers still wear black robes and white wigs in court.

Professional Conduct

Aussies are famously nonconfrontational. Phrases like "class struggle" never took hold in the country, despite its softly socialist structure, but words like

BUDDY BELL

Hundreds of thousands of young girls had their first experience with cosmetics courtesy of Bonne Bell and products like Lip Smackers. Less well known is the fact that the owners of Bonne Bell, the Bell family, have a long-standing relationship with Australian and American tennis, and recently relocated their main operations from Cleveland, Ohio, to Sydney, Australia.

"The things we've learned the hard way!" laughs CEO Buddy Bell, when reflecting on the move. "It's been an incredible adventure, but I wish we had known more about it before it began."

Bell's grandfather, Jesse Bell, started the company back in the 1920s, and has been sponsoring tennis for years. In 1974, he put together a head-to-head prize match featuring Aussie Evonne Goolagong and American Chris Evert, which was played in Cleveland. Today, the company's marketing director, Lesley Gibbs, is the mother of U.S. teen tennis sensation Nicole Gibbs.

After many years of success Down Under, but sensing an opportunity to take their success to a new level while enjoying an expat experience, the Bells decided to relocate to Sydney for a few years,

moving to the northern suburbs. With them came their business, courtesy of Australian legislation that accelerates visas for business relocations. So for the past few years, this well-known American cosmetics brand has been managed from Sydney (mirroring the management of the Murdoch media empire, including 20th Century Fox, also from Sydney).

The Bells say that, from a business standpoint, the transition has been smooth, but that there were challenges adapting to Australian lifestyle, from schools to making friends. New Australians typically report that Aussies are more reluctant to from friendships with short-term expats than almost any other group, an experience the Bells confirmed.

"They think that the minute they make a friendship, that you are going to leave." But they report that, with time, friendships form and hassles are worked through.

"It's definitely been worth it," says Bell, "not only for business, to be able to focus on building up our Australian operation, but for the incredible opportunity to live here. We'll never forget it, long, long after we're back in the States."

"reconciliation" and "arbitration" are a part of daily life. Aussies like harmony, at home and at the office.

Having said that, Aussies kid each other all the time, with insults that are a form of affection. So you will find yourself tested, perhaps in a job interview, or speaking with a recruiter, or in the job itself. "Another stupid bloody Yank" someone might call you. It will sound (and feel) like an insult, but it's really just a test. "That's right, they asked me to come to keep you company," you might reply. Never take an insult; give it right back, but paint a smile on it and make sure everyone can see that you are playing along and assimilating.

Aussies are highly egalitarian, and while respectful toward the boss they do not like to be obsequious, and you shouldn't be either. Aussies can't stand the office tattletale or snitch; don't become one, no matter how much you want to please the boss.

Aussies tend to take public transport and arrive to work on time. Because Australians have personal lives that are important to them, they tend to leave on time, too, and place a high premium on getting the job done efficiently while in the office. Untidy desks are not appreciated, five-minute calls should take five minutes, and 10 o'clock appointments should begin at 10 o'clock, not five after.

Labor Laws

Generally speaking, Australia has a very strong tradition of employee rights and employer responsibilities. In the past 25 years, the Labor Party has been generally in power in most Australian states, and in power at the federal level about 60 percent of that period. The general drift of legislation has been to expand and safeguard worker rights.

The doctrine governing employees is a controversial set of laws known collectively as WorkChoices. The former Liberal government introduced these in 2005, and it lost the federal election of 2007 in large part because of the controversy over their implementation. "WorkChoices is dead," said the new Liberal Party leadership, and the Labor government will be dismantling and changing the structure over the next several years, primarily to expand workers rights.

For now, WorkChoices remains largely intact, and many of its features are likely to survive.

Under WorkChoices, the nation formed a single industrial relations structure, which replaced a collection of federal and state systems that had evolved over the years.

The nation established an Australian Fair Pay Commission to set minimum standards in areas such as pay, hours, and leave.

The legislation also limited, controversially, the right of certain individuals to join unions and to qualify for collective agreements as opposed to individual agreements on pay, benefits, and conditions. It also extended the Australian Workplace Agreement to establish that collective agreements between employers and unions would last five years, compared to three in the previous structure. However, union membership remains strong in Australia, with 30 percent of the workforce belonging to a trade union, compared to 12 percent in the United States.

WorkChoices also increased controls on strikes and other industrial actions, exempted small businesses from unfair dismissal laws, and required secret ballots for strikes, elections, and other union activities. Controversially, the legislation exempted all companies from unfair dismissal laws as long as dismissals could be shown to have been based on a reasonable operational concern. As interpreted by the courts, finding employees to work at lower wages constituted a reasonable operational concern, and many Australians felt less secure because of WorkChoices laws.

WorkChoices does not apply to all corporations at this time, only to federally recognized or chartered corporations such as banks, the government itself, and corporations in the federal territories and in the state of Victoria.

Other states have retained many of the structures of the past, which included strong unfair dismissal protection, with a tribunal to hear complaints and the burden on the employer to show fair dismissal. Also, previous arrangements, still in force in all states except Victoria, require new collective agreements to be subject to the No Disadvantage Test, which means that the new agreement, taken as a whole, cannot disadvantage the employees in comparison to the old agreement.

WORK CHOICES PROVISIONS

In Australia, the Australian Fair Pay and Conditions Standard operates in five areas relating to pay, hours, and leave. There are five basic provisions, which form a minimum standard for Australians.

Hours

Australians work a maximum of 38 hours per week, although this can be averaged over a 12-month period. Employees can be asked to work "reasonable" additional hours and can refuse "unreasonable" requests. Reasonability is based on health, safety, hours previously worked, the operational structure of the

© MITCHELL CHESHER

Volunteerism is an important part of Aussie work life and retirement life, as illustrated here by the Lions service club.

business, and the notice given for the request. Overtime is generally paid at twice the hourly rate and is usually welcomed in small doses by Aussies.

Annual Leave

Australians are entitled to four weeks paid annual leave. Part-time employees earn leave on a pro-rata basis depending on how many hours they work, but casual (seasonal) labor does not earn paid leave. Workers who regularly have shifts on Sundays or public holidays receive an extra week. Also, employees can request to "cash out" up to two weeks of their leave every 12 months, to earn extra money instead of taking holidays, but employers are not required to agree.

Personal and Carer's Leave

Australians are entitled to 10 days of paid sick or carer's leave each year, with caring limited to an immediate family member or member of the household. This leave accumulates, and there is no limit on the amount of sick leave that can be accumulated or used in a given year. There are limits on carer's leave (10 days per year), but two unpaid days of extra carer's leave per emergency occasion are available.

Parental Leave

Australians are entitled to up to 52 weeks of unpaid parental leave, which can be taken by one parent or shared, and is taken at the time of birth (or adoption in the case of an adopted child under the age of five). Any employee who has worked for each 12 months for an employer is eligible for parental leave, and in this case even small enterprises are covered by this provision. Mothers are also entitled to six weeks of paid maternity leave immediately following the birth of a child, if they have accumulated 12 months' service with an employer.

Minimum Pay

The Australian Fair Pay Commission is responsible for establishing the federal minimum wage, classifications, and pay scales in the Australian Pay and Classification Scales, as well as the timing and frequency of pay reviews. The commission also sets minimum wages for trainees, apprentices, and juniors, but all adult full-time workers must be paid the federal minimum wage even if their job is not covered in a commission classification. The federal minimum wage is currently $13.74 per hour and is generally increasing by 3–4 percent per year.

Self-Employment

Australia does not have a strong entrepreneurial culture in comparison to the United States, but it is generally more open to self-employment and entrepreneurialism than Europe. The climate for self-employment is generally improving; many financial institutions, for example, are making it easier to obtain mortgages and other consumer finance based on self-employment.

The gamut of self-employment opportunities includes:
- Sole trader or sole proprietorship; e.g., a consultancy
- Small start-up business; e.g., services
- Franchise
- Large start-up business; e.g., manufacturing

Generally speaking, the sole trader route is only viable in the case of a wealthy private individual who can qualify for a business investor visa, or for the spouse of someone coming in on a business or professional visa. In this sector, there are opportunities to affiliate with larger firms as a "business finder," including headhunters and financial services firms. One route that has been popular with expats is to establish a real estate practice catering to other expats; again, this is typically the case when the businessperson has obtained a visa through a spouse, and this is viable only in Sydney and Melbourne.

In Australia, an investor or business owner can obtain a visa on the strength of an investment in Australian bonds or a business. Business owner (provisional) visas allow a person with business interests in the country to obtain a four-year residency visa, which can be converted to permanent residence after two years for business owners or four years for investors. The visa will also extend to a spouse and children under 18.

Investors have to purchase at least $750,000 in Australian bonds to qualify. Business owners face a more daunting set of criteria, which include establishing a successful business background, age under 45 years, an annual revenue in existing businesses of at least $500,000, net assets of at least $500,000, and competence in English. States and territories have business investment programs with slightly lower requirements, such as a ceiling of 55 on age and assets of $300,000.

Australia, like most countries, maintains a fairly robust government support system for planning small business activities, including seminars on starting businesses. Finance is just as tough to find in Oz as anywhere else, maybe harder, as Australia generally has a highly risk-adverse banking culture on smaller investments.

The federal government maintains a small-business office, the Small Business Development Corporation (www.sbdc.com.au), with field officers who answer questions and give local presentations.

One of the best routes to starting a business in Australia is franchising, which is a growing field and one foreigners often have excellent results with, as many of them involve international brands. The franchising route requires upfront investment, and they generally require a long-term commitment to be financially viable. The Franchise Council of Australia (www.franchise business.com.au) offers information on more than 800 franchises, which typically involve upfront payments of $20,000 to $250,000. The same business categories—primarily food, consumer goods, and services—apply to franchises in Australia as in Europe and the United States.

FINANCE

Although Australia is not "within cooee of" (is very far from) the western nations of Europe and North America, it is remarkably similar in terms of finance, and one of the great advantages of the country is the fact that the local economy is well-linked to the West with highly comparable systems.

Australia uses the Australian dollar for its currency, which in recent years has almost reached parity with the American dollar in exchange rates. However, this can't be counted on. In the early 1970s, the Australian dollar was worth as much as $1.50 in U.S. dollars, and by the mid-1990s was worth around US$0.50. Those are the extremes, and the Australian dollar has generally been valued in the US$0.70–0.85 range in recent years.

One of the first differences you will notice is how advanced Australia is in the all-online aspect of bill paying. It's a good thing, because the cost of living is high in the major cities, and you'll pay a lot to enjoy the incredible delights of Sydney, especially if you are aiming for a house in one of the better

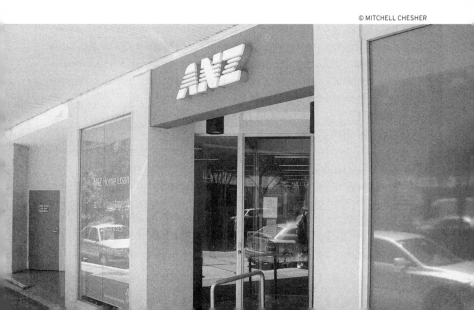

sections of town or near the waterfront. Aussies, particularly older ones, will say "dear" when something is "expensive," and "Sydney is dear" in every sense of the word.

Cost of Living

In the most recent Mercer Consulting cost of living rankings, Sydney ranked 21st among the most expensive cities in the world, ahead of every U.S. city except New York. Melbourne ranked 60th, and Adelaide ranked 96th. By comparison, Los Angeles ranked 42nd and London was 2nd. The reason? The weak U.S. dollar, which makes all U.S. cities cheaper by comparison when currency is taken into account. The downward trend of the U.S. dollar is expected to continue for some time, which will make Australian cities even more expensive by comparison. But as long as you are being paid in local dollars, the trend will not affect Americans except when on home leave—the United States will seem incredibly cheap when traveling on Australian dollars.

HOW MUCH MONEY DO I NEED?
Minimum Standards
Outside of Sydney, life can be relatively affordable, but a good basic standard is to use $400 per week as a starting point for a minimal lifestyle for an individual, and add a third for Sydney and Melbourne and about 10 percent for Brisbane. This would include a shared, modest flat in an accessible, relatively safe outlying suburb, basic utilities, a public transit card for commuting, and money for food and low-cost entertainment. In Australia, rent is quoted by the week, and most of your budget will follow this for simplicity's sake, compared to monthly budgeting in the United States. This includes an allowance for a broadband Internet connection that will cost you about $30 per month, but this will enable you to connect to Skype, the expat's friend for unlimited computer-to-computer international calling.

Average Standards
Commencing again with a "base case" in regional cities, use a figure of $1,200 per week as a starting point for an average lifestyle with a family of four, and add a third for Sydney and Melbourne and about 10 percent for Brisbane. This would include a three-bedroom house (on an 80 percent mortgage) in an accessible, safe, and well-regarded suburb, utilities, one child in an average-range private school and one in public schools, one car, and money for food and average entertainment with about $200 per month toward budget travel

COMPARING COST OF LIVING

Every few years, Mercer Consulting releases a study showing the comparative cost of living between various cities around the world. New York City is
used as a base and assigned a value of 100. Cities that are more expensive
than New York are rated higher than 100, and cities cheaper to live in are
rated lower than 100. Housing, transport, energy, education, food, and entertainment are among the major components of the index. The 2004 Cost
of Living Survey from Mercer HR Consultants gave a comparison between
Aussie cities, which can be used to determine the comparative cost not only
to New York and other international cities, but between Aussie cities too.

City	Rating
Sydney	91.8
Melbourne	77.5
Brisbane	72.7
Adelaide	72
Perth	70.7

Source: Mercer HR Consultants, 2004

around Australia. In some countries, private schools are a luxury item enjoyed
only by wealthy families, but attendance is far more common in Australia,
with about 33 percent of secondary school-age kids in private schools.

Add about $10,000 in capital costs for electrical appliances and another
$5,000 for the furniture—computers are expensive in Australia, for sure, but
given the cost of transport and the different voltage of the Aussie system, a
capital investment in basic conveniences such as a washer/dryer, microwave,
fridge and the usual entertainment appliances will set you back handsomely
in this high-tariff market.

Luxury Standards

Commencing again with a "base case" in regional cities, $2,000 per week cov-
ers a top-flight lifestyle for a high-flying couple; add a third for Melbourne,
10 percent for Brisbane, and 40 percent for Sydney. This would include a two-
bedroom townhouse in a top inner-city suburb (on a 50 percent mortgage),
utilities, a top private school for one child, two "status" cars, and money for
dining out and other city delights such as the occasional trip to the opera or
concerts, and about $500 per month toward travel around Australia.

Add about $15,000 in capital costs for electrical appliances and another
$15,000 for the furniture and you have the beginnings of a great lifestyle. For
the truly well-off, investments in waterfront real estate in the $5 million-plus

range are not unheard of in Sydney, but this hits the capital budget far more than the day-to-day expenses.

MONTHLY EXPENSES
Housing and Utilities

Some expats will have housing provided by an employer at a corporate flat, in which case rejoice! For sure, housing is the fastest-rising expense in Australia over the past two decades, and since waterfront is a finite resource, down by the main rivers and harbors of Aussie cities the costs can be daunting for the new arrival. In Sydney, be prepared for sticker shock unless you are arriving from New York City, with $1,000 per week a good starting figure at the top end for a good flat in an excellent location, down to a minimum of around $100 per week plus shared expenses for a room in a house in an outlying area.

Food and Other Necessities

If you are used to the U.S./U.K. traditional measures in gallons and pounds, the meat and veggie prices will seem astronomical while milk and juices seem like a bargain; they are quoted in "kilos" (kilograms, about 2.1 to the pound), and "litres" (about 3.8 to the gallon). In general, the food price structure is a little different, with basic goods such as flour and meat generally inexpensive, while finished goods (basically, anything in a bottle or can) are quite "dear" by other countries' standards. This is because Australia is one of the world's great breadbasket economies, producing prodigious amounts of livestock and grains on a per capita basis, but it lacks the local population to spread out the cost of equipment for high-end food processing. A single person can live very well on $100 per week, with a high percentage of fresh foods and proteins; fruits are pricey. American goods are widely available, so there's rarely a need for care packages from home except for sweets and thick ketchup if you feel you need it.

Medical

In Australia, basic health care is public and free, but the key word is "basic," not "free." Expect cruel waiting times for nonelective procedures. Accordingly, many Australians choose private health care. There is "excess" coverage for items such as dental, optometry, and physio that are typically not covered by the Medicare system, and it runs about $55 per month for a single person. Private hospital coverage runs about $80 per person per month for standard care. In smaller cities such as Perth, Brisbane, and Adelaide, it costs about 10 percent less.

Schooling

A recent article in the *Sydney Morning Herald* said 10 percent of families that send their children to independent private schools spend half their take-home pay on education. Nevertheless, 33 percent of all students attend a private school. For an independent school (that is, nonreligious), allow $16,500 per year per child with about 90 percent of that representing tuition. Top-end schools cost more than $20,000 per year per student. Catholic schools run about half of that, while public school expense will be less than $1,000 per child per year including meals.

Entertainment and Travel

All entertainment in Australia is relatively expensive, because the attendance base is low. A good local rugby team in Sydney will be doing well to attract 20,000 fans per week through the turnstiles. Boutique numbers mean boutique costs—as a baseline, expect to pay $14 for a movie ticket, and add about 40 percent to the U.S. cost of most entertainment for a rough sense of the price. Travel depends on preferred style and required distance, but generally internal air travel is an expensive premium compared to the highly competitive U.S. and European short-haul markets, so a budget of $5,000 per year will cover a pair of weeklong vacations in the interior or along the coast for a family of four, but add an extra $1,000 if flying.

Shopping

In Australia, shopping is very much like in most Western countries except for generally higher prices for clothes and manufactured goods, about 20–30 percent more as a rule of thumb. In the cities, boutiques are arranged in "arcades"; historically, these were narrow passages connecting main city streets, but many of them are relatively spacious although often crowded. Traditional malls are a growing phenomenon, especially in the suburbs. The true essence of Aussie-style living is to patronize the farmers markets, where fresh produce and fine goods are available from stalls operated usually on a given weekday. The crush of people and the dazzling arrays of great fresh food make these a must-do. Credit cards are widely accepted, although American Express is less so.

In the suburbs, most shops close by 6 P.M.; they are open late only on Thursday nights, typically until 9 P.M. This brings throngs of two-breadwinner families out for grocery shopping and can really be a zoo. Bargain supermarkets where you box or bag your own purchases and buy generic brands can substantially lower the food bill, but the crowds cost time and aggravation. Most shops close on Saturday afternoon and all day Sunday, which makes the cities peacefully quiet as the nation turns to sport and barbecues for the weekend.

© MITCHELL CHESHER

The retail sector in Australia includes mega malls, but also a lively small retail sector that still hugs the main driving corridors in the suburbs of major cities.

Keep in mind that, in Oz, specialty meat, fish, and "fruit and veg" shops still exist, although they are rarer each year. The "fruit and veg" shop is also known, especially to older Aussies, as the "greengrocer."

Electronics are cruelly expensive, as are cars. Serious consideration should be given to bringing computers, iPods, etc., with you when you make the move, despite the fact that the power plugs in Sydney deliver 240 volts. Cars are also prohibitively expensive—generally 20 percent higher than in the United States, or more, but U.S. cars can't be imported because Aussie cars have right-hand drive. The best you can hope for is a company car, or a car allowance from your employer to help defray the initial expense.

Banking

Aussie systems are highly electronic and online-oriented, so if you are doing a lot of online bill-paying at the moment, you will find it a snap to convert to the Aussie approach to banking and bill-paying.

OPENING AN ACCOUNT

Opening an account could hardly be easier. You just bring a copy of your passport and a minimum deposit, which is typically around $500. There are traditional banks as well as what are known as building societies, similar to savings and loan banks in the United States. Building societies tend to be well structured for the average family in terms of basic services, and often offer a higher rate of interest on deposits as well as friendly service. St. George is the largest of this type. Traditional banks offer a broader range of commercial and investment services but have higher fees. They tend to have larger branches and be more impersonal. The state-owned Commonwealth Bank is the largest of this type, followed by National Australia, ANZ, and Westpac.

INTERNATIONAL ACCOUNTS

The most typical form of international transfer is still the bank wire, for which fees of $30 to $50 per wire are typical. Paypal is increasingly popular as a low-cost, online payment medium and works well for international transfers.

CURRENCY

Australian currency is based on the Australian dollar, which in recent years has been nearing parity with the U.S. dollar. The coins are worth 5 cents, 10 cents, 20 cents, 50 cents, $1, and $2, and are easy to distinguish from each other and generally heavier and larger than American coins—$20 in coins can really weigh you down! Old-timers may still refer to 10 cents as a "bob," an old term for shilling, which was a part of the money system until 1966. Notes are available in denominations of $5, $10, $20, $50, and $100. Each note is a different color and size to allow blind people to distinguish them. An American wallet may need to be redesigned to fit the larger notes.

ATMs, CREDIT CARDS, AND CHECKS

Bank machines are widely available, except in remote rural areas, and they are used for deposits, withdrawals, and some bill paying. All major banks have online bill-paying systems, and they are widely used for utilities and other recurring household bills.

American Express is accepted at hotels and major restaurants, but Visa and Mastercard dominate the Aussie market and are far more widely accepted.

Foreign checks are a big no-no. Even if drawn in local currency, they will take 30 days to clear. Generally, the check is dying out and being replaced by smart cards. A smart card combines aspects of credit and debit cards, and typically has a 3x5 mm security chip embedded in the card.

Taxes

AUSTRALIAN INCOME TAXES

On income taxes, there is good news and bad news. The good news is that in Australia there is only a federal income tax obligation, and there is no need to file state or local income tax returns in any state. The bad news is that you still have a foreign tax obligation and will need to file a tax return for the country you are arriving from.

Australian taxes are due to be filed by October 31 each year, based on a July 1 through June 30 tax year. When arriving in Oz, you will need to obtain a tax file number, which you can get online (www.ato.gov.au) or at a local tax office. For sure, use a tax professional for your taxes because do-it-yourself tax software is not well designed to handle forms from two countries.

Taxes are collected on a pay-as-you-go basis, so in many cases the filing will produce a return.

SALES TAX

Australia has a general sales tax, or goods and services tax, known as the GST. This rate is set at 10 percent and is applied by merchants to almost all your transactions for goods, although services are currently exempt from GST. This revenue, like income tax, is collected by the federal branch of the government and is then shared with states on a negotiated basis, and the state in turn then funds local government.

Investing

The Australian economic structure is very similar to the U.S. structure, with two exceptions. First, Australia has a federally supervised pension scheme, called superannuation, which works somewhat like a 401(k) plan but has some effective and worthwhile differences. Second, Australian immigration law places investors at the head of the class for visas, so redistributing your wealth is a terrific way to reduce the hassle of moving to Australia.

SUPERANNUATION

When you work in Australia, you will receive superannuation, or an employer-funded pension. Employers must contribute 9 percent of your earnings base into your superannuation fund, which you can manage yourself or have the state manage. Temp workers are excluded, plus military and foreigners, but contract workers are generally covered.

STOCK MARKETS AND MUTUAL FUNDS

Stocks and mutual funds are broadly similar to the U.S. market. The Australian market has less liquidity than the U.S. system, and stocks are generally

SUPERANNUATION IS NOT FROM *MARY POPPINS*

It sounds like supercalifragilisticexpealidocious, and sometimes feels as complex, but "super" is a pension scheme a little like a 401(k).

In Australia, your employer has to make a contribution to your superannuation scheme at least once every three months. Individuals can make contributions on a tax-deferred basis. Your "super" is managed by one of more than 300,000 superannuation funds operating in Oz, of which about 300 are majors with more than $50 million in assets. You choose the manager of your funds. The employer contribution is 9 percent.

You can begin to access the funds as early as age 55.

"Super" is, in fact, a "super" way to manage a pensions program. The government offers a guaranteed pension (based on a means test) to all older persons, plus a pensioner may access his or her compulsory contributions to superannuation, and of course there are also the voluntary contributions made by the employee.

believed to be more volatile. There are several types of funds available: closed-end funds, funds, and index funds. Since Australians are forced to save money for retirement but have some discretion in management, the country has more invested in funds than any other country in the world; Aussies hold an average of more than $48,000 per person in mutual funds.

COMMUNICATIONS

Australia is a remote country, and nothing has occupied more attention for more people over more years than the design, care, and feeding of the national communications infrastructure. Defense Minister Sir Jim Killen once famously quipped that Indonesia could conquer Australia "on a Sunday morning with a phone call," so weak and unattended were Australia's defenses on weekends. But Australia's telecommunications networks are always shipshape and state-of-the-art; notably, Sir Jim thought the Indonesians would call instead of invade, a tribute to the reliability of the phone system.

In Australia, you can generally expect that services will be top level, and thoughtfully provisioned in remote areas, although the "packages" you buy (wireless minutes, for example) sometimes are not well constructed. The handsets, devices, computers, and other electronic gizmos will set you back what will feel like an equivalent sum to the national debt, and customer service will feel slower and less responsive than you are accustomed to seeing. Excellence comes at a high price in the happy halls of Telstra, Australia's

state-owned telecommunications system, and your gratitude and compliance are kindly required.

Telephone

In 1995, Australian telecommunications were deregulated, and 18 companies have services of some kind provisioned in Oz. Telstra and Optus are the main landline companies. Telstra, the government-owned telephone company, is the choice of the vast majority of Aussies, and it definitely has the broadest coverage (in case you find yourself, or friends and family, in outlying areas).

Generally speaking, for a basic Telstra plan, expect to pay $50 per month, plus $0.10 per local call and $1 per long distance call (maximum 20 minutes), with $0.20 per minute for calls to Telstra mobile phones and $0.37 per minute for non-Telstra mobile phones. International calls start at $0.39 for the call, plus $0.21 per minute, capped at $1.49 for 20 minutes.

AREA CODES AND NETWORKS

For telephone calls, Australia has a short and easily remembered system of calling codes, much easier than the complex set of area or city codes used in the United States or other countries. Area codes are organized by state, with some exceptions around border areas. Mobile phones have their own area code of 4. When dialing from inside Australia, you add a 0, so that Sydney's area code is 02 instead of 2.

AREA CODES
- 2 – Central East: New South Wales, Australian Capital Territory, parts of northern border areas of Victoria
- 3 – Southeast: Tasmania, Victoria, and parts of southern border areas of New South Wales
- 4 – digital GSM mobile phones
- 7 – Northeast: Queensland
- 8 – Central and West Region: South Australia, Northern Territory, and Western Australia

NETWORKS
For mobile calling, Australia operates three types of networks, which will work with a wide variety of devices, and there is a very good chance a U.S. device will operate in Australia if you have an international roaming plan. Check with your service provider. Upon moving to Oz, it may be possible to keep your existing phone, and simply insert a new SIM card to be recognized by your new carrier. Here are the providers that serve the most common networks, GSM-900, GSM-1800, and CDMA-800:

- **GSM-900**
  Singtel Optus
  Telstra
  Vodafone
- **GSM-1800**
  3-Com (some cities)
- **CDMA-800**
  Telstra

By stepping up to $90 per month, you get all your local and long-distance calling included, and Telstra calls are $0.05 per minute. Bottom line: For an average household you will be looking at $100 per month for a solid, basic phone service.

INTERNATIONAL VALUE PACKS

A must for international calling are value pack options, especially if a lot of your calls will be to the "old country," as is usually the case. For $5 per month on a fixed basis, you can call the United States for $0.02 per minute, which will slash your budget considerably.

CALLING CARDS

Telstra has a wide range of prepaid or billable calling cards, which can be used remotely, but the long-distance is a killer diller on these babies—$0.31 per minute to the United States plus a $0.75 connection charge.

Convenience stores have cards with better rates. A friend writes, "Forget Telstra, Optus, Vodafone, and the rest. They are still living in the dark ages. You have several options—walk to the nearest convenience store. But when they say 120 minutes—[it's] not necessarily so."

VOIP

For long-distance service, most expats choose to sign up for Skype at www.skype.com. It is a VOIP (voice over Internet protocol) service that offers free, unlimited computer-to-computer calling. Even dialing from your computer to a landline costs less than $0.10 per minute. Making 10 calls per month, using 200 minutes, you should expect to save nearly $50 per month on long distance. Skype sells handsets that plug into your computer's USB drive yet look and work like traditional phones. Earphones are also available for purchase, or you can simply use your computer's built-in speaker system. Skype includes integrated text chat and file sharing, so you can have a truly robust telephony experience for very little cost. If you happen to have an Apple computer, you can try the iChat service, which includes a built-in multiparty audio/video service, so you can have unlimited video chat (computer-to-computer) for free.

VOIP services in Australia are clear and have very few dropouts and call drops, but VOIP is in its early days, so do expect the occasional dropout. VOIP is less reliable in mobiles but is the focus of mobile companies such as 3. One of the downsides of VOIP is that you do need to prefill your account with a credit card or Paypal, and putting your account on auto refresh is advised if you do not want calls to terminate on you if you forget to refill. Also, a friend advises "they do have a tendency to call you with special offers. But once you tell them a couple of times they will stay off."

MOBILE PHONES

The larger mobile companies are Optus, Virgin Mobile, Vodafone, Telstra, and 3. Telstra is by far the biggest, although the others are all well-known except perhaps 3, which focuses on exotic 3G services.

As in the United States, mobile service generally comes with subsidized phones and contracts. A Telstra package with a 24-month contract and a midrange phone is around $60 per month, which includes $50 for voice and $10 for data, which is burned at $0.56 per minute and $2 per MB, and $0.25 per SMS text message. Understandably, Australians have widely adapted to the text message to keep from going broke.

As in most countries, customers typically buy their handsets through the carrier, but you can always buy the service plan and a new SIM card. Ringtones are available in a wide assortment of styles, the same as in advanced mobile countries.

A popular option is the prepaid mobile, which can be purchased outright (no contract) for $99–209 depending on the phone. It comes with $10 of call credit and six months of network access. At that point, fill the phone with as much credit as you like, which you burn at $0.38 per minute for voice, $2 per MB for data, and $0.25 per text message. You can buy specialized plans that optimize your value for text messages, and generally calls and texts to numbers on the same carrier network come at highly discounted rates, with some packages offering unlimited calls and texts to a calling circle of up to five numbers on the same network.

BRINGING YOUR EXISTING PHONE

Australia is a GSM country, and G3 services are available but will require a compatible handset. A typical CDMA phone from the States will not work. The good news is that GSM is getting more and more popular in the United States, so there's a good chance that a handset will be compatible. But keep in mind

An exception to the "buy in Oz" rule is the iPhone, which you will need at this time to buy elsewhere and bring to Oz, and use on a roaming basis with your existing plan. Note that Telstra is likely to be the only carrier to be compatible with an iPhone unless you unlock the phone (not recommended; staying with Mother Telstra is a safer choice), but your iPhone will work in Oz if you bring one.

For your initial visit, and even when starting out, Telestial (www.telestial .com) offers a good Australia SIM card, with free incoming calls and local-rate outbound calls, all prepaid and no contract. You start with $209 airtime credit and burn minutes at $0.39 each, and it gives you a local Australian number.

Internet and Postal Services

INTERNET

The "big provider" is Big Pond, Telstra's service, which offers dialup, ADSL broadband, or broadband over cable when bundled with the Foxtel cable service. Big Pond also features wireless broadband and satellite broadband to service remote areas.

Dialup is getting to be quite rare these days in Oz, but plans will set you back $10 per month for a 12-month contract, and with Big Pond you can expect a good email system including spam filtration, web-mail access, and good solid technical support, although make sure you have some time blocked out if you call in, as wait times can be daunting at more than 30 minutes.

Broadband via ADSL is typical these days and starts at $30 per month on a 256/64 Kbps service for 200 MB in data transfer (very, very light usage, little more than checking a home page daily and handling email). Minimum is a 12-month contract. A typical "robust" plan offers ADSL 2, which gives a blazing 20 Mbps in selected urban areas and 8 Mbps/384 Kbps elsewhere. That service will cost $150 per month for a 60 GB transfer, enough for the heaviest user, or $90 per month for a 12 GB transfer limit for a medium user not transferring too many high-intensity video files. Special offers may discount up to half the monthly cost for the first year of a two-year contract. Home networking systems for up to five computers can be available free from Telstra.

Wireless Internet access is good in the cities, useless in most remote areas, and runs $85 per month for 1 GB of transfer using a Super G fast network, which requires compatible mobile 7.2 cards, which are sold separately. Super G offers up to 3.0 Mbps/1.3 Mbps. For remote areas, broadband satellite is the way to go. It requires a dish that is pointed north (not south, as in the United States). For a midrange 512/128, 2 GB data transfer plan, the monthly cost is $250 with a cost of $0.15 per extra MB. It's a bit of a rip-off.

POSTAL SERVICE

The postal service (Australia Post) is coming along, slowly, and services have improved from a dreadful state in years past. But generally speaking, mail should be used only when absolutely necessary. For bills, pay online. For cards and notes, use email.

Postage is incredibly complex, determined based on size, weight, thickness, and destination distance. Sizes come in unusual codes: DL, C6, C5, C4, and B4 (from 220 x 110 mm, or about 8 x 4¾ inches to 353 x 250 mm, or about 14 x 10 inches). A standard envelope (the DL size), standard thickness, weighing 3 ounces, traveling from the Sydney CBD costs $0.50 for nonguaranteed first business day service, or $4.30 for express mail that is guaranteed the next business day.

Packages over ¾ of an inch thick (20 mm), weighing more than 500 grams (1.1 pounds), or larger than 260 mm x 360 mm (12 x 14 inches) are considered parcels. A 1 kg (2.2 pound) package that is 12 x 12 x 12 inches will travel Sydney to Melbourne in two business days for $9.40 or $13.70 for Express Post (guaranteed next day).

FedEx services are available for international service only.

Media

Australian media is remarkably well-known around the world, considering Australia's small population and physical remoteness. Many financial television watchers around the globe are used to daily market updates from Sydney, and many programs from Australia are adapted for American audiences, such as *Wheel of Fortune* and the now-defunct *A Current Affair*.

The Australia-U.S. transfer has become particularly acute since the entry of Australia's News Corp into U.S. broadcasting with its acquisition of 20th Century Fox in 1984. The Australian-owned FOX and FOX News networks have become highly recognizable around the world, as well as Aussie-owned premium service such as SkyTel, which is the main satellite television service in Australia.

NEWSPAPERS

Australia has a highly robust and competitive newspaper market, although the Internet age and the general decline of newspapers have been felt in Oz as well. But expats will be surprised by the wide variety of papers available, their competitiveness, and the racy, lurid style of their headlines and story mix.

There are two newspaper chains of note, the Murdoch and Fairfax chains. The Murdoch tabloid newspaper style will be familiar to those who have experienced Murdoch papers such as the *New York Post* or London's *News of the World*. They are sensationalistic, typically rough-hewn conservative, aimed at the mass market, tabloid-sized, and generally the circulation leaders. The *Herald Sun* in Melbourne and the *Telegraph* in Sydney are the leading Murdoch tabloids. The Fairfax chain produces the establishment, tony, broadsheet-style *Sydney Morning Herald* and *Melbourne Age*. They are generally the number two papers in circulation but have the higher advertiser rates reflective of their upscale readership.

In addition to the local papers, Australia has two national newspapers, *The Australian,* a respected broadsheet published by Murdoch; and the *Australian Financial Review,* a daily financial tabloid published by Fairfax. Accordingly, the typical Australian capital city has 3–4 daily papers to choose from, excluding free city weeklies and weekly community "advertisers."

RADIO

Australia has had a relatively quiet radio market owing to its small population and conservative licensing policies. No stations were launched (excepting some FM experiments) between 1932 and 1976, and although the country has been catching up, only a limited range of stations can be supported by the small population, especially in rural areas. In the cities, FM is well established as the dominant band, and it has a mix of formats ranging from religious stations to alternative rock. News and opinion tends to still exist mostly on the AM band. National radio networks have built up around key radio brands Triple J, Triple M, the MIX, and Hit Music, which have affiliates in all major Aussie cities. Talk radio is dominated by four stations owned by the Fairfax media empire.

The Australian Broadcasting Corporation (ABC, or "Aunty") is the government's broadcast, which is quite independent of the government of the day, and it produces a news service, a country radio network (DiG Country), a classical music service, and an NPR-like service, Radio National. SBS radio is the multicultural radio service serving in major immigrant languages. A number of religious broadcasters appear on the dial, primarily fundamentalist Christian.

Call signs begin with numbers that reflect the station's state, so that 2MMM is the Triple M station in Sydney, while 3MMM is in Melbourne. 4MMM is the Triple M affiliate in Brisbane, 5MMM is Adelaide, while 6MIX is the Perth affiliate.

TELEVISION

Australian free-to-air television consists of five national television networks. The ABC is the government channel; it runs a BBC-type service offering serious fare, including many documentaries.

SBS is the multicultural television service that grew out of a desire by the government to explain the first national health scheme to new immigrants. It shows multilanguage programming including foreign films, features news with a stronger international element, and airs international sports such as soccer.

The three commercial networks are the Seven, Nine, and Ten networks, named for the channels they occupy on the VHF spectrum. The Nine Network, controlled by the Packer family, has consistently been the leader, especially in sports, while the Seven Network has been its most persistent rival. The Ten Network was launched in the 1960s to increase local content, and it consistently trails in ratings. All commercial networks have a mandated percentage of local content, but they tend to purchase syndicated international shows to save on cost. Most well-known U.S. shows appear on one of the networks.

CABLE AND SATELLITE

Foxtel is the primary cable and satellite broadcasting system in Australia. It is a joint venture between News Corporation, Consolidated Media Holdings (owner of the Nice Network), and Telstra. Foxtel produces a standard cable service, a high definition service, a mobile service featuring 12 channels that can stream on wireless devices, an on-demand service, and a Tivo-like personal digital recording service called Foxtel iQ.

The basic Foxtel service starts at $38 per month for 30 channels, including Discovery, CNN, CNBC, Fox Sports, and Nickelodeon. Sport, movie, and Showtime services can be added on for $16–18 per module per month, and there are specialty packages for extended music, entertainment, adult, and documentary options for $17 per module. Full channel access runs about $106 per month, or you can build your own lineup starting at $38 for 30 channels. Multiroom access is available for a $24.95 installation cost and an additional $19.95 per month per outlet, while Foxtel iQ costs $15 per month.

The Foxtel service serves approximately 1.4 million homes, or about 25 percent of the population, compared to 90 percent in the United States.

MAGAZINES

Australia has a vibrant magazine market despite its small population. The primary chains are the Fairfax magazines and ACP. Most well-known international titles are here, but keep in mind that they are Australian editions produced under license, so local content will be more heavily featured. Prominent magazines include the *Women's Weekly, Woman's Day, Cleo, Cosmopolitan, New Idea, Ralph, FHM, Rolling Stone, Better Homes and Gardens,* and Time Inc. titles such as *People* and *Money.*

Magazines are coming under pressure from the Internet, both in advertising and circulation, and Aussie magazines increasingly represent the interests of the advertisers who fund them. Extensive product placements and advertiser-friendly storylines have become more common.

TRAVEL AND TRANSPORTATION

More than 60 percent of Aussies live in one of the six major cities, and distances between Outback towns can be daunting, dry, and desolate—for this reason, although car ownership is high on a per capita basis, Aussies take a lot of group transport. It's fitting for a culture that had to learn how to cooperate to survive in a dry, generally unfertile climate—but it makes travel and transport an important topic to master, as just getting in your car and turning on the GPS is not quite sufficient in Oz.

By Air

Given the distance between the major cities, the preferred means of interstate transport is by air, but generally Australians do less domestic travel than

Americans, whether for leisure or business purposes. As a result, there has always been a shortage of good domestic carriers to compete with the national airline, now known as the domestic service of Qantas. The major competitors now are Virgin Blue and Jetstar, which focus on low-cost services. Regional service is provided by a number of smaller airlines offering prop or small-jet service to regional cities, especially in New South Wales and Queensland. But when it comes to international travel, there are a large number of carriers who provide service to Australia owing to the popularity of the Land Down Under as a vacation destination, as well as to the insatiable desire of Aussies for international travel.

The major international gateway and the most important airport is Sydney's Mascot airport, about 13 kilometers south of Sydney's CBD, but all of the Australian capital cities except Hobart feature international services. The second most important airport is Melbourne, which also offers direct non-stop service to the U.S. west coast, and Brisbane and Cairns also offer direct service to the United States, although Cairns service requires a stop. Direct nonstop service across the Pacific reaches Honolulu, Vancouver, San Francisco, and Los Angeles, and flight times are around 13 hours to LAX and about an hour more to Vancouver and San Francisco. Service to Honolulu is around 10 hours. Round-trip airfares can range from a minimum of US$900 to more than US$5,000 for a full-fare economy seat in peak season (around Christmas); booking well ahead of time and avoiding the Australian summer, the U.S. summer, and domestic Australian school holidays is the best way to keep airfares low. October, November, and May are classic times to get a deal on travel. Business class fares can range US$3,000–8,000, and first class is generally around 30–50 percent higher. Typical flight patterns involve evening departures from the United States and an early morning arrival in Sydney, but the clock will have advanced an extra day due to crossing the international date line. Trips to the States typically involve early evening departures and late morning arrivals, with the curious effect of crossing the international date line and sometimes arriving before the official departure time.

Most Australians book online, and services such as Expedia Australia (www .expedia.com.au) and Flight Centre (www.flightcentre.com.au) are popular sites for both domestic and international needs. Airline websites such as www.qantas.com.au and www.virginblue.com.au are even more popular.

From the United States and Canada, direct service into Australia is provided by Air Canada, Air Tahiti Nui, Continental, Hawaiian Airlines, Qantas, and United Airlines, with Qantas connecting into the American Airlines U.S. domestic market. Continental provides service to Cairns from Guam, connecting

DAILY LIFE

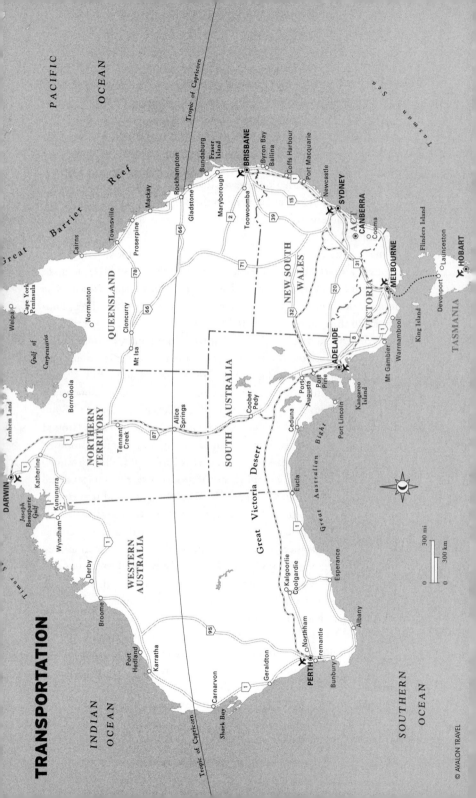

on to Honolulu or Houston. Air Tahiti Nui connects through Papeete, while Air Canada operates service to Vancouver. Hawaiian serves Honolulu. Qantas and United serve San Francisco and Los Angeles.

By Train

Australia has a national rail service, Australia Rail, that offers long-distance travel, but the vast majority of travel is organized by the states in the form of state rail services throughout the countryside and commuter rail services in the city. Each state has a network of country rail, which is used primarily for freight but offers a low-cost alternative to air travel for those who don't like to fly, or for areas not served by airports, or for short journeys where rail is competitive compared to the time needed to get to an airport, check in, and get through security.

Brisbane, Adelaide, Perth, Sydney, and Melbourne have commuter rail, and Hobart periodically looks into it and may eventually establish light rail for its northern suburbs. But the main cities offer extensive rail for commuters, and in many parts of town it is the major conveyor of commuters to the CBD. Most rail networks are the hub-and-spoke type; that is, they converge on the CBD, so getting from suburb to suburb can be daunting unless they are linked by the same rail line. In Sydney, to give a sense of the scope of rail options, there are more than 2,300 scheduled rail services on weekdays, carrying more than 900,000 passengers per day, or nearly 20 percent of the state's population moving among 302 city stations in the network. All cities offer day tickets, weekly and monthly commuter passes, and à la carte ticketing for one-time travel. In Australia, note that "round-trip" travel is called "return." All state rail authorities have schedules and route maps online.

By Bus

Like rail service, buses are used for national and statewide service, but overwhelmingly are used by commuters and students in the major cities. The bus networks are extensive in all capital cities as well as Canberra. For example, the state of New South Wales operates 15,000 bus services each day, carrying more than 600,000 passengers per day. About half of buses are accessible to the disabled at this stage, and about half are air-conditioned. All major state authorities have online websites with timetables and routes. As with rail, fares can be paid on a one-off basis, or with day, weekly, quarterly, or annual passes. There are family passes for day travel and discounts for seniors and other pensioners. A standard annual commuter pass in Sydney will cost $1,280, while a "single" (one-way) trip costs $1.80 at a minimum. Travel is costed on the basis of sections, as is typical in most cities worldwide, with a maximum of 16 sections in Sydney, which will cost $5.80 per single ticket. Children and pensioners receive 50 percent discounts as a rule of thumb.

By Ferry and Hovercraft

Adelaide, Perth, Brisbane, Sydney, and Melbourne all offer ferry services, but Sydney's are the most extensive by far. Sydney Ferries transports more than 14 million people per year around Sydney Harbour via more than 110,000

COMMUTING BY FERRY

A book on Australia would not be complete without mention of commuting by ferry. Adelaide, Melbourne, Brisbane, and Perth say that commuting by ferry is a stress-free and "festive" way to travel. In Sydney, it is simply majestic.

The Sydney ferries started back in the 1860s, when there was no bridge across Sydney Harbour. They were privately run until 1951. The Manly service was independently run until 1974. Services run from Manly, the eastern suburbs, Taronga Zoo, the Parramatta River, and the inner harbor. All ferries arrive at Circular Quay, after passing by the Sydney Opera House and turning into the Quay just before the Sydney Harbour Bridge. Parramatta and some inner harbor services, as a bonus, pass under the bridge.

Sydney ferries are named for the ships of the First Fleet that arrived in Sydney in 1788, while most of the "cats," or high-speed catamarans, are named for Australia's greatest female athletes.

© MITCHELL CHESHER

Sydney ferry on the harbor

individual services. The ferries are passenger only, and they run between Circular Quay in the heart of Sydney's CBD to the inner harbor suburbs, primarily on the north shore. It is the most elegant way imaginable to commute, passing the Sydney Harbour Bridge and the Opera House twice each day, and the ferries are crowded but not teeming with passengers. Fares are available on a single, return, ten-tripper, day pass, weekly, quarterly, or annual pass basis. A bus/ferry pass in Sydney providing a bus down to the ferry wharf and passage to Circular Quay runs $1,280 per year.

All state ferry systems provide online timetables, route maps, and fares.

By Car

DRIVING

Auto ownership is high in Australia on a per capita basis, but commuting is generally to be avoided if possible unless you need a car for work or you have a very short commute. Every city in Australia except Canberra has a traffic problem, and Sydney and Melbourne are just awful despite extensive freeway-building efforts. A commute from Sydney's northern beach suburbs can take more than an hour in heavy morning rush hour traffic and is start-and-stop most of the way. It's better to suffer the hour on a bus working a crossword puzzle or reading a morning paper, although at heavy rush hour times, seats are generally hard to find. Weekend travel, particularly on Sunday, is much lighter unless in the vicinity of beaches, sporting venues, or other recreation or entertainment centers.

Australia does not have an extensive freeway system but is rapidly expanding what it has. Generally, commuters will travel at 50–60 kph on suburban streets, 60–80 kph on arterial roads connecting suburbs and used as secondary commuting routes to the CBD, and 100–130 kph on limited-access freeways.

Designated drivers are an absolute must in Australia, which has practically no tolerance for drunk driving. The national blood alcohol limit is 0.05 percent, there's a zero limit for most learners and provisional drivers, and random breath testing takes place at roadblocks.

Speed limits are enforced with motion-detecting speed cameras that take a picture of your license plate and send you a very, very steep fine. With as few as two offenses where a major speed violation of more than 15 kph is involved, you may lose your license and be forced to take the driver's test again; you will drive for up to three years with a provisional license that restricts your speed.

Driver's Licenses

In Australia, licenses are handled on a state by state basis, as in the United

GREEN Ps, RED Ps

Over the last 20 years, Australia has been tightening up the rules for obtaining a driver's license. If you have a current license and have held it for more than five years, you are eligible to simply exchange your foreign license for an Aussie one upon passing the written test. Otherwise, it can get complex.

The rules from state to state are different, but in general all drivers will have to obtain a learner's permit for a minimum of three months. After passing the driving and written test no earlier than 17 years of age, the driver is issued a provisional license for a minimum of one year, which restricts blood alcohol, speed, use of freeways, and type of engine driven.

In New South Wales and Victoria, where the vast majority of relocations are, the news is worse. You have to hold the learner's permit for one year and complete 120 hours of approved driver instruction. Taking the driver's test no earlier than at 17, after passing the test you hold a class 1 provisional license for one year (displaying a P plate on your car when driving), and a class 2 provisional license for two years (displaying a Green P plate while driving). There are restrictions on passengers, speed, engine type, road type, and blood alcohol. And if you receive a traffic ticket while holding a provisional license, you start over again. Also, those who receive too many points for traffic violations lose their licenses and have to go back to Red or Green P plates.

The good news in all this is that traffic fatalities have dropped in New South Wales to 7.6 per 100,000 persons per year, from 19.9 in 1950.

States. However, as a general rule, licenses are harder to get and harder to keep. As an immigrant to Australia from the United States, Western Europe, or New Zealand, you should not have to take a practical driving test if you hold a current license from the home country, but you will have to take a written test.

You can practice the written test online and take it an unlimited number of times until you pass, although you have to pay a fee of around $30 every time you take it.

A new driver will need to take a practical test as well as a written one, and you can't generally take the practical test until you are 17 years old. Learner's permits are generally available up to 12 months prior, and driving education is often available through the public school system, as well as private commercial tutoring. New drivers must complete 120 hours of driver education and hold the learner permit for a year before applying for the P1. In New South Wales, upon passing your test you will be given a provisional license for one year, which requires you to display a Red P plate and observe special restrictions on freeway access, speed, passengers, and alcohol. After a year, you can obtain a new Green P provisional plate, which relaxes some of the road and speed restrictions. After two years on the Green P, you may obtain a full license

Rules of the Road

The major difference in Australia is quite obvious: Aussies drive on the left, and drivers are on the right side of vehicle and use their left hand to shift gears. Other major differences include the aforementioned rules regarding licensure and alcohol, plus the mandatory use of seatbelts, a prohibition against U-turns at traffic lights, and roundabouts.

Roundabouts, which have replaced many stop signs and traffic lights, can cause confusion. The general rule is that you give way to your right, enter to your left, continue around until you come to the road you need to continue on, and exit the roundabout to the left. Don't forget to signal when exiting a roundabout; failing to signal is an Aussie no-no.

If driving in remote areas, remember that Australia is a very underpopulated country and there is not always a friendly service station just around the corner. Don't allow your fuel level to get low unless you are sure you know where you are, and carry a spare tire, water, a first-aid kit and spare fuel ("petrol") or at least a gas can when traveling in remote areas. Try to avoid driving at night when you are tired, and for sure keep an eye out for animals. Kangaroos may hop across the road in front of you, and when you hit a large 200-pound kangaroo with a much lower center of gravity than your car, it is your car that may be the worse for the encounter.

RENTING, LEASING, AND BUYING A CAR
Driving and Renting a Car

The major global rental-car brands, such as Avis and Hertz, operate out of the major airports and have some city locations as well. A compact car will cost approximately $55 per day in Sydney and Melbourne in the off-peak season. Cars, by the way, tend to be much smaller in countries outside the United States. You do not need a special driver's license for rental cars while you are in Australia.

Buying a Car

In Australia, a car purchase can be done privately or through a Licensed Motor Car Trader (LMCT). The latter is more expensive, but you have a cooling-off period during which you can cancel the purchase, as well as a warranty on the car if it is sold for more than $3,000. If you buy privately, make sure you check on the title and have a mechanic examine the vehicle. The best place to find private cars for sale is the http://carsguide.news.com.au site, operated by the Murdoch media empire, or through the local papers. Saturday is the day to find the most car ads.

In Australia, registration is through the state motor authority. Insurance is competitive, and the leading provider is NRMA (National Roads and Motorists' Association), which is the Australian equivalent of AAA. Cars are smaller in Australia, and foreign makes are a little more unusual. Parts are sometimes hard to obtain. Most cars are in the $10,000–30,000 range on the secondary market. In the new market, a Toyota Camry retails for $28,400, for comparison purposes; Australia's most popular car, the Holden Commodore, costs $31,500. GM-Holden, Toyota, and Ford are the best known makes.

TAXI SERVICES

Taxis are widely available, especially at airports. The cost will be about double what you are used to if you are living in a U.S. city outside of New York. In general, taxis are an acceptable and common option to/from the airport, but they are less reliable for getting around the city and are not cost effective. It's better to simply get used to public transportation if you are not renting a car.

- Sydney CBD from Mascot airport: $27–35, 15 minutes
- Melbourne CBD from Tullamarine airport: $40–50, 20–25 minutes
- Brisbane CBD from Brisbane airport: $30–35, 25 minutes
- Adelaide CBD from Adelaide airport: $20, 15 minutes
- Perth CBD from Perth airport: $30–35, 15 minutes

PRIME LIVING LOCATIONS

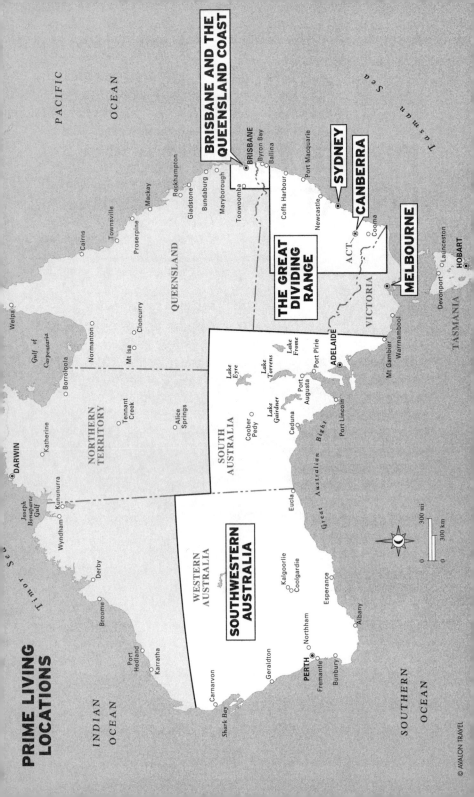

PRIME LIVING LOCATIONS

BRISBANE AND THE QUEENSLAND COAST

SYDNEY

CANBERRA

MELBOURNE

THE GREAT DIVIDING RANGE

SOUTHWESTERN AUSTRALIA

PACIFIC OCEAN

Tasman Sea

INDIAN OCEAN

SOUTHERN OCEAN

Timor Sea

QUEENSLAND

NORTHERN TERRITORY

WESTERN AUSTRALIA

SOUTH AUSTRALIA

VICTORIA

TASMANIA

Gulf of Carpentaria

Joseph Bonaparte Gulf

Great Australian Bight

Byron Bay
Ballina
Port Macquarie
Coffs Harbour
Newcastle
Coma
ACT

BRISBANE
Toowoomba
Maryborough
Bundaberg
Gladstone
Rockhampton
Mackay
Proserpine
Townsville
Cairns
Weipa
Normanton
Borroloola
Mt Isa
Cloncurry
Tennant Creek
Alice Springs
Katherine
DARWIN
Kununurra
Wyndham
Derby
Broome
Port Hedland
Karratha
Carnarvon
Shark Bay
Geraldton
Northham
PERTH
Fremantle
Bunbury
Albany
Esperance
Coolgardie
Kalgoorlie
Eucla
Ceduna
Coober Pedy
Port Augusta
Port Pirie
Port Lincoln
ADELAIDE
Mt Gambier
Warrnambool
MELBOURNE
Devonport
Launceston
HOBART

Lake Eyre
Lake Torrens
Lake Gairdner
Lake Frome

300 mi
300 km
0

© AVALON TRAVEL

OVERVIEW

When tourists visit Australia, they tend to head for Sydney or the Gold Coast, and extended visits tend to take them to the Outback for a taste of Australian country culture, as well as wonders such as the opal mines, Uluru (Ayers Rock), or the Olgas rock formations. But for the purposes of exploring a life in Australia, tourism considerations generally go out the window because tourist life and "real" life in Australia are considerably different.

In this section, we have chosen out six regions of the country that are the most important to different types of potential expats and immigrants. These are the main cities of Sydney and Melbourne; the political capital in Canberra; the leisure capital of Brisbane on the Gold Coast; the southwestern cities of Adelaide and Perth, home to regional industries such as automotive, wine, and mining; and the intriguing areas along the Great Dividing Range.

© MITCHELL CHESHER

SYDNEY

The vast majority of immigrants, especially from the United States, end up in Sydney, which has the biggest economy, the most jobs, and the diverse needs that often require foreign talent. Plus, Sydney is the most self-consciously internationalized city in Australia and takes a distinct pride in its diversity, as well as in the energy and pace the immigration brings to city life. Also, the highly internationalized finance industry, which brings many people to Australia, is based here.

Sydney is the New York of Australia in almost every respect: the financial capital, the population leader, the oldest city, and set, like New York, beside a famous harbor with a famous bridge and a famous landmark—the archetypal Sydney Harbour Bridge and the famed Sydney Opera House. Like New York, it is the most self-consciously internationalist of Australian cities, and sees itself as a player on the world stage as a "world city," a status confirmed by the incredible economic and prestige-gaining success of the 2000 Olympic Games.

Sydney has its critics, especially in other Australian cities, though rarely for its splendid weather and never for its spectacular setting. Residents in other cities feel that their own regions are more "typical" or authentically Australian, and like New York, Sydney is thought by other cities to be brash and domineering. Many people think of it as the most American of Australian cities, and perhaps the most American-influenced city in the world outside of North America.

Conservatory of Music, set amidst the Botanical Gardens, overlooking Sydney Harbour

Earlier criticisms of Sydney life, which centered around its wretched traffic and the high cost of living, are typical of bustling major cities, but Sydney has gone to considerable lengths to improve its traffic with an extensive freeway-building cycle. Its public transportation system, also, is quite extensive, and many Sydneysiders live without cars even though Australia is among the top in the world in per-capita car ownership.

For sure, Sydney is famous because of a harbor second only to Rio for sheer beauty. Add to that a fast-growing and dynamic economy, great weather, and a closer proximity to the U.S. west coast, and you have a recipe for high immigrant interest. It's overwhelmingly the top choice among those who express an interest in Australia, and for many immigrants is all that they know from countless TV shows and documentaries that take advantage of its scenic setting.

More than 1.3 million of Sydney's inhabitants were born overseas, the most of any city in the world and dwarfing all other Aussie cities in this category. In fact, more overseas immigrants live in Sydney than the total population of cities such as Brisbane, Adelaide, Canberra, and Hobart. No matter how popular Sydney is for tourism, for immigration it is even more so.

MELBOURNE

Second only to Sydney is the large metropolis of Melbourne, which is famously home to a vast population of southern Europeans and also attracts a large population of students and academics who flock to some of the country's most revered institutions in the University of Melbourne and Monash University. Many corporate relocations take place in Melbourne, which is home to many of Australia's largest industrial and agricultural companies.

Melbourne does not match Sydney for pace or financial importance, but it is widely considered the cultural capital of the country, and academics that can manage a posting to Melbourne University will be glad for the experience. Melbourne is also the most important city for Australian sports, and is the heartland of Australia's own Aussie Rules football, which is played in front of huge crowds weekly at VFL Park and smaller club stadiums around the city. Melbourne is also home to the Melbourne Cricket Ground, generally felt to be the most important sporting venue for Australia's national sport. The city is filled not only with galleries, museums, and music-filled nightclubs, but also with extensive Victorian parks and a well-protected selection of Victorian architecture, especially in the inner-city suburbs. Interestingly, for all of the attention that Sydney receives, especially in the wake of the Olympics, Melbourne has been growing faster than Sydney in population and income since

2000. One of the reasons is the generally lower cost of living than in Sydney, although Melbourne is one of the 50 most expensive cities in the world according to analysts. In fact, according to a prominent demographer, Melbourne will pass Sydney in population in 2028 if current population trends hold.

The city is the traditional home of the film and television industry in the country. Also, it is known for its historic tram system.

As a corporate relocation point, Melbourne is popular, owing to the fact that five of the ten largest companies and two of the four largest banks are headquartered in the city.

For all these reasons, Melbourne remains a highly popular immigration point and nearly 25 percent (900,000) of its inhabitants were born overseas.

BRISBANE AND THE QUEENSLAND COAST

Tourism professionals and retirees tend to focus their immigration search on the tiny strip of land comprising Brisbane and the Gold Coast of Queensland. There, tropical weather and massive government investment have produced a swath of resorts, golf courses, and condo complexes that complement the extensive collection of white-sand tropical beaches. The city is also famed as the gateway to the Great Barrier Reef.

It is absolutely the number-one destination to be considered for retirement relocations, by those seeking a warmer climate or a more "laid-back" culture.

The region comprises three areas. First, there is the attractive city of Brisbane itself, with urban dwellers occupying towers along the Brisbane River. To the south, the Gold Coast is the more established beach center, but far more commercial too. The glistening beachside condo towers would not be out of place in Florida or Hawaii, and year-round good weather coupled with some affordability (compared to established markets in the United States) makes it a compelling alternative to similar locations in the northern hemisphere.

To the north lies the comparable but lesser known Sunshine Coast, which tends to attract price-takers plus those who want a quieter beachside lifestyle than the bustling Gold Coast provides.

CANBERRA

Next to Melbourne, the national capital of Canberra is home base for many relocatees—typically expats more than permanent immigrants—serving in diplomatic posts, attending or teaching at the Australian National University, or serving in nongovernmental organizations (NGOs) or lobbying firms based in the capital.

Canberra has a population of only 323,000 and is also by far the newest

© AUSTRALIAN CAPITAL TOURISM

Canberra city parkland

of the major Australian urban centers, dating back to 1913, with most of its development since World War II.

There was an old Australian cartoon that featured a stern judge pronouncing "I sentence you to live in Canberra," but times have changed. Its planned city, lakeside setting, and extensive preservation of bushlands and green belts have made it one of the greenest and most pastoral of cities. It is the largest Australian city situated in the bush, rather than by the coast, which gives it not only distinctive scenery and weather but proximity to the bush that makes it quite authentically Australian. It also has the best auto traffic situation of any city in Australia.

THE GREAT DIVIDING RANGE

The Great Dividing Range is an area of increasing interest for retirees, telecommuters, and those who have part-time requirements to be in the vicinity of Sydney.

The range comprises several sections. In the north, the mountains come quite close to the coast, and to their east and along the coastline is the northern New South Wales tourism, surfing, and second-home center of Byron Bay; to the west of the Northern Tablelands are regional agricultural centers such as Tamworth and Armidale.

West of Sydney are the Blue Mountains, a spectacular collection of eroded plateaus that provides excellent retirement opportunities, second homes, or even commuter homes for those working in the tourism industry in the mountains or who have work in the far western suburbs of Sydney. South of Sydney, the range is composed of a series of low rolling hills that have small towns dotted with boutique wineries, B&Bs, artist retreats, and second homes, plus a colony of retirement homes around the small-craft marina-based towns like Ulladulla, Mollymook, and Bateman's Bay.

Near the New South Wales and Victoria border lies the terminus of the range, in the Australian Alps. Numerous ski lodges and homes are situated near the ski centers of Perisher and Thredbo.

SOUTHWESTERN AUSTRALIA

Unlike the other sections of *Prime Living Locations,* which focus on small and distinct sections of the country, southwestern Australia refers to an enormous section of the country about the size of Texas. In a practical sense, though, it's divided between the metropolitan areas and surrounds of Adelaide, in South Australia, and Perth, capital of Western Australia.

Beautiful as the southwest is (and popular with tourists), relocations typically occur in these two cities because of industry-specific job hires or transfers; Adelaide is a major center for the auto industry and is the primary center for Australia's famed wine industry. Perth is home to the mining industry and is a major center for oil and gas exploration.

Adelaide is situated in the south-central region of the country, about 480 kilometers northwest of Melbourne, and is the gateway to the famed Barossa Valley, Australia's primary wine center. The parklike city has long-ago outstripped its original greenbelts, which once served as the city border and now are an inner-city ring, but it remains one of the prettiest urban designs in the country.

Perth, which is popular with U.K. expats as well as mining corporations, is the "big leagues" when it comes to iron, bauxite, and other primary mineral recovery companies. Oil and gas exploration continues to take place offshore, and overall Western Australia has ridden a resources boom that has made it Australia's third-largest and fastest-growing city, where execs can commute from beachside suburbs to jobs in buildings along the majestic Swan River, without the commuting hassle that haunts those who choose Sydney and Melbourne.

Both Adelaide and Perth are two of the most highly urbanized cities. More than 70 percent of the population of Western Australia lives in the Perth metro area, and the same ratio holds for Adelaide and the state of South Australia. By contrast, 60 percent of the population of New South Wales lives in Sydney.

SYDNEY

Sydney is my hometown, but it doesn't take a hometown perspective to acknowledge the city as one of the most beautiful, most beloved, and most exciting cities in the world. The original European penal settlement, dating to 1788, Sydney (pop. 4,297,100) has been the leader among Australian cities in population, economy, and fame almost throughout its history, but since the completion of its famed Opera House in 1973 it seems to be reaching new heights with every decade.

Almost every tourist to Australia passes through Sydney, and as the financial capital of the country, much of the money passes through it as well. Home to more than 20 percent of the country's entire population, Sydney has more of an impact on national life than the leading cities of most other countries. It is the most bold, lively, and entrepreneurial of Australia's cities, and is self-consciously international in its outlook. It is famed for its welcoming attitude toward Americans in particular, who find many similarities between Sydney and California, yet revel in its architecture, the friendliness of its people, and a harbor that is rivaled for beauty only by Hong Kong's and Rio de Janeiro's harbors.

© JAMES M. LANE

Sydney has capitalized on its proximity to the United States and Southeast Asia (in comparison with Melbourne) by passing its traditional rival in finance and industry. Increasingly, major corporations are based here, as are the major media organizations. Most corporate relocations tend to focus for this reason on Sydney, but also, those who are simply in love with Australia tend to gravitate here for its fun nightlife, outstanding beaches and surf, and a subtropical Mediterranean climate that never seems to get too hot or too cold.

Sydney is famed for its extensive network of ferries and harbor JetCats, but it also sports a highway and public transportation infrastructure that was greatly strengthened during the lead-up to the 2000 Olympic Games. Accordingly, it has become an easier city to get around despite its fast growth. Sydney is the home of Australian rugby as well as the Sydney Cricket Ground, and fields the ever-popular Sydney Swans in the Australian Football League (Australian Rules football).

Bottom line: More than 1.3 million of Sydney's inhabitants were born overseas, a number that is light-years beyond that of any other city, and in fact exceeding the overseas relocation statistics for almost every city in the world. So you'll feel right at home. In fact, the number of people living in Sydney who were born out of the country is larger than the entire population of any other Australian city besides Melbourne, Perth, and Brisbane.

THE BRIEF STORY OF SYDNEY

Europeans first visited Sydney when the 1770 expedition of Captain Cook charted the southeastern Australian coastline and discovered Botany Bay. For his trouble, Captain Cook is occasionally featured on Australian commemorative currency.

But it was the American Revolution that brought settlers to Australia, because the practice of transporting convicted criminals to America ceased at that time, and Australia was identified as a dumping ground for convicts in the 1780s, leading to an initial expedition to Botany Bay led by Captain Arthur Phillips in 1787.

Landing at Botany Bay on January 26, 1788, a day now celebrated as Australia Day, the convicts and soldiers rapidly discovered a shortage of fresh water and eventually resettled a few miles north at Sydney Cove. Today, Sydney Cove is known as Circular Quay, and it remains the home base of Sydney's extensive ferry fleet.

Convict transportation continued until 1850 in Sydney, but, increasingly, the country began attracting free settlers. Some moved inland and entered the farming or ranching business, while others stayed on in Sydney, which served as the center of government, finance, law, education, health, trade, and services. Sydney was one of the great Pacific trading seaports of the clipper era, along with Shanghai, Hong Kong, and San Francisco.

In 1823, the settlers earned limited self-government, and Sydney became the capital of the colonial legislature of New South Wales. Many fine 19th-century government buildings are still in evidence around the central business district, and particularly along Macquarie Street, which is named after the state's most admired colonial governor, Lachlan Macquarie.

Federation came in 1901, and Sydney briefly served as capital of the new Commonwealth of Australia. The city was hit hard by casualties in World War I, and Anzac Day (April 25), which commemorates the landing of the Australian troops at Gallipoli in 1915, is still the subject of a solemn ceremony at the War Memorial in Hyde Park. The city was also hit very hard by the Great Depression, which crippled the global trade that brought Sydney its livelihood. But the opening of the Sydney Harbour Bridge in 1932 was a highlight.

After suffering minor attacks from submarines in World War II, Sydney began an era of great expansion after 1945. The population boomed, and Sydney's unique beach culture flourished amid considerable prosperity. The Sydney Opera House opened in 1973, and Darling Harbour was redeveloped in the 1980s as Sydney became known as one of the most beautiful seaside cities in the world. The city played host to the 2000 Olympic Games with a unique blend of sports, Australian friendliness, and indigenous Australian culture that charmed the world.

The Lay of the Land

In Sydney, everything is centered on the harbor, which runs east–west and divides the city into its southern and northern halves, which are joined by the Sydney Harbour Bridge.

The central business district (CBD)—what Americans would call downtown—is on the south side of the harbor about 15 kilometers from North Head and South Head, which mark the entrance to the Pacific Ocean. The CBD is approximately one kilometer wide and five deep. It is bordered on the north by Circular Quay, which is the ferry hub; on the west by Darling Harbour, which is a shopping and dining district; on the south side by Central Station, which is the rail hub; and on the east side by the trendy inner city suburbs of Woolloomooloo and Darlinghurst.

Fashionable areas for living include the inner-city suburbs such as Balmain, Paddington, and the aforementioned Woolloomooloo (pronounced "wuh-luh-muh-LOO" or simply "The Loo"). Other fashionable areas include the eastern suburbs, which follow the harbor all the way out to the eastern beach suburbs such as Coogee and Bondi Beach; the northern suburbs, which include the inner harbor suburbs of Mosman, Neutral Bay, and Kirribilli; the North Shore suburbs, which consist of 10 suburbs from North Sydney to Hornsby that hug the North Shore commuter rail line; and 10 Northern Beach suburbs, which reach from Manly Beach to Palm Beach.

The city has extensive suburban areas to the west and south, which offer more affordable and spacious living.

The metropolitan area is bounded by Botany Bay in the south, the Nepean River and Blue Mountain foothills in the west, the Hawkesbury River to the north, and the Pacific Ocean to the east.

The city is quite hilly near the inner harbor but never mountainous, and it contains an astonishing amount of greenery. Suburban homes are often hardly visible from the street due to the extensive array of eucalyptus trees and bushes, and many suburbs border national parks or other reserved lands.

CLIMATE

Sydney is blessed with one of the most famously enjoyable climates in the world, with mild winters and summers that keep Sydneysiders outside throughout the year and in the oceans nine months a year without a wetsuit.

Sydney records snowfall once a century, most recently in the mid-1980s,

AVERAGE TEMPERATURES AND RAINFALL

	Rainfall (mm)	Daily High (°C)	Daily Low (°C)
January	103	26	18
February	111	26	19
March	131	25	17
April	130	22	14
May	123	19	11
June	129	17	9
July	103	16	8
August	80	17	9
September	69	20	11
October	83	22	13
November	81	23	15
December	78	25	17

Source: Australian Bureau of Meteorology

and temperatures near freezing are highly uncommon. The outlying western suburbs are typically 5–10 degrees colder, and beyond the western suburbs lie the Blue Mountains, which typically do receive snowfall in the winter.

Sydney is quite dry in the winter and humid subtropical in the summer, so afternoon rainfall is common in the summer months, especially in the month of February. In the summers, there is often a buildup of temperature and humidity throughout the day until the sudden arrival of strong (often gale-force) winds from the south—called the "Southerly Buster"—which can drop the temperature by as much as 10°C in 15–30 minutes, resulting in a cool, pleasant Sydney summer evening.

Sydney receives so much sunshine throughout the year that dryers are not common in homes and buildings, and heating and air-conditioning units are uncommon except in office buildings, apartment blocks, and newer homes. Older Sydney homes rely on electric space heaters in the colder evenings of the winter, and even in the height of summer, air conditioning is not typically needed.

Where to Live

There are 38 local government areas in the Sydney metropolitan area, but these can be divided into eight recognizable areas to live. New arrivals will, depending on budget, want to live in the more convenient northern and eastern suburbs if working in the city. Commuting is not unpleasant by public transport, but it can be lengthy, so living close to work is advisable if feasible. U.S. expats generally congregate in the eastern suburbs, but there is no expat enclave in this most international and cosmopolitan of cities.

Excellent, comprehensive sources for real estate listings, units for rent, and information on suburbs, schools, shopping, and more is available through the major real estate agencies, which are active in all parts of the city and throughout Australia. LJ Hooker (www.ljhooker.com.au) and Real Estate Australia (www.realestate.com.au) offer the best resources.

CENTRAL BUSINESS DISTRICT AND INNER SUBURBS

The central business district (CBD) has only recently become popular as a place to live, but it is a lively gathering point not only during the week but also through the weekend, with lively clubs, galleries, shops, and restaurants. The inner ring of suburbs that surrounds the CBD includes Pyrmont to the west and Woolloomooloo ("The Loo"), Darlinghurst, and Kings Cross ("The Cross") to the east.

These are stylish, artsy places to live, and feature gentrified, Victorian row houses that are narrow but deep, often with charming gardens or conservatories in the back. Some of them are subdivided by floor, others available in their entirety. These are districts for singles, empty-nesters, culture vultures, and those who simply have to be as close to the CBD as possible. While the residents are not all young, they are very outgoing, and noise can be a factor. Kings Cross is the traditional home of Sydney's red-light district, and late-night revelers and derelicts are out and about at all hours in certain patches of the Cross. Choose carefully in this district. Overall, the inner suburbs offer a fun experience of the most cosmopolitan side of Sydney, if you can accept the occasional noise and lack of wide open spaces that come with inner city living. Residents of San Francisco, New York, and other highly urbanized cities will find this district to their liking.

Median home prices for the CBD are $715,000 for houses, $540,000 for units, and rentals average $510 per week.

EASTERN SUBURBS

The eastern suburbs encompass an area stretching nearly to the eastern edge of the CBD all the way to the Pacific Ocean, about 15 kilometers as the crow flies but a world away from the CBD culturally, and highly varied from suburb to suburb. Commuters have a choice between buses and the Eastern Suburbs Railway, which proceeds from the CBD to Bondi Junction.

Along Sydney Harbour are suburbs such as Point Piper and Double Bay, which are the most expensive areas to live in all of Australia. These suburbs have a number of houses available for long-term rental (in Oz you "let" an apartment, rather than "rent", although Aussies recognize both terms), but purchase is generally prohibitive unless you are in Australia for the long haul or have considerable corporate assistance. The recent drop in the value of the U.S. dollar hasn't helped much in this respect.

Away from the harbor, there is the artsy enclave of Paddington, which is well known for its eclectic boutiques, galleries, and cafés. Paddington offers a bit more breathing room and elegance than the immediate inner ring of suburbs around the CBD but has much of the same Victorian row-house architecture. It appeals to many professionals.

Farther east, there is the majestic, rather inaccessible and expensive beach suburb of Vaucluse, which follows the harbor right to South Head, which marks the entrance to the Pacific Ocean. Down south from Vaucluse is a series of eastern beach suburbs that are just delightful and highly prized as places to live. Bondi Beach is the most famous, but Coogee, Bronte, and Clovelly appeal to affluent renters and buyers. Bondi Junction is considered the heart of the eastern suburbs and has a strong commercial and professional base as well as extensive shopping, including a major mall.

Slightly inland, suburbs such as Randwick and Kensington are more affordable. Kensington is home to the University of New South Wales, and attracts both students and professors, while Randwick is home to the Sydney Cricket Ground and the Sydney Sports Stadium and is generally more of a middle-class and working-class location, along with adjacent Maroubra.

Median home prices for the eastern suburbs are $1,250,000 for houses, $575,000 for units, and rentals average $540 per week.

LOWER NORTH SHORE

On the northern side of the harbor are several inner harbor suburbs, which are strong both for prestige and amazing views of Sydney, the Harbour Bridge, and the Opera House. The suburbs are built into sloping harborside hills, so there are a lot of view opportunities that are non-waterfront. Commuters from these suburbs have the option not only of bus service but also the magnificent ferry system which is just a really memorable way to commute, passing the Opera House every day of your life en route to Circular Quay.

On the north side of the Harbour Bridge are Kirribilli and North Sydney. North Sydney is a mini-CBD with tall commercial towers as well as houses and apartment complexes. It's 10 minutes from the CBD by rail or bus. Kirribilli is home to Kirribilli House, the Sydney home of the governor-general or, recently, former prime minister John Howard. The suburb is pricey and features incredible views. The atmosphere is low-key compared to the trendy eastern suburbs.

East of North Sydney is the trio of Neutral Bay, Cremorne, and Mosman. Each is served by its own ferry service, and many commuters walk or take a short bus trip down to the harborside jetty for the commute. They all feature many elegant homes, many with spectacular views of the city, plus extensive blocks of apartments ("flats") that also feature views. Each of these suburbs is far more tranquil than the eastern suburbs, but they do have a bustling commercial area along Military Road with some excellent restaurants. Mosman is the largest of the three, and is home to Taronga Park Zoo. Sailing enthusiasts favor Mosman, which is home to marinas at The Spit and Mosman Bay.

On the western side of the Harbour Bridge are the quiet, affluent harborside suburbs of Gladesville and Hunters Hill, which are well liked as locations for affluent, professional families and those looking for both views and space.

Median home prices for north Sydney are $1,000,000 for houses, $533,500 for units, and rentals average $500 per week.

UPPER NORTH SHORE

The upper North Shore generally follows the North Shore rail line from North Sydney to Hornsby, taking in Waverly, Wollstonecraft, St. Leonards, Chatswood, Pymble, Wahroongah, and Hornsby, among others. Willoughby, Ryde, and Lane Cove are also considered a part of the upper North Shore. This area is popular with expats looking for larger, newer (if not new) suburban tile-roofed, single-story homes that are far more affordable than the inner suburbs, yet still convenient to the city, safe, and upscale. Professionals and corporate executives often head up this way. Chatswood has become a corporate center in recent years, which has added to the appeal of these areas. The rail trip into the CBD is 15–45 minutes depending on how far "up the line" one is. Along with the eastern suburbs, this area is home to more well-known private schools than any other district.

Median home prices for Chatswood are $980,000 for houses, $495,000 for units, and rentals average $470 per week.

MANLY AND THE NORTHERN BEACHES

There are 39 suburbs that are loosely referred to as the northern beaches, which is a peninsula bordered also by French's Forest and Kuringai National Park, and feels a world away from the city. The 39 suburbs surround Manly, Freshwater, Harbord, Curl Curl, Dee Why, Collaroy, Narrabeen, Newport, Whale, and Palm Beaches. Generally speaking, the homes in this area feature Pacific views and appeal to professionals who would rather host a Sunday barbecue than spend the weekend at fashionable restaurants or galleries.

The beach suburbs, as a rule, have more access to the water than the harborside suburbs. The harborside has homes built right along the harbor, many of them spacious, expensive, and exceedingly private. By contrast, golf courses, public parks, marinas, shops, and restaurants dot the beachside areas.

This is the home of Australian surfing, and hundreds of surfers will be on the water in ideal conditions at North Narrabeen and Manly. For the quintessential beachside experience, this area is a good choice, although rentals are pricey and commuting to the city is a beast that can take an hour or more from the far northern beaches.

Median home prices for Manly are $1,605,000 for houses, $640,000 for units, and rentals average $600 per week.

THE INNER WESTERN SUBURBS

The inner western suburbs, along with the North Shore and eastern suburbs, are without question the most popular locations for expats. These areas include

the road to Sydney's CBD from the beach suburbs

Glebe, Newtown, Erskineville, Leichhardt, and Marrickville. The inner west is known as a center of the GLBT community in Sydney, especially in the Newtown area. Like the eastern suburbs, the inner west offers a combination of trendy, artsy suburbs for affluent singles and empty-nesters, as well as more middle class areas toward the west and south in Canterbury and Strathfield.

Median home prices for Leichhardt are $677,500 for houses, $450,000 for units, and rentals average $425 per week.

GREAT WESTERN SUBURBS

The outer western suburbs are not generally in favor with affluent expats owing to commute issues, but execs working in the west or those looking for affordable housing will be drawn out this way. Sydney has been expanding in this direction for some time, so new construction will tend to be in the far northwest or southwest, which means the most modern and spacious homes can be found in this area. Bankstown, Baulkham Hills, Parramatta, Penrith, and Campbelltown are the best known out of 14 different local areas that form the vast western suburbs.

A cultural stereotype has built up over the years in Sydney called the "Westie," generally a lower-class, uneducated, usually unemployed youth who makes poor fashion choices. "Trailer trash" would be the closest American equivalent to this expression, which reflects the generally higher unemployment and lower graduation rates in the west. The stereotype is a less-than-attractive side of Sydney culture, which is known to reek occasionally of snobbishness.

Median home prices for Parramatta are $420,000 for houses, $307,000 for units, and rentals average $290 per week.

SOUTH SYDNEY

South Sydney refers to an area including the St. George and Sutherland shires, and more than 90 individual suburbs. Noise from Sydney Airport and traffic congestion have prevented this district from attracting a lot of affluent expats, but St. George is generally home to more middle-class immigrants than any other area in Sydney, and South Sydney is the home of the Greek and Italian communities in Sydney, which were established by extensive immigration in the 1950s and 1960s. Many of these areas are on or near Port Hacking or Botany Bay and offer more affordable water views than any other part of the city. Cronulla is a particularly attractive suburb that has excellent surfing spots along a collection of eight small beaches.

Median home prices for Cronulla are $970,000 for houses, $395,000 for units, and rentals average $370 per week.

Daily Life

MEDIA RESOURCES

Sydney is very much a vibrant newspaper town, and residents still choose from three morning daily papers: the establishment *Sydney Morning Herald,* the racier *Daily Telegraph,* or the "national newspaper," *The Australian.* The *Australian Financial Review* is a daily business tabloid.

PRIME LIVING LOCATIONS

SYDNEY RADIO STATIONS

AM

- 576 kHz 2RN ABC
- 630 kHz NewsRadio ABC
- 702 kHz 702 ABC Sydney
- 873 kHz 2GB Macquarie Radio Network (News/Talk)
- 954 kHz 2UE Fairfax Media (News/Talk)
- 1017 kHz 2KY Sky Channel (Racing/Sports Radio)
- 1170 kHz 2CH Macquarie Radio Network (Easy Listening)
- 1269 kHz 2SM Easy, Talk, Sport, and News
- 1476 kHz 2KA Country Music

FM

- 88.7 MHz Cool Country FM
- 92.9 MHz ABC Classic FM
- 96.9 MHz Nova 969
- 102.5 MHz 2MBS
- 103.2 MHz Sydney's 103.2
- 104.1 MHz 2DayFM
- 104.9 MHz Triple M
- 105.7 MHz Triple J
- 106.5 MHz MIX FM 106.5

TWO EXPLANATIONS OF CRICKET

Since you are looking at moving to the most sports-mad country on earth, it's best to learn a little about cricket.

THE REAL EXPLANATION

Think of a baseball game, only instead of four bases there are two, and you start with a batsman at each. When a ball is hit, they each run to the other base, and if they reach safely, the batsman who hit the ball scores a run. A batsman gets one strike and unlimited balls, and stays in as long as he is not "given out." He can be "bowled" (when the ball crashes into the wicket, which has the same function as a strike zone in baseball), caught, run out (caught before reaching the "crease," the equivalent of a base), or given out by the umpire for using his legs to block a ball from striking the wicket, called "leg before wicket" or "LBW." Each inning consists of 10 outs, and there are two innings, for a total of 20 "wickets" (same as outs) instead of 27 as in baseball.

Since batsmen can stay in until they are out, and they continue to amass runs, scores of 100 runs by a batsman (a "century") are not unusual, although a century is a high mark of achievement. Matches last five days at the international level, but there is a one-day version, and school cricket is played over one day.

THE COMIC EXPLANATION

From a tea towel popularly distributed over the years, origin and author unknown: You have two sides, one out in the field and one in. Each man that's in the side that's in goes out, and when he's out he comes in and the next man goes in until he's out. When they are all out, the side that's out comes in and the side that's been in goes out and tries to get those coming in, out. Sometimes you get men still in and not out.

When a man goes out to go in, the men who are out try to get him out, and when he is out he goes in and the next man in goes out and goes in. There are two men called umpires who stay out all the time and they decide when the men who are in are out. When both sides have been in and all the men have been out, and both sides have been out twice after all the men have been in, including those who are not out, that is the end of the game.

Cricket is the national summer sport of Australia.

© MITCHELL CHESHER

The city is remarkably well-wired for Internet service, and wireless Internet access is the norm for the CBD as well as major commercial centers in the suburbs. Online guides exist for practically every topic under the sun: The sites maintained by major newspapers and television, such as www.news.com.au and www.smh.com.au, are good starting places. The Channel Nine network site is a joint venture with MSN (http://ninemsn.com.au), while the rival Seven Network is a joint venture with Yahoo (http://au.tv.yahoo.com/tv).

HEALTH CARE

Sydney forms the center of New South Wales's extensive health system. There are four basic health regions under the state government's health scheme: Northern Sydney/Central Coast; South Eastern Sydney/Illawarra; Sydney South West, and Sydney West.

Most of the best known hospitals are relatively near to the CBD, including Sydney Hospital, Royal North Shore, and Royal Prince Alfred, with more than a dozen major public and teaching hospitals throughout the city. Among the finest are those affiliated with the two major universities: the Prince of Wales, affiliated with the University of New South Wales, and Royal North Shore, affiliated with the University of Sydney.

Though the specifics of Medicare are extensive, in general the government will cover 75 percent of in-patient costs and 80–100 percent of outpatient costs through the public health system, but more than 40 percent of Australians choose to supplement this with private health insurance.

Private insurance covers a higher percentage of costs, allows more freedom of choice in practitioners, and can shorten waiting times for services, especially those of a nonemergency basis. Public hospitals have been known to experience severe backlogs of patients, and even emergency care has been subject to delays, often unacceptable ones. For peace of mind, go with a private health insurance supplement to Medicare—called Medibank—if you find that your family budget can afford it.

Major hospitals are found throughout the city, but please note that "surgery" is the term for a doctor's office. Doctors are called "doctors" as elsewhere in the English-speaking world, but registered nurses are usually addressed as "sister" whether they have religious affiliation or not; "nurse" is a term used for both registered nurses and aides.

SCHOOLS

The Australian school system is quite different from the American system, and despite Sydney's reputation as the most American of Aussie cities, the differences can be daunting, so be careful in planning the transition to Aussie schools for your younger ones.

The most important decisions you will face with children in transition are how to deal with the different school year (January–December) and whether to enter your children in private or public schools. Generally speaking, it's better to try to advance your children "ahead" if you are planning on leaving Australia before they finish high school, else they may find themselves being "held back" on return to the northern hemisphere and graduating a year behind their natural class. If planning to stay in Oz for the long term, consider putting your children back to give them fewer academic challenges while adjusting to Aussie life, as well as ensuring they are as mature as possible when entering high school.

Like the United States, Sydney has a K–12 system followed by a three-level tertiary system awarding bachelor's, master's, and doctoral degrees, but the similarities end about there.

In Sydney schools are divided into K–6 primary schools and high schools, which are attended by students from years 7–12. There is no equivalent of middle school or junior high school, although younger high school students typically have specialized administrators that look after them.

The Sydney school year consists of four terms, which run from late January to mid-December. There is a relatively short summer break of around six weeks, punctuated by three two-week breaks between terms during the year.

Schooling is free and mandatory through the public school system through year 10; at the end of year 10, students are awarded the School Certificate, which is based on statewide examinations in English and mathematics plus school-run examinations in elective subjects including natural science, social sciences, languages, and fine arts. A substantial minority of students discontinue studies at this time and enter the workforce.

Students who return for years 11 and 12 will prepare for statewide examinations in all their subjects, known as the Higher School Certificate (HSC) exams, conducted at the end of year 12. Subjects can be chosen at the 1, 2, 3, or 4-unit level, which refers to the relative number of course hours (around 1.7 hours per week per unit of class time), and choose a minimum of 11 units (but typically 12–13), with a course called 2-unit English and one 2-unit natural science or mathematics course mandatory.

Primary and secondary students will generally follow, minimally, a strict dress code by American standards, and most schools require school uniforms. In Sydney, the state schools tend to be coeducational, but competitive "magnet" or "selective" schools are in many cases segregated by gender, such as Sydney Boys High and Sydney Girls High.

Selective schools are generally enrolled in year 7 based on results from comprehensive statewide tests.

Sydney has a very extensive private school network, and far more students attend private schools in Sydney than is normal for the United States. In Sydney, there are two main associations for boys' schools: the older and more prestigious Great Public Schools (GPS) and the Combined Associated Schools (CAS).

Foreign students generally have an easier time gaining admission to CAS schools such as Barker, Knox, Cranbrook, and St. Aloysius, although entrance at year 7 is possible for all schools but is based not only on competitive examination but family history.

Admission to private schools is possible at any time, but generally placements are far more difficult to obtain after year 7 due to limited availability.

There are not only private Catholic schools—ranging from local institutions to prestigious secondary schools—but also Presbyterian private schools such as The Scots College and Knox Grammar (both boys only), and Anglican schools such as Sydney Church of England Girls Grammar School ("Sceggs") and Sydney Church of England Grammar School ("Shore"). There are also nondenominational schools such as Newington, Wenona, The Kings College, and Sydney Grammar.

To confess, my own school was Sydney Grammar and I recommend it highly for its splendid, classical educational environment, although a dodgy sports record, high fees, and cramped location in the heart of the city are justly cited by its detractors.

Sydney is home to a series of state technical colleges and universities, and three outstanding major universities in Macquarie University, the University of New South Wales, and Sydney University. University is generally less mandatory in Australia than in the United States, but tertiary education continues to grow in importance. Students generally select their major concentration—arts, commerce, science, law, or medicine—directly out of high school. BA, BS, and BCom degrees are typically awarded after three years, although students can take a fourth year to graduate with an "honors" degree.

The Sydney Institute focuses on technical and vocational courses. New South Wales has an extensive TAFE (Technical and Further Education) network of colleges, and these focus on tourism, construction, visual arts, computers, and other technical subjects. Study is often completed in association with a formal apprenticeship period in the trades.

SHOPPING

Sydney has traditional large department stores in the CBD such as David Jones or Myer, but generally shopping is conducted at large suburban malls such as Bankstown Square in the southwest, Chatswood Mall in the north, Warringah Mall along the northern beaches, Westfield Shopping Town in the eastern suburbs. Boutique-style shopping is found throughout many of the eastern suburbs, especially Paddington. Manly, the queen of the northern beaches, has an extensive outdoor area for art exhibitions and sales.

In the CBD itself, narrow, vibrant "arcades" were tunneled in the 19th century between the main north–south streets of Sydney, and the Strand Arcade, which connects Pitt Street and George Street, is an excellent example of Victorian architecture and modern glitz.

Most Sydneysiders look for meals and drinks in the arcades with occasional "spree" or holiday shopping, while reserving their main shopping for the suburban malls.

Traditionally, Australian shops were open until noon on Saturday and closed on Sunday. To cater to working families, shops have been traditionally open until 9 p.m. on Thursday evenings, and even though weekend shopping is generally available now, Thursdays are still a bustling night for shoppers.

Sunday remains a quiet day, and bars are generally closed, although increasingly there is Sunday service at pubs and hotels.

Getting Around

PUBLIC TRANSPORTATION

Sydney is blessed with an extensive public transportation system—one of the most comprehensive of its kind in the world. There is bus and rail service throughout the metropolitan area, along with extensive ferry services in the harbor. Commuters typically take public transportation to the CBD owing to traffic congestion, and many Sydneysiders—particularly those who live along major bus or rail lines or in the inner-city suburbs—live a happy car-free existence. In the outer suburbs, commuting is still possible and typical via the city bus system, but cars become more of a necessity than a luxury the farther from the CBD one lives.

The central focus of the rail system is Central Station at the south end of the Sydney CBD. There is a six-stop city loop, which is sufficient for all CBD commuters. One of the stops on the loop, Wynyard Station on the northwest side of the CBD, is also the major bus station for the CBD, while at the north end of the loop is Circular Quay, which is where all the Sydney ferries terminate. Bus-rail transfers are typically made at Wynyard and ferry-rail connections at the Quay.

From the eastern and western suburbs, commuters choose between bus and rail service—rail service typically requires more walking to the station but a

© MITCHELL CHESHER

Major bus stops, like this intersuburb connection in Sydney, are covered to shade Aussies from the strong sunshine.

faster transit speed than city bus service, and commuters work out (depending on their home location) which option is best for them.

From the North Shore, commuters living along the North Shore line typically commute via rail, while in other outlying suburbs—particularly the northern beaches—bus service to the CBD or a major rail station is the only option. Commuters in the inner harbor suburbs take the ferry service if the ferry wharves are walkable from their homes. It is a spectacular ride, which takes commuters past the Opera House and Harbour Bridge every day, and is one of the major arguments for living in the expensive inner harbor suburbs.

In addition to the CBD, Sydney has several regional business centers including Parramatta, Chatswood, and north Sydney, and these are well served by rail and bus.

Commuters typically purchase weekly or monthly rail, bus, or ferry passes, which can be purchased online.

HIGHWAYS

Sydney's highway structure has undergone major transformation in the past 10 years, especially in the years leading up to the 2000 Sydney Olympic Games. However, the highway structure is still not as good as in a typical American city, and commute times and traffic can be daunting for those commuting by car.

Like England, Sydney has an M and A naming convention for its highways. Major highways carry the M designation and a number (M1, M2, etc.), while secondary highways carry the A designation (A1, A2, etc.).

Sydney's speed limits are expressed in kilometers per hour (kph) and are typically 50 kph in congested suburban areas, 60 kph for primary suburban roads, 80 kph for highways, and 100 or 110 kph for motorways.

Speed limits are monitored by speed cameras, which have a tolerance of between 5–10 kph over the speed limit. Above that limit, the camera takes a photograph of your license plates and the government sends you a ticket by mail, which costs you $100–400 depending on the severity of the speeding infraction. If you receive two speeding infractions in a three-year period your driver's license is suspended. To regain your driving privileges you must take a new driving test and go through the provisional license system and display "P" plates.

Sydney's roads are also closely monitored for infractions such as driving without seatbelts and drunk driving. Sydney has mobile "booze buses" and random breath testing, and it is said that your chances of being pulled over for a random breath test on a Saturday night are 1 in 6. Tolerance is 0.05 percent rather than 0.08 percent as in most U.S. jurisdictions, and penalties for driving under the influence are severe.

SYDNEY AIRPORT

Sydney's major airport is found approximately eight kilometers south of the CBD on the shores of Botany Bay in the suburb of Mascot. The airport is served by all major Asia-Pacific airlines and is the hub of Qantas, the national airline. Qantas is a member of the OneWorld alliance and has extensive code sharing arrangements with American Airlines for flights to L.A., San Francisco, and Honolulu, and United Airlines also serves Sydney from Los Angeles and San Francisco.

Sydney has separate domestic and international terminals. Transfers cost $4 and are made by a five-minute bus ride. Qantas has a separate terminal joined to the main international terminal.

Sydney's airport security arrangements are roughly equivalent to U.S. standards, but its strict standards regarding plants and animals will be surprising to new arrivals. The country has draconian laws in this respect. Generally speaking you simply should not bring plants or animals to Australia, even beloved pets, unless you are prepared to meet extremely tough standards.

The airport has excellent duty free shopping, and is highly convenient to the city by taxi, car or rail. Airport Link trains run every 10 minutes and have you in the CBD rail system in 13 minutes, while it is less than 15 minutes by car into the CBD in light traffic.

MELBOURNE

Melbourne (pop. 3,850,000), Australia's second-largest city, is in every imaginable way the rival, contrast, and counterweight to Sydney. Where Sydney is full of flash, Melbourne is full of substance; for Sydney's harbor there are Melbourne's gardens; for Sydney's ferries there are Melbourne's trams; for Sydney's rugby there is Melbourne's Aussie Rules; for Sydney's mercurial economy built on world finance, trade, and stock flotations there are Melbourne's rock-solid, large-scale, traditional corporations operating in agriculture and natural resources. Sydney may be the country's leading "world city," but many observers have felt that Melbourne is more authentically an "Australian" city. It is entirely fitting that BHP Billiton, the world's largest natural resources company and one that for many years billed itself as "The Big Australian," is based in Melbourne.

Cooler in physical temperature than its rival city to the northeast, Melbourne is cooler in temperament as well. The city is more rooted in its past, more traditional in its outlook, and occasionally has been described as "staid"

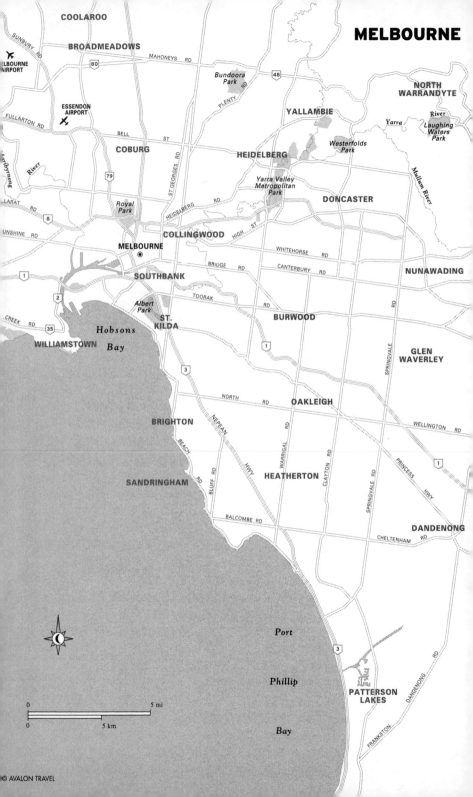

by critics who would call Sydney "flighty." It is built around a set of beautiful suburbs that feed into a CBD that, despite Melbourne's reputation as a slow mover, has been transformed in recent years with the redevelopment of the Docklands into a beautiful mixed-use commercial and residential crown jewel in an already beautiful crown. A 2004 survey by the Economist Intelligence Unit ranked Melbourne as the second best city in the world to live in for expatriates (behind Vancouver, Canada), edging Sydney and Perth on the basis of a lower crime rate and better weather (although to be frank it is a little rich to give Melbourne a perfect score for weather, as the survey did).

For many years following the 1850s Victorian gold rush, Melbourne had the upper hand over Sydney in wealth, population, and global reputation, and the city is the beneficiary of a magnificent legacy of Victorian-era construction and city landscaping and development. Plus, during those years Melbourne established its unrivaled collection of universities such as Monash and the University of Melbourne that have kept Melbourne all these years at the top of the list for academics.

Those who come to Melbourne typically do so owing to corporate or academic appointments, because the weather is less appealing for retirees, yet those who come for reasons of career often finding themselves staying for reasons of the heart. It is a lovely city, well-loved by those who value its many treasures.

THE BRIEF STORY OF MELBOURNE

The city of Melbourne sits at the point where the Yarra River empties into Port Phillip, and was occupied for nearly 40,000 years. At the point of European contact in the 1830s, the Wurundjeri people occupied the Yarra Valley, and the tribe transferred the land of modern-day Melbourne in return for an annual rent of "40 blankets, 30 axes, 100 knives, 50 scissors, 30 mirrors, 200 handkerchiefs, 100 pounds of flour, and 6 shirts," in what was known as Batman's treaty, for it was negotiated by Tasmanian farmer John Batman. Subsequently, the British government nullified the treaty, and a swarm of squatters descended on the area. The resulting confusion over land titles led to the formation of British administration at Melbourne in 1837, and ultimately the colony of Victoria was separated from New South Wales in 1851. The city itself was named for the British prime minister, Lord Melbourne.

Just after the establishment of Victoria, gold was discovered just north of Melbourne, in Ballarat, and what remains until this day the biggest gold rush in history was on. The population of Victoria swelled from 76,000 to 540,000 by 1861, and more importantly, a miner's movement for reduced fees and political representation led to un uprising at the Eureka Stockade in 1854 that is credited as the birthplace of representative democracy. Ten thousand miners massed in meetings that ultimately led in the short run to a doomed Eureka Rebellion, but in the long run to universal male suffrage in elections for the lower house of the Victorian parliament.

The miners who participated in the Eureka Stockade uprising were known the "Diggers," and soldiers in the Australian Army are still known by that name. The Diggers took an oath of allegiance, "We swear by the Southern Cross to stand truly by each other and fight to defend our rights and liberties," and raised a flag featuring the Southern Cross constellation against a blue field. The Southern Cross today forms a part of the Australian national flag.

As the port of entry to the gold fields, and the banking center for the mining industry and ultimately the financing center for Australia's agricultural industries, Melbourne became one of the largest and richest cities in the British Empire. The term "Marvellous Melbourne" was coined by journalist George Sala to reflect the gorgeous Victorian architecture, terrace houses, and gardens of the city. A worldwide economic downturn in the 1890s hit the city hard, and although Melbourne served as the national capital of Australia from 1901 to 1927, Sydney caught up with Melbourne in population during this time.

Melbourne served as Allied Headquarters for the Pacific Theater in World War II, and after the war a resources boom and the 1956 Olympic Games re-established the city as a prosperous leader of the country. Melbourne continued to serve as the banking and corporate center of the country until the 1970s, when Sydney's ties to the United States became more important than Melbourne's ties to London.

A dedicated effort since a tough recession in the early 1990s has resulted in prosperous times for Melbourne in recent years, and since 2000 the city has been growing in population and economy faster than any major city in the country.

An overview of Melbourne would be woefully incomplete without a mention of sport. Where Sydney disappears to the beach on weekends, Melbourne heads for the cricket, the footy parks, or the racecourses. Melbourne Cricket Ground is the most prestigious venue for international matches, and the Telstra Dome packs in more than 50,000 for Aussie Rules football. Aussie Rules draws the biggest crowds of any type of sport in the country, and its great champions are remembered in song and story. In racing, the Melbourne Cup horse race is run at Flemington Racecourse in November, and it is such a big deal that it is a public holiday in Melbourne, and across the country business shuts down for a few minutes while the race is run. It seems like half the country has a wager down on race day.

The Lay of the Land

The Melbourne CBD is situated on the north bank of the Yarra River as it makes its final turn toward Port Phillip Bay. The Hoddle Grid, laid out in 1837 and subsequently expanded, demarcates the 48-block traditional city area, bounded by Southern Cross Station in the west, the Queen Victoria Market in the north, Parliament House to the east, and the Yarra River on the south.

The city includes numerous major landmarks within walking distance, including Parliament House, the daily farmers market at the landmark Queen Victoria Market, and the Melbourne Cricket Ground.

The metropolitan area is of the low-density, sprawl type typical of cities that expanded after the development of railroads and automobiles. The suburbs radiate primarily to the north of the city, in the Yarra Valley, but also wrap around the shores of Port Phillip Bay to the southeast and, to a more limited extent, the southwest.

There are five recognized areas of Melbourne, each with a number of independent shires and cities, and numerous suburbs within each city or shire: the city, the northern suburbs, the southeastern suburbs, the southwest suburbs, and the western suburbs. In all, there are more than 500 recognized suburbs in the metro area.

PRIME LIVING LOCATIONS

AVERAGE TEMPERATURES AND RAINFALL

	Rainfall (mm)	Daily High (°C)	Daily Low (°C)
January	48	26	14
February	48	26	15
March	50	24	13
April	58	20	11
May	56	17	9
June	49	14	7
July	48	13	6
August	50	15	7
September	59	17	8
October	67	20	10
November	60	22	11
December	59	24	13

Source: Australian Bureau of Meteorology

CLIMATE

Melbourne generally has a mild climate but is famous for its fast-changing weather, which can produce four seasons in one day under certain conditions. The city experiences frosts and fogs in winter but has not had a snowfall since 1951, although a sleet storm struck in 1986. The city, while quite cool in winter, is notoriously hot and dry in summer, with temperatures known to exceed 40°C with a maximum in the city of 45.6°C in 1939, equivalent to 114°F. The city is noted for its clouds and rain, with 146 rain days per year and only 48 clear days. But the spring and fall are known for mild and delightful weather.

Where to Live

CITY OF MELBOURNE

The Melbourne CBD and the traditional inner-city suburbs include the City of Melbourne, the Docklands, the City of Port Phillip, and the City of Yarra. Within Port Phillip are well-known suburbs such as Port Melbourne, South Melbourne, and the seaside town of St. Kilda, home of Luna Park. Yarra is home to Fitzroy and Richmond.

The inner city appeals to those who want shorter commutes, better access to public transportation, or an opportunity to live in suburbs like the Docklands or St. Kilda that are undergoing a real transformation. There are opportunities to do well from an investment point of view as well as be in a "trendy" area. The Docklands has been recently transformed in the Victoria Harbour area into a series of apartments and commercial buildings that are attractive and have some fantastic views of the city, although some people feel they are very "apartmenty."

St. Kilda was a seaside resort at the high end in Victorian times, and then went through a seedy red-light district period, but it has emerged as a yuppie area, with a lot of gentrification possibilities. Fitzroy has been gentrified, and the Brunswick Road area is definitely an area to look at if you are seeking great cafés, boutiques, and bars. People refer to it as a "style capital." Richmond also has a café and boutique setting, and at 20 minutes from the CBD it's a quick commute, but keep to the Swan Street area.

Elsewhere in the inner suburbs, South Yarra is a coveted address, and Chapel Street is arguably the bistro and fashion center of the city. There are many Victorian-era mansions and a large selection of high-end homes. South Yarra adjoins the Royal Botanic Gardens and Fawkner Park, which makes it also a favorite with those who want some wide open space. All of this, plus a 15-minute commute into the CBD, makes South Yarra the "most livable suburb"

view of Melbourne's business center

according to the *The Age,* although they weren't rating it for affordability—the median home price is double the average for the metro area. For a yuppie life, with cafés, parks, beach proximity, and lots of young professionals, Port Melbourne, Middle Park, Elwood, and Albert Park form a good sector to try for.

SOUTHEASTERN SUBURBS

The southeast is the most popular part of the metro area, and the suburbs can stretch out a bit, so commuting can be an issue in the outlying areas. Aside from the inner city, more people will go on and on about the southeastern suburbs than any other part of town. Perennial favorites include Berwick, Cranbourne, Bentleigh, Caulfield, and Ormond, always in vogue. Berwick is noted for being home to a number of private schools.

Cranbourne, Beaconsfield, Pearcedale, Hastings, Langwarrin, Lillydale, and Healesville are places to look for larger homes. Armadale has been rated in the top five suburbs in Melbourne. Bentleigh, East Bentleigh, Cheltenham, McKinnon, Mentone, Parkdale, Mordialloc, Aspendale, and Chelsea are well worth a look in terms of raising a family—good schools, proximity to the bay, friendly, and safe. The latter five are 45–60 minutes from the CBD. East Bentleigh is more affordable than Bentleigh, where prices can go over a million dollars. Monash University is in this part of the city, so many students find themselves concentrating in this part of town. Rental range is $400–700 per week.

THE MELBOURNE CUP

"The race that stops a nation" goes the slogan for this race, and for once the promotion department isn't kidding. Eighty percent of Australian adults put a bet down on this horse race, run the first Tuesday in November at Flemington Racecourse. The date puts it in competition with the American presidential elections, but there isn't really any competition at all, except on the racecourse, where horses from Australia, New Zealand and Japan compete for $5 million in prize money in the most prestigious two-miler in the world.

The Cup is a public holiday in Melbourne, and also in the Australian Capital Territory. But don't try to accomplish anything, anywhere, during the half hour around the race, because the whole country stops to watch. Before the race, the closest equivalent to the red carpet at the Oscars or Ascot is the Spring Carnival, which just about keeps the Australian couture hat business, in business. As many as 120,000 spectators crowd the racecourse on the day, but viewing it with friends, family, coworkers, or fellow students is just as fun. Office "sweeps" are conducted for small stakes, and winning the "pool" is cause for a bit of a celebration, and perhaps a few drinks at the pub thereafter.

NORTHERN SUBURBS

The northern suburbs are not the choicest sections of the city, but there are some excellent opportunities, especially if you are concerned about the prices and commute times from the southeastern suburbs. Watch out for the hot northern winds in the summer if you are very far away from the bay and river. Craigieburn has fans, for affordability, schools, and more space both in houses and yards. Greenvale is as close as one can get to the city and still have big lots (around an acre), plus convenience to Tullamarine Airport (which is in the northwest of the city). Sunbury is out toward the airport and is a pleasant and affordable location. Rental range is $150–400 per week.

EASTERN SUBURBS

Like the southeastern suburbs, the east is very popular and attractive. The farther you go out, the more commuting issues there are, but prices are lower and properties bigger. Balwyn, Balwyn North, Camberwell, Caterbury, and Hawthorn are highly popular. Balwyn and North Balwyn are slightly more affordable, with the median prices double or triple the Melbourne average in the others. These are safe, good for families, and are convenient to parks and malls. The state school in North Balwyn gets rave reviews, with the downside there being incovenient access to trains. Way out east in the Yarra Ranges, Mount Evelyn has acreage and good-size homes in natural settings for less than the average price in the city, but prices are increasing quickly. Rentals range $300–600 per week.

WESTERN SUBURBS

Out west are some bargains, fewer traffic hassles, and good schools. Caroline Springs and Cairnlea are worth a good look in that respect. But it's not the prestigious side of town, nor are the trendy nightspots for young professionals out this way. Point Cook, about 20 minutes west of the CBD, has a lot of new construction, good prices, and is not only close to beaches but has lots of infrastructure for young families. Many people swear by Williamstown, which has an older style of architecture, coffeehouses and cafés, gardens everywhere you look, and a beach. Rental range is $200–500 per week.

A YANK WHO CAME AND WENT AGAIN

Dan Butler is a commodities trader from Seattle who moved to Australia, among several countries he has lived in, including the Ukraine, the Czech Republic, and the United States. I recently asked him to write down for me the three reasons he moved to Oz, the three reasons he loved it, and the three reasons he left.

REASONS I MOVED TO AUSTRALIA
- I was looking for some adventure.
- I had some contacts there from trading on an overnight trading desk.
- There seemed to be more opportunities for a ne'er-do-well trader on Wall Street (which was me).

REASONS I LOVED AUSTRALIA
- Climate, birds, flowers, weather, beach . . .
- Food
- Friendly people
- Clean, safe, bright, sunny
- The memories that I have every day since I left

Oh, only three reasons? Forget that – there are too many.

REASONS I LEFT AUSTRALIA
- I was laid off and wanted to do something different in Eastern Europe for a little while.
- I thought I would be back in a year or two.
- I am a bloody silly bugger when it comes to life choices.

PRIME LIVING LOCATIONS

Daily Life

MEDIA RESOURCES

Melbourne has two newspapers, the more conservative *The Age* and the racier tabloid *Herald-Sun,* but Melbourne also receives the national newspaper, *The Australian,* as well as the daily *Australian Financial Review.* The *Herald-Sun* is owned, along with *The Australian,* by News Corp. The rival Fairfax company publishes *The Age* and the *Financial Review.* The best "resource" day is Saturday, when the papers run their main classifieds for homes, flats, and cars. As with all major Australian cities, there are numerous free community newspapers available through Fairfax Community News. There are also newspapers in Greek and Italian that cater to the large immigrant communities.

There are more than 50 radio stations available in every popular format as well as a number of community and niche stations. Also, Melbourne receives all five major free-to-air television networks (the commercial Seven, Nine, and Ten Networks, and the government-run SBS and ABC), as well as major cable and satellite services from Optus, Foxtel, and Austar.

An excellent online guide to Melbourne is the official city guide (www.thats melbourne.com.au). It has everything from nightlife, dining, and shopping

MELBOURNE RADIO STATIONS

AM

- 621 kHz Radio National
- 693 kHz 3AW Fairfax Media
- 774 kHz 774 ABC Melbourne
- 927 kHz Sport 927
- 1026 kHz NewsRadio ABC
- 1503 kHz 3KND South Eastern Indigenous Media Association
- 1611 kHz 3XX 80s and 90s Music Radio (Melbourne 1611 AM)

FM

- 87.6 MHz Kiss FM 876 Dance Culture radio
- 87.6 MHz GB Radio from the U.K. (Melbourne east)

- 87.6 MHz FM 876 Network Melbourne's 87.6 FM Network
- 93.9 MHz Bay FM
- 98.7 MHz 3RPP Mornington Peninsula
- 101.1 MHz MIX 101.1 (formerly known as 3DB/3TT/TT-FM) ARN
- 101.9 MHz FOX FM
- 103.5 MHz 3MBS Music Broadcasting Society of Victoria
- 104.3 MHz Gold 104
- 105.1 MHz Triple M
- 105.9 MHz ABC Classic FM
- 107.5 MHz Triple J ABC

to some excellent material on sport, parks, and other recreation. The *Herald-Sun* and *The Age* both have websites; the former is longer on flash and fun and the latter on newsy substance. Both have city guides, events, and things to do around town.

HEALTH CARE

Medical care is free in Victoria through the federal Medicare system but requires long wait times, especially for elective items. Nearly half of Australians take out supplementary health insurance so they have more choice in doctors and more options to speed up appointments.

The Victorian health system is similar to that of the rest of Australia, including a network of hospitals, community health centers, home and disability care, a health screening system, and a dental system.

The teaching hospitals in Melbourne are the Royal Melbourne, in Parkville, and the Austin & Mercy complex in the northern suburbs, while the other majors are the Royal Children's, Royal Women's, St. Vincents, the Queen Elizabeth, and the Flinders Medical Center (associated with Flinders University), all in the 300–700 bed range. Health.vic.gov.au is the major online portal that covers the services provided by the state government in the health area.

SCHOOLS

The Victoria school year runs from January to December and has four terms, with 1–2-week holiday breaks for Easter, winter, and spring, and a longer, six-week summer break. Private schools generally have fewer school days.

In Queensland, children are required to attend school between ages 6 and 15. Primary school is years 1–6, and high school is years 7–12.

There are more than 50 private schools in Melbourne, and private schooling is more typical in Oz than in the United States. The premier secondary boys' schools belong to the Associated Public Schools, which includes Brighton Grammar, Carey Baptist Grammar, Caulfield Grammare, Geelong College, Geelong Grammar, Haileybury, Melbourne Grammar, St. Kevin's College, Scotch College, Wesley College, and Xavier College. Brighton, St. Kevin's, and Scotch College are boys-only. For the top of the pack, most people would suggest Melbourne Grammar. Premier girls schools include Melbourne Girls Grammar, MLC, Loreto, Camberwell Girls Grammar, PLC, and St. Margarets. Among public schools, Mac Robertson Girls and Melbourne High School are at the top in terms of academic results.

Melbourne is home to the University of Melbourne and Monash University, members of the elite "group of eight" Australian "unis" (universities;

pronounced "YOU-knees"). Monash is the largest university in the country in terms of enrollment, and it's ranked 43rd in the Times Higher Education Supplement ranking of the top 200 universities in the world. The University of Melbourne is ranked 27th in the world, second only to the Australian National Universiy among Australian universities. Both universities are truly well-known internationally, and those interested in pursuing academics in Australia are advised to put Melbourne at the top of the list. Deakin and La-Trobe Universities are also highly praised and offer comprehensive options in all major fields of study.

The other tertiary option in Victoria is the TAFE (Technical and Further Education) path, which offers technical and vocational education, often in conjunction with apprenticeship programs or other employer-sponsored education in areas such as tourism, computers, construction, and visual arts. There are 20 TAFE institutions in Victoria. TAFE courses can lead toward a diploma but not a bachelors degree.

SHOPPING

In the CBD, the main shopping experience is the Queen Victoria Market, which is on the northwest side of the CBD and is open daily except Monday and Wednesday. The market is the largest open-air marketplace in the southern hemisphere. Just across the river in Southbank is the Crown complex, featuring entertainment as well as a high-end shopping environment. Bourke Street Mall runs between Swanston and Elizabeth Streets and is home to major department stores such as Myer and David Jones. The Melbourne General Post Office was converted into a high-end shopping experience, similar to what has been done in Sydney, and the boutique and café environment is frankly a better showcase for one of the city's best-looking Victorian structures.

Factory outlets can be found at Australia on Collins, which has more than 64 outlets in residence in the CBD.

Getting Around

PUBLIC TRANSPORTATION

The transit system in Melbourne is known as Metlink, which unifies the buses, trains, and tram services.

There are 17 rail lines linking the suburbs with the city, and all of them come into a loop around the CBD. The Flinders Street Station is the main station and a well-used meeting point for Melburnians. Outside of the loop, four lines serve the southeast, four serve the east, six serve the north, and three serve the west. The trains operate in two zones for train fare purposes. Melbourne also has 300 bus routes. But Melbourne is best known for its distinctive trams, the second-largest network in the world and including 500 trams that serve 1,813 tram stops. The fleet was privatized and modernized in the late 1990s. Trams, buses, and rail feature weekly and annual passes for commuters, and also combinations. Riding a tram is a distinctive Melbourne experience akin to riding the cable cars in San Francisco: As in San Francisco, well after the wonder has worn off, a pretty good way of getting around town remains.

HIGHWAYS

Like England, Melbourne has an M and A naming convention for its highways. Major highways carry the M designation and a number (M1, M2, etc.), while secondary highways carry the A designation (A1, A2, etc.).

The main highways are the Princes Highway, the Hume Highway, the Western Highway, and the Nepean Highway.

Commuting in Melbourne is generally a nightmare, but it's marginally better from the north and west. Cars are a choice for only about 8 percent of commuters, but riding in from southeast Melbourne during morning rush hour, you'd think the whole country was on the one road.

Melbourne's speed limits are expressed in kilometers per hour (kph) and are typically 50 kph in congested suburban areas, 60 kph for primary suburban roads, 80 kph for highways, and 100 or 110 kph for motorways.

MELBOURNE AIRPORT

Melbourne's Tullamarine Airport is northwest of the city 25 kilometers from the CBD. There is no rail link from the CBD as yet, but there is bus service from the airport, plus taxi, limousine, and rental car. The Airports Council International named Tullamarine one of the top five airports in the world in the 15–25 million passengers per year category. The airport is served by 26 airlines, including six focused on domestic traffic.

PRIME LIVING LOCATIONS

BRISBANE AND THE QUEENSLAND COAST

Brisbane, Australia's third-largest city and well-known globally in its own right, is the gateway to the tropical beaches of the northern coast and to the Great Barrier Reef. It is absolutely the number-one destination to be considered for retirement relocations, by those seeking a warmer climate or a more laid-back culture. The Brisbane River runs past the CBD and past the eastern suburbs to Moreton Bay, and at that point there are more than 100 miles of attractive destinations in either a northern or southern direction along the Pacific Coast. Brisbane is the gateway to Australia's main beach tourism area, the Gold Coast (featuring Surfers Paradise), but is also home to a growing cadre of entrepreneurs in information technology and financial services.

Real estate and tourism are proven sources of wealth for Brisbane, as well as old-line industries such as paper, oil refining, and ship and rail car construction. The metropolitan area holds 1.8 million people, who enjoy a famed

© ISTOCKPHOTO.COM / SCOTT HAILSTONE

warm, subtropical climate; the population has nearly doubled since 1980 as more and more people begin to discover the outstanding arts, cultural, and sporting venues and events. Like most Australian cities, Brisbane has a sophisticated public transport and highway infrastructure that features signature ferries and jet catamarans that cruise the Brisbane River.

The expat moving to Brisbane should keep in mind that the city has some traffic congestion issues. Because of its beautiful setting along the Brisbane River, it really is a city made for inner-city urban living. The apartment towers are relatively new, and the small size of the CBD makes it great for walking around. There's lots to do on evenings and weekends, whether you are on the south side of the river in South Bank or on the north side in the Chinatown Mall area, or elsewhere in the hip, trendy Valley section of town. There are good private schools in the inner-city environs.

The outlying areas are quite beautiful, however, and very decentralized. You won't see the Victorian terrace or row houses here, as virtually all the homes are detached and have some breathing room. Brisbane is fairly affordable for seaside living near the shores of Moreton Bay, especially compared with the skyrocketing values of Sydney waterfront.

Many expats coming to the area are looking for second homes or retirement, and that brings them to the Gold Coast to the south of Brisbane or the Sunshine Coast to the north. The Gold Coast is far more established, but far more commercial too. The glistening beachside condo towers would not be out of place in Florida or Hawaii, and year-round good weather—and some affordability compared to established markets in the United States—makes it a compelling alternative to comparable locations in the northern hemisphere.

All Australian states have their local character. If you find Queenslanders refreshingly plain-spoken, you won't be the first. It's the most casual of the states, and one that takes pride in being different and, to some extent, isolated. If that and the great weather, great golf, and Great Barrier Reef are your "cuppa" (cup of tea), by all means approach Queensland with confidence and enthusiasm. The locals won't all remind you of the charismatic Steve Irwin, but you'll meet enough to know that his personality was not entirely a creation of television.

THE BRIEF STORY OF BRISBANE

The area surrounding Brisbane had been occupied since time out of mind by the Turrbal peoples, but the first European sighting occurred during the 1770 expedition of Captain Cook, who named Morton's Bay after the president of the Royal Society, Lord Morton. A geographer misspelled the name, calling

it Moreton Bay, and gave no name at all to the excellent freshwater river that would eventually be named the Brisbane River. Queenslanders have been feeling misunderstood ever since.

Brisbane was originally founded in 1825 as a penal colony for repeat offenders, an unusual beginning for a town and region that would become synonymous with tropical sunshine and retirement in later years. The city and river were named for Sir Thomas Brisbane, who was the governor of New South Wales and sponsored an expedition by John Oxley to the area in 1823. It was the best decision the dour Scottish governor ever made.

The location was chosen for the Brisbane River's abundance of fresh water, after an earlier attempt the previous year to establish a penal colony slightly to the north, at Redcliffe, foundered because of a shaky water supply.

The new colony was located in a floodplain area surrounded by numerous hills, and it flourished as a penal colony until free settlers began arriving in 1838. The Brisbane government had been instrumental in exploring the agricultural potential of the vast continent, and in Queensland the original focus of the colony was agriculture. The city of Brisbane became a regional center serving the interests of plantation owners who were opening up vast tracts of Queensland to sugar and pineapple cultivation, among other crops.

In 1859 the growth of the population and the distance from Sydney led to the formation of Queensland, which was named for Queen Victoria. The colonial line was essentially drawn to transfer everything north of Brisbane, although the official border was drawn somewhat to the south and to follow the course of the Darling River headwaters. Brisbane was made the capital, and the ensuing years were ones of growing prosperity, especially after the rise of sugar cultivation in the mid- to late 19th century.

Even after federation in 1901, Queensland continued to be beset by the problems of isolation, and the state embraced aviation early in its history; Queensland was the original home (in 1920) of the Queensland and Northern Territory Air Service, now known around the world as Qantas.

Increasingly, important mineral discoveries made Brisbane a center for industrial and mining corporations as well as an agricultural hub. Today, the state remains the center of the Australian aluminum industry, and as the closest major port to Southeast Asia, the city is home to several major electronics firms who use Brisbane for entry of imports. The port is the major exit point for sugar and exports significant amounts of coal and container cargo.

Following World War I, Brisbane benefited from increasing attention to Queensland's abundant sunshine, spectacular beaches, and proximity to the Great Barrier Reef. The tourism industry began a major build-up with the

PRIME LIVING LOCATIONS

building of the Surfers Paradise Hotel in 1925. The term "Gold Coast" dates from the 1940s and was applied by real estate developers who were referring to the lucrative financial opportunities rather than the abundant sunshine. Today, tourism ranks with mining as the most important state industry, and the Gold Coast is an urbanized stretch of hotels, golf courses, and condo towers that continue from Beenleigh, just south of Brisbane, and extend 65 kilometers to the New South Wales border.

Queensland has always gone its own way in managing its affairs, which has resulted in many observers comparing the state, for Americans, to the state of Texas. For example, the state Labor government in 1922 appointed a "suicide squad" of politicians to the state's unelected upper house, the Legislative Council, and they voted themselves out of existence. Queensland remains the only unicameral state in Australia.

The city passed one million in population in the 1970s, and the Gold Coast is now the most important tourism and second-home mecca in the country, rivaled only by Cairns along the northeast coast.

The city continues, as Queensland's capital, to play host not only to spectacular events such as the Commonwealth Games, Goodwill Games, and the 1988 World's Fair, but also to an independent style of brash politics that often pits the urban strength of the Labor Party against the rural strength of the conservative National Party. Numerous maverick politicians such as Sir Joh Bjelke-Petersen, Pauline Hanson, and Senator Barnaby Joyce hail from the Sunshine State, as does Australia's current prime minister, Kevin Rudd. Perhaps the most famous Queenslanders globally are golfer Greg Norman and the late naturalist Steve Irwin, who popularized the state through frequent documentaries for the Animal Planet television network.

The Lay of the Land

Brisbane is set on a floodplain several kilometers inland from the mouth of the Brisbane River, and the central business district is situated around an S-shaped bend in the river. Accordingly, the city is highly subject to periodic flooding. The central business district is compact and typically covered on foot. It has the most thoughtfully named street grid in all of Australia, with the streets in the CBD running parallel to the river named after men and the cross streets after women. It's basically impossible to become lost. The southern bend in the river is commanded by the Botanic Gardens and the main government building. Overall, it's quite beautifully presented.

Numerous bridges cross the river and connect the north and south of the city, dominated by the William Jolly Bridge to the southwest of the CBD, which connects the CBD with the artsy South Bank area. The Story Bridge to the northeast of the CBD connects Kangaroo Point with Fortitude Valley, known as "the Valley." The Valley is a shopping and restaurant hub and home to the Chinatown Mall area, which is a cool Asian-themed area.

The city is surrounded by a series of low mountains and hills, reaching around 30 meters in elevation, while the Brisbane River snakes from the northeast to the southwest.

The 189 recognized suburbs are grouped loosely by their relation to the CBD and are known as the southern, eastern, northern, and western suburbs.

CLIMATE

Brisbane is blessed with a warm, sultry but not suffocating climate with tons of sunshine in between the frequent summer rainfall. However, as in all parts of Australia the rainfall is not even, but rather alternates between periods of drought and some years of deluge and flooding. For the past few years, Brisbane has been affected by a severe drought, which has resulted in stage 6 water restrictions, the highest ever imposed for a major Australian city. In stage 6, all outdoor water use is banned except by special permit, and there is no use of sprinklers; the target consumption is 26 gallons of water per person

PRIME LIVING LOCATIONS

AVERAGE TEMPERATURES AND RAINFALL

	Rainfall (mm)	Daily High (°C)	Daily Low (°C)
January	159	29	21
February	158	29	21
March	141	28	19
April	93	26	17
May	74	23	13
June	68	21	11
July	57	20	10
August	36	22	10
September	46	24	13
October	75	28	18
November	97	28	18
December	133	29	20

Source: Australian Bureau of Meteorology

per day. Swimming pools may not be refilled under this restriction. However, Brisbane typically receives abundant rainfall, especially in the summer, with an average of more than 15 centimeters per month.

Where to Live

BRISBANE CBD

The Brisbane inner city and the CBD have two very good districts to live in: the South Bank area and the Valley. Fortitude Valley is more than one square kilometer in area on the north edge of town and on the north side of the river. For generations, this was the main downtown shopping area, but with the rise of suburban malls, the area went downhill and ended up as a red-light district, but it was revived in the 1980s and '90s with eclectic boutiques, music, restaurants, and several historic buildings converted to residential apartment buildings. It's the heart of Brisbane's nightclub scene and really a lot of fun.

South Bank, or more formally South Brisbane, is linked by the pedestrian and bike-only Goodwill Bridge and the Victoria Bridge to the CBD; also there's the CityCat ferry service or the South East Busway. South Bank was an industrial area without much merit until it hosted the World Expo '88, during which time it was completely transformed as a cultural center for the city. Like the Valley, it is full of restaurants but not as heavy on the music and definitely stronger on galleries. Also, it has the South Bank Parklands, which are the old Expo site. A number of corporations have settled

cycling along the river in Brisbane

in to the area, and a lot of health and education workers try to base here to be close to Griffith University and Mater Hospital, plus the Queensland Cultural Center.

Both South Bank and the Valley have a high percentage of immigrants, around 30 percent.

Median home prices for the Brisbane CBD are $537,000 for houses, $448,000 for units, and rentals average $390 per week.

NORTHERN SUBURBS

The northern suburbs begin with the areas around the inner city and the river, such as Newstead, which is among the most expensive places to live in the city. It's a locale for affluent yuppies and empty-nesters. Farther north, along the Doomben railway line it generally gets more hilly and has some great CBD views. The more affluent areas are east of the railway line, whereas the west side of the line has middle- and working-class families; the Italian community is strong up here. Going farther north along the line, Albion features a lot of big, expensive suburban homes. Continuing further north, there are family-oriented neighborhoods, such as Bald Hills, that have a lot of newer homes and more of a bush setting. There is a popular beach community at Sandgate, which is also a popular weekend getaway in the summer.

Median home prices for Newstead are $585,000 for houses, $477,000 for units, and rentals average $420 per week.

EASTERN AND SOUTHERN SUBURBS

East of the city along the Pacific and Gateway Motorways are some good areas, especially if you like a bit of room and some feeling of the Aussie bush or are on a budget. There are also well-liked and well-developed suburbs such as Belmont, which has a lot of bushland and some big lots. Sunnybank encompasses a number of smaller suburbs and is set in a rolling hillside area. It's popular with immigrants, especially from Southeast Asia.

In the south, Woolloongabba is home to the Brisbane Cricket Ground, while St. Lucia is the home of the University of Queensland. There are a ton of Asian and Middle Eastern immigrants in the Moorooka area, which is very affordable. Carina, Carina Heights, and Carindale are the more affluent suburbs in this part of town; they are convenient to the large Westfield Carindale shopping center.

Median home prices for Belmont are $555,000 for houses, $434,000 for units, and rentals average $380 per week.

PRIME LIVING LOCATIONS

WESTERN SUBURBS

Heading west of the city, Mount Coot-tha is home to the Brisbane Botanic Gardens and the planetarium, but generally the western suburbs follow the rail line toward Ipswich. West End is getting pricey but has a number of apartment towers of recent vintage. Indooroopilly ("Indo") is home to the biggest shopping center in the West and has a lot of students and professors spilling over from the University. Then there's the planned area known as the Centenary suburbs, including Jindalee. Finally, Ipswich is about 40 minutes by train from the CBD.

Median home prices for Indooroopilly are $590,000 for houses, $383,000 for units, and rentals average $340 per week.

GOLD COAST

The Gold Coast is perhaps the prime living location in Queensland for expats, home to more than 500,000 people who crowd into a 65-kilometer stretch of condo towers. The beaches are incredible, and the temperatures and humidity in the summer are moderated by the offshore winds. It is crawling with tourists, hotels, and casinos, but of course tourists come for good reasons.

The heart of the Gold Coast is Surfers Paradise ("Surfers"), which is loaded with soaring apartment towers. It is home to schoolies week, which is very much like spring break for U.S. cities like Daytona Beach. Immediately south of Surfers is Broadbeach, which is a low-rise area and home to the state's biggest shopping mall, Pacific Fair. It offers a lot of the advantages of Surfers but without the crowds and the towers.

Median home prices for Surfers Paradise are $1,300,000 for houses, $370,000 for units, and rentals average $330 per week.

SUNSHINE COAST

The Sunshine Coast is the northern "echo" of the Gold Coast, with fabulous beaches and a lot of tourism. It is less developed in terms of towers and has more golf courses as well as several popular attractions, such as Steve Irwin's Australia Zoo. The Sunshine Coast consists of the Caloundra, Maroochy, and Noosa districts, with Noosa being the northernmost. Noosa is highly prized for swimming and surfing, and is especially popular with older surfers who ride longboards. Maroochy is the more important commercial area and is home to the University of the Sunshine Coast. Caloundra is primarily residential and suburban shopping.

Median home prices for Maroochydore are $433,000 for houses, $375,000 for units, and rentals average $330 per week.

SURFERS PARADISE

Two years ago, Surfers Paradise was voted one of the best beaches in the world by the Travel Channel, but that just means the secret is out.

The city in fact was not named for the surf, but for the Surfers Paradise Hotel, which launched in the 1920s in a town then known as Elston. The Gold Coast, as a region, was known as the South Coast until a newspaper article called it the "golden strip of the south coast."

The collection of condo towers by the beach, along with the action at places like the Conrad Jupiters Casino, is one of the reasons that Brisbane is referred to as Brisve-gas by many Aussies (the others call it Brisbane to strangers and "Brizzee" among themselves). Surfers has the complete collection of whale-watching cruisies, fishing charters, surf boards, boogie boards, body boards, and Jet Skis. At night, it lights up into a dizzying collection of nightclubs and bars.

It's an accidental name but no accident that it has become one of the most popular tourism destinations, not only for foreigners, but among Australians. Tell them you are going to "Surfers" and they'll say "good on ya."

NORTHERN NEW SOUTH WALES, INCLUDING BYRON BAY

South of the Gold Coast is the New South Wales border, a growing area of interest for those who are seeking the same lifestyle benefits of the Gold Coast and Sunshine Coast but with less pizzazz and perhaps more affordability. Byron Bay has been a beach mecca for many years, and has in recent years seen extensive and beautiful development with a far more naturalistic look and far less congestion. It's really worth a look for those considering the Gold Coast area but who look askance at the more rococo excesses of Surfers. The M3 motorway leads right through the area, and while not exceedingly convenient to Brisbane it is less than two hours away, so it's acceptable for the occasional flight in or flight out.

Median home prices for Byron Bay are $650,000 for houses, $432,000 for units, and rentals average $380 per week.

Daily Life

MEDIA RESOURCES

Brisbane has the one newspaper, the *Courier-Mail,* which has a Sunday edition known simply as *The Mail,* but Brisbane also receives the national newspaper, *The Australian,* as well as the daily *Australian Financial Review.* The *Courier-Mail* is owned, along with *The Australian,* by News Corp. The rival

BRISBANE RADIO STATIONS

AM

- 612 kHz 612 ABC Brisbane (Talk/News/Information)
- 693 kHz 4KQ ARN (Classic Hits)
- 792 kHz Radio National ABC (Information Variety)
- 882 kHz 4BH Fairfax Media (Easy Listening)
- 936 kHz ABC NewsRadio ABC (News)

FM

- 97.3 MHz 97.3 FM MIX
- 103.7 MHz 4MBS (Classical)
- 104.5 MHz Triple M (Classic Hits)
- 105.3 MHz B105 FM (Music Variety)
- 106.1 MHz ABC Classic FM
- 106.9 MHz Nova 106.9
- 107.7 MHz Triple J

Fairfax company produces an online-only *Brisbane Times,* which competes with the *Courier-Mail*'s online site. As in all major Australian cities, there are numerous free community newspapers, including the *Brisbane News.* There are more than 20 radio stations available.

Brisbane receives all five major free-to-air television networks (the commercial Seven, Nine, and Ten Networks, and the government-run SBS and ABC), as well as major cable and satellite services from Optus, Foxtel, and Austar. An excellent online guide to Brisbane is www.ourbrisbane.com.

The Gold and Sunshine Coasts have their own free community newspapers, but residents generally depend on Brisbane major media.

HEALTH CARE

Queensland Health is the government health service, and it supervises the eight public hospitals in Brisbane. There are four private hospitals as well. The state has free, universal public hospital treatment, although special services such as TV and phone are extra, and dental service is extra as well. The state operates numerous outpatient clinics, which are also free but can have waiting periods of up to 12 months.

General practitioners are not part of the Queensland Health system—nor are private specialist practices and hospitals that charge for service but do not have the long waiting periods. But GP services are covered by Medicare, and private care can be covered through the Medibank private insurance scheme.

Though the specifics of Medicare are extensive, in general the government will cover 75 percent of in-patient costs and 80–100 percent of outpatient costs through the public health system, but more than 40 percent of Australians choose to supplement this with private health insurance.

Private insurance covers a higher percentage of costs, allows more freedom of choice in practitioners, and can shorten waiting times for services, especially those of a non-emergency basis. Public hospitals have been known to experience severe backlogs of patients, and even emergency care has been subject to delays, often unacceptable ones. For peace of mind, go with a private health insurance supplement to Medicare—called Medibank—if you find that your family budget can afford it.

Major hospitals are found throughout the city, but please note that "surgery" is the term for a doctor's office. Doctors are called "doctors" as elsewhere in the English-speaking world, but registered nurses are usually addressed as "sister" whether they have religious affiliation or not; "nurse" is a term used for both registered nurses and aides.

SCHOOLS

The Queensland school year runs from January to December and has two semesters broken into two terms each, with holiday breaks for Easter, winter, spring, and summer. Private schools generally have fewer school days.

In Queensland, children are required to attend school between ages 6 and 15. Primary school is years 1–7, and high school is years 8–12.

There are more than 50 private schools in Brisbane. The premier secondary boys' schools include Anglican Church Grammar School, Brisbane Boys, Brisbane Grammar, Brisbane State High, Ipswich Grammar School, St. Joseph's, Gregory Terrace, The Southport School, and Toowoomba Grammar. Premier girls' schools include Brisbane Girls Grammar, Brisbane State High, Clayfield College, Moreton Bay College, St. Aidans, St. Hildas, St. Margarets, St. Peters, and Somerville House.

Brisbane is home to the University of Queensland, one of the elite group of eight Australian universities. It is ranked among the top 50 universities in the world. Griffith University has five campuses and has 33,000 students in the Brisbane and Gold Coast area, and the Queensland University of Technology is the other major university in Brisbane. University of the Sunshine Coast is located in—you guessed it—the Sunshine Coast.

The other tertiary option in Queensland is the TAFE (Technical and Further Education) path, which offers technical and vocational education, often in conjunction with apprenticeship programs or other employer-sponsored education in areas such as tourism, computers, construction, and visual arts.

MIDDIES AND SCHOONERS

Drinking age is 18 in Australia, and although the draconian drinking and driving laws (which have saved countless lives) have cut down dramatically on Aussie beer consumption, Australia remains at fourth on the global list with an average of 109.9 liters a year per capita, or just shy of two kegs per man, woman, and child in the country.

Beer comes in several sizes: Officially there's the pony, the seven, the middy, the schooner, and the pint, but generally these days it's schooners and pints. The 10 ounce (285 milliliters) is probably only for those who have to drive but feel obliged to have one "with the group."

By and large, schooners are the typical Aussie size, at 15 ounces or 425 milliliters. For some reason, in Adelaide a schooner is about the size of a middy, and you need to order a pint. Beer comes in cans and bottles, and the major brands vary by city, but they are all generally lagers. In Sydney, you'll find Toohey's and KB Lager; Melbourne has Victoria Bitter (VB) and Carlton Draught (pronounced "draft"); Adelaide has Coopers; Perth has Swan; and Queensland has the estimable XXXX ("four-x").

There is not exactly a federal law requiring you to drink beer, but going to the pub with friends or colleagues is a time-honored tradition. If you prefer cocktails (mixed drinks), go right ahead, or if you don't like to drink, have a non-alcoholic Clayton's. The world record for fastest consumption of beer was held for many years by one Robert James Hawke of Perth. Bob Hawke went on to become one of the most popular prime ministers of Australia.

More than 250,000 Queenslanders each year take TAFE courses. TAFE courses can lead toward a diploma but not a bachelors degree.

SHOPPING

In the CBD the two main shopping areas are the Chinatown Mall area in the northeast and the 600-meter-long Queen Street Mall in the heart of the CBD, which is also home to Myer Center and is highly convenient to Central Station and the Transit Centre. The Eagle Street Pier on the river has a good shopping area.

The outdoor weekly Valley markets sprawl across Brunswick Street and Chinatown Mall on weekends in the Fortitude Valley district. The markets offer food, fashion, and jewelry, while during the week there are boutiques on Ann Street and Brunswick Street. South Bank also has outdoor weekend markets, and there is a Fresh Market at Rocklea on Saturday morning.

Factory outlets can be found at Brisbane Airport and Jindalee, and there are a dozen major suburban shopping centers dotting the city, with the biggest of them in Chermside, Mt. Gravatt, Carindale, and Indooroopilly ("Indo").

Getting Around

PUBLIC TRANSPORTATION

Brisbane has an excellent public transport system including rail, bus, and ferry. The buses generally come into the city at Queen Street; the trains come into Central Station and Roma Street; and the ferries come in at several locations with the well-known, high-speed CityCat connecting the University of Queensland with Brett's Wharf.

There are 10 rail lines in all, and all of them come into the CBD and stop at Central Station, Roma Street, and South Bank. Five lines head south of the city, including a line out to the Gold Coast, and five head to the north, including service to the Brisbane Airport northeast of the city. More than 100,000 people ride the trains daily. Bus-train link services are available, and TransLink is the bus service; it offers suburban service and a free city loop bus.

HIGHWAYS

Like England, Brisbane has an M and A naming convention for its highways. Major highways carry the M designation and a number (M1, M2, etc.), while secondary highways carry the A designation (A1, A2, etc.).

The main highways are the Pacific Motorway (M3), which heads south to the Gold Coast, and the Bruce Highway, which heads north toward Cairna. The Gateway Motorway is a toll road that connects the Sunshine and Gold Coasts with a Brisbane bypass. The Ipswich Motorway heads into the southern suburbs, and the Western and Centenary Freeways connect Brisbane with the western suburbs. Traffic congestion is problematic, especially at the Brisbane River bottlenecks, and Brisbane is constructing a tunnel under the river to relieve the pressure.

Brisbane's speed limits are expressed in kilometers per hour (kph) and are typically 50 kph in congested suburban areas, 60 kph for primary suburban roads, 80 kph for highways, and 100 or 110 kph for motorways.

BRISBANE AIRPORT

Brisbane Airport is northeast of the city and is connected via the Airlink rail line from the CBD as well as the Gateway Motorway. The airport is served by 22 airlines, primarily Southeast Asian and Pacific Island carriers as well as Qantas, Virgin Blue, and Air New Zealand. Several airlines offer service to the Middle East via Singapore. The airport is currently undergoing a major expansion that will be complete by late 2008, which will add gates, parking, shops, baggage claim carousels, and additional arrival and departure facilities.

CANBERRA

Canberra (pronounced "CAN-bra") is one of the smallest capital cities in the world, with a population of only 323,000. It reminds many of a charming "company town," only in this case the "company" is the sprawling Australian federal government. Over the years it has become home to a number of institutions outside the formal bureaucracy, such as the Australian National University, the National Museum, and the National Gallery, but overwhelmingly people are drawn to Canberra because of government-related work opportunities, or work in business related to government contracts or lobbying activity.

The city is also by far the newest of the major Australian urban centers, dating back to a ground-breaking ceremony in 1913, and most of its development has taken place since World War II. Its development was undertaken for bureaucratic rather than commercial reasons, so the city is maligned for feeling "manufactured" but also has grace notes of genuine beauty in its planned lakeside setting and extensive preservation of bushlands and green belts. It is also the only major Australian city that is set in the bush, rather than by the

© AUSTRALIAN CAPITAL TOURISM

sea coast, which not only gives it distinctive scenery and weather but makes it more authentically reminiscent of the Australia described in pioneer-era bush ballads. In short, it's a bucolic city with a highly educated populace that seems to be insulated from the boom-and-bust economic cycles of the other cities. It also has, hands-down, the lightest traffic of any city in Australia. It's a pleasure to drive there.

Canberra is set among low hills on an elevated plateau beside the Molonglo River, about 145 kilometers inland from the east coast; the river was dammed to form Lake Burley Griffin, which dominates the center of the city and serves as the foreground to Parliament House. The central city was originally designed by Walter Burley Griffin as a series of hub-and-spoke areas, and with the exception of major roads that form the "axes" of Griffin's design, long stretches of straight road are difficult to find in Canberra, which makes it pleasing to the eye but not always intuitive to navigate.

The city enjoys four distinct seasons owing to its distance from the moderating sea breezes of the coast. It is decidedly low-rise and decentralized. One of the primary appeals of the city is its location just two hours away from the ski slopes of the Snowy Mountains, Australia's only ski resort area, and Canberrans are also often found spending weekends on the southern New South Wales coast, usually somewhere around Bateman's Bay, which is two hours from the city by car.

There is a city bus service, but it is used by only about 5 percent of the population, about the same number who bike or walk to work. The typical Canberran gets around by car, using the uncongested parkways that connect the major suburban areas with the city center.

For the expat, a move to Canberra will likely result in more "culture shock" than moving to any other major Australian city, simply because of the low density, low population, and the fact that 40 percent of the population works for the federal bureaucracy. The town feels "sleepy" on first arrival, and some expats never get over that feeling, although others quickly begin to take advantage of the proximity to coast, snow, and bush to use Canberra as a base to explore a huge slice of Australiana that can be undertaken in day-long and weekend trips.

One major change from most other cities: Canberra features 99-year leases, rather than freehold property. If you would rather not get into that sort of an ownership structure, by all means lease a house or rent an apartment ("let a flat"). Otherwise, there's nothing to be alarmed about; it's just the legal structure of land ownership in the Australian Capital Territory, and all properties are the same.

If Canberra is sleepy, it is also home to 95 embassies and high commissions and, as such, is decidedly international in its population and outlook. Canberra is the most educated and affluent city in the country, and the embassy and

PRIME LIVING LOCATIONS

street scene in Canberra's city center, known as "Civic"

consular staffs bring an internationalist outlook (not to mention a pretty good range of ethnic dining) that will keep any good conversationalist on his or her toes. It's by far the city where expats feel the least out of place, and the formal support of embassies adds to the sense of security. Of course there is also informal support from local groups that are found in all major Australian cities.

Aside from government work, temporary workers find themselves occasionally posted to Canberra for government contract–related work, or for exchange-style programs for students and professionals. Cheap, temporary housing is never in plentiful supply, and although Canberra has a lower cost of living than Sydney or Melbourne, it is not inexpensive by overall Australian standards, and coming to Canberra after a stint in Adelaide can be a bit of a shock. The city is the third most expensive in Australia for housing cost.

Culturally, although Australian national museums and galleries are still in their emerging stages, the city is home to a wide variety of outstanding institutions, especially considering the city's size, and there are plenty of national sports teams to follow, although the adored national cricket team will have to be enjoyed three hours up the road in Sydney. Nightlife is far more restrained than in Sydney or Melbourne, but Canberra is highly regarded for its clubs, such as the Wig and Pen or The Private Bin. The clubs are generally located near Garema Place or City Walk. Younger people tend to focus on cafés, clubs, and pubs in the Manuka and Kingston areas.

THE BRIEF STORY OF CANBERRA

The area that forms the Australian Capital Territory was historically home to two Indigenous Australian tribes, and occupation went back thousands of years; European contact occurred in the 1824 when employees of grazier Joshua John Moore built a small homestead in the area. Moore purchased the land in 1826 and named his property Canberry. Appropriately for a capital city, the name means "meeting place."

Other families soon established the Yarralumla and Duntroon properties, which gave their names to the modern-day governor-general's residence and the national military college.

The region seemed destined for complete, happy obscurity when a controversy over the location of the national capital erupted between Sydney and Melbourne after federation in 1901.

Originally the town of Dalgety in the Snowy Mountains was selected, but Sydneysiders protested that it was too close to Melbourne, and everyone agreed it was too far from the Sydney-Melbourne train line. (Dalgety has less than 100 residents today; they really missed out!) Canberra was selected as a compromise site, because it was less than 300 kilometers from Sydney, close to the rail line, had been thoroughly surveyed, and had access to fresh water. At the time Canberra was selected, the Australian Capital Territory was home to 1,714 people and 224,764 sheep.

The state of New South Wales ceded 2,330 square kilometers for the new Australian Capital Territory, which continues today to be under-populated bushland, except for the capital city itself. Canberra is home to more than 95 percent of the territory's population on about 30 percent of the ACT's land.

The federal government took its time moving up to Canberra. Architect Burley Griffin submitted his plan in 1911, and groundbreaking took place in 1913, but the provisional Parliament House was not completed until 1927, and the first embassy did not appear in Canberra until 1940. Several government departments did not make the transition to Canberra until after World War II, and Lake Burley Griffin was not completed until 1963.

After the war, development of Canberra accelerated, and the government created housing projects to provide homes in North Canberra and South Canberra for the growing population. Several new towns, such as Belconnen and Woden, were developed, and further development included three satellite tracking stations operated for the U.S. space program. Neil Armstrong's first step on the moon was transmitted by the Honeysuckle Creek tracking station. The city grew in population from less than 200,000 to more than 300,000 people between the 1960s and '90s.

Canberra received a significant facelift in 1988 at the time of the Australian Bicentenary, and a permanent federal Parliament finally replaced the provisional building, which had been used for 70 years.

Also in 1988, the Australian Capital Territory was given full self-government powers and elected its first Territorial Legislature, after gaining limited self-governing powers in 1974.

The Lay of the Land

Canberra is 290 kilometers from Sydney along the Hume Highway, and the surrounding area is filled with rolling low hills, typical Australian bushland, and a bowl of slightly larger hills that surround the city itself.

The city is centered around the seat of government, which is Parliament House. The Parliament complex sits just south of Lake Burley Griffin and has a dominating view of the low-rise city. The lake itself runs east–west and divides the city into its traditional areas of North Canberra and South Canberra. Two scenic bridges traverse the lake and connect the city, although there are now multiple alternative routes that connect the northern and southern sections of the city.

The city is planned in a series of circles, and broad avenues connect the circles. So the streets are not in a typical city grid pattern, and the first few times driving around the city, it's a great idea to keep a map handy, as side streets tend to be somewhat bewildering until you get a little oriented.

© AUSTRALIAN CAPITAL TOURISM

Canberra parklands

PRIME LIVING LOCATIONS

AVERAGE TEMPERATURES AND RAINFALL

	Rainfall (mm)	Daily High (°C)	Daily Low (°C)
January	63	28	12
February	54	27	12
March	53	25	10
April	50	20	8
May	48	18	5
June	40	12	0
July	42	11	0
August	46	12	2
September	52	16	5
October	65	20	7
November	63	23	9
December	53	26	20

Source: Australian Bureau of Meteorology

There are seven major suburban areas, and the primary diplomatic area is Yarralumla, which is immediately northwest of Parliament. The main downtown area is officially known as City Centre but generally called "Civic" and is located on the north side of the lake.

CLIMATE

Owing to its bush location, Canberra is cooler and drier than typical major Australian cities. The rainy season is in the spring and early summer (October–January), while the driest part of the year is the late fall and early winter.

Where to Live

CIVIC AREA

The Civic area is not highly populated, with about 1,500 urbanites in residence, but it is well worth considering as the most urban and lively place to be in the city. Canberra's building codes limit buildings to 13 stories, so there are no "urban canyons" to contend with, but rather a great collection of shops and restaurants along Northbourne Avenue, which is the main road in Civic.

Civic is also home to Canberra Centre, which is Canberra's primary shopping mall and is a three-story sunlit but indoor 300-retailer shopping mecca. It includes a multiplex movie theater complex.

Canberra's City Walk is a pedestrian mall that features an attractive and fun collection of shops and restaurants; the picturesque Garema Place has extensive outdoor dining and is adjacent to City Walk.

Median home prices for Civic are $610,000 for houses, $380,000 for units, and rentals average $370 per week.

North Canberra

Immediately north of the Civic area is North Canberra, which includes slightly older, more commercial suburbs such as Braddon and Ainslie. This area tends to cater to working-class families, young urban professionals who like the convenience to Civic, and apartment dwellers who like the broad assortment closer to Civic. Farther north, in Dickson and Lyneham, there are more traditional family-oriented suburbs with single-family homes and numerous parks and sporting grounds ("ovals"). Acton, which is along the northwest shore of Lake Burley Griffin, is home to the Australian National University (ANU), and the population is primarily students.

Median home prices for Braddon are $650,000 for houses, $375,000 for units, and rentals average $370 per week.

Belconnen

In the northwest district, Belconnen is home to Canberra Stadium, which features the Canberra Raiders rugby team, as well as the University of Canberra. The district dates back to the 1970s, and most buildings were constructed in the 1980s. The center of activity is the Belconnen Town Center, which features

PRIME LIVING LOCATIONS

DEEP SPACE TRACKING CENTER

One of the most interesting relocation options is getting NASA to send you to Canberra to work at Deep Space Stations 34, 43, 45, and 46. Constructed in 1965, DSS 46 received the first images of Neil Armstrong walking on the moon in 1969, and DSS 45 tracks deep space missions such as *Voyager 2*'s encounter with Uranus and the *Cassini* mission to Saturn.

On any given day, the station will be tracking 20 or more space missions, including the *Mars Observer, Spirit,* and both *Voyager* spacecraft. *Star Trek* fans will be delighted to learn that "VGER," the name of the artificial life complex that threatened humankind in *Star Trek: The Movie,* is in fact the working call sign of the *Voyager* spacecraft. *Voyager 1* and *2* are currently both beyond the solar system and are expected to reach the nearest planetary system in 40,000 years. That's a long relocation, for sure.

a large Westfield shopping mall and several blocks of residential apartments around parkland and the shores of Lake Ginninderra. The combination of iffy facilities and distance from Civic and the diplomatic sections of town makes this an area that is more visited (for the stadium) than lived in.

Median home prices for Belconnen are $395,000 for houses, $335,000 for units, and rentals average $330 per week.

Gunghalin

Gunghalin is the far northern district of the city and is home to several excellent golf courses, primarily The Lakes. The district is brand spanking new and there are a number of home sites available for longer-term residency plans; houses for resale are in most cases less than 10 years of age and tend to be larger than in the older parts of the city.

One major cultural shocker: The suburb of Mitchell, which lies at the border of the North Canberra and Gunghalin districts, features legal prostitution (it was decriminalized more than 10 years ago but is limited to Mitchell and the South Canberra suburb of Fyshwick). Mitchell is also home to a number of other adult entertainment options, and accordingly the district has tended to provide a higher degree of expat shock than others. But for some, it certainly offers a distinctive experience not typical of the countries that new arrivals have come from.

Median home prices for Gunghalin are $465,000 for houses, $337,000 for units, and rentals average $330 per week.

South Canberra

South Canberra is the part of town most people from outside of the country know first and know best. Yarralumla is the area along the south shore of Lake Burley Griffin, and it's home to most of the diplomatic missions, of which there are more than 90. Many of them are quite beautiful. Those that are not in Yarralumla are in O'Malley or Deakin. Embassies are also in some cases located in commercial office buildings, and the residences of ambassadors are not restricted as to their location.

The most affluent suburb in Canberra is Red Hill, located in South Canberra. Red Hill is home to, not surprisingly, a pretty hill for walking on the west edge of the suburb, as well as the prestigious Canberra Grammar School. If you are looking for a mansion in Canberra on a huge block of land, head for Red Hill's Mugga Way.

Median home prices for Yarralumla are $955,000 for houses, $710,000 for units, and rentals average $700 per week.

© AUSTRALIAN CAPITAL TOURISM

South Canberra seen from Civic across Lake Burley Griffin

Woden

Farther south of the city is the Woden Valley and the Woden district, which is home to Canberra Hospital and to O'Malley, the third of the diplomatic areas of Canberra. Twenty-five embassies call O'Malley home, mostly smaller countries or ones with shorter diplomatic histories. Woden Town Centre is in Philip, which adjoins O'Malley and is home to a Westfield shopping center as well as the Lovett Tower, Canberra's tallest building—although it is a little like calling the 2,228-meter-high Mount Kosciuszko one of the world's Seven Summits. Aside from the diplomatic delights of O'Malley, Woden is a pleasant, middle-class area that is home to a number of townhouses.

Median home prices for Philip are $572,000 for houses, $335,000 for units, and rentals average $330 per week.

Weston Creek

Southwest of South Canberra is the small enclave district of Weston Creek. The district dates back to the 1960s, and many of the buildings were built in the 1970s and 1980s. It's a younger, slightly less affluent area that features primarily houses and town- or row houses. Weston is home to one of the few bilingual schools in Australia, Lyons Primary School, which features Italian and English instruction. It primarily caters to English-speaking students and is a distinctive option for parents with younger children. Weston Creek is on the edge of Mount Stromlo, from which there are excellent views of the city. Owing to the distance from commercial areas, Weston Creek is not a typical choice for new arrivals, but adjoining the bush it offers a more rural version of Canberra living.

Median home prices for Weston are $469,500 for houses, $385,000 for units, and rentals average $380 per week.

Tuggeranong

About 10 percent of Canberrans live to the extreme south of the city, in Tuggeranong Valley. There are 19 suburbs, of which the most affluent are Fadden and Macarthur. The most affordable are Richardson and Hume, while Greenway is midrange. All of Tuggeranong is relatively low density; the younger, less affluent suburb Chisholm is the most crowded at 1,823 persons per square kilometer. The center of activity is the Tuggeranong Town Center, alongside the small, pretty (if artificial) Lake Tuggeranong. It includes a large shopping mall, the Tuggeranong Hyperdrome.

Median home prices for Greenway are $450,000 for houses, $360,000 for units, and rentals average $350 per week.

Daily Life

MEDIA RESOURCES

For Canberra news, the *Canberra Times* is the main daily newspaper, although *The Australian* offers fairly good coverage of Canberra because of its national political coverage.

CANBERRA RADIO STATIONS

AM

- 666 kHz 666 ABC Canberra
- 846 kHz 2RN ABC
- 1008 kHz 2KY Racing narrowcast
- 1053 kHz 2CA Capital Radio Network
- 1440 kHz 1SBS SBS Radio Multicultural

FM

- 88.7 MHz Racing Radio ACT TAB
- 91.9 MHz 1WAY FM Canberra Christian Radio Limited
- 92.7 MHz ArtSound FM Music and arts
- 98.3 MHz 2XX Canberra's Double X
- 101.5 MHz Triple J ABC
- 102.3 MHz ABC Classic FM ABC
- 103.9 MHz NewsRadio ABC
- 106.3 MHz Mix 106.3 Austereo/ARN

CityNews is a free, glossy weekly newspaper. The websites http://outin canberra.com.au and http://canberraeguide.com will provide a great online start for things to do, see, and eat in the city. Another popular online destination is http://canberra.citysearch.com.au.

For television, the three main television networks (Seven, Nine, and Ten) are available in the form of Prime, WIN, and Southern Cross Ten, in addition to the two government channels ABC and SBS. Foxtel provides the main satellite service, and cable comes from TransACT. More than 10 radios stations offer programming in most formats.

HEALTH CARE

The main health service in Canberra is ACT Health, and the main portal for information is HealthFirst, which is online (http://healthfirst.net.au) or accessible by phone (tel. 02/6207 7777); calling connects you with a nurse to discuss any health topic, from stings and bites to general health questions.

As in all of Australia, Medicare card holders receive free care in public hospitals and subsidized care from specialists or general practitioners outside of hospitals. The waiting lines for public care can be daunting, and to experience a typical waiting time from the United States, private health insurance supplements such as Medibank are the order of the day.

The two major public hospitals in Canberra are the 170-bed Calvary Public Hospital, which is in the Belconnen district to the north of Civic, and the 500-bed Canberra Hospital in Woden.

SCHOOLS

The Canberra school year runs from January to December and has four terms, with holiday breaks for Easter, winter, spring, and summer.

In the ACT, children are required to attend school between ages 6 and 15 and may leave after year 10. Primary school is years 1–6, and high school is years 7–10, with "college" offerings in years 11 and 12. However, new "super-schools" are offering K–12 education on a single campus. Home schooling is permitted but requires a provisional six-month registration period.

There public schools in Canberra are going through a major consolidation throughout the 2007–2008 period to reduce the number of public schools from 96 to 57. There are more than 40 private schools, many of them ethnic or religious in nature. Canberra Girls Grammar (in Deakin) and Canberra Grammar (in Red Hill) are both south of the city and are generally at the top.

Canberra is home to the Australian National University, one of the elite group of eight Australian unis. It's highly regarded as a research institution.

ANU is on the northwest shore of Lake Burley Griffin and has 13,900 students from 94 different countries. It is the most likely university in Australia for an overseas student to attend. The University of Canberra attracts 10,000 students and is located in the north of the city.

The other tertiary option in the ACT is the Canberra Institute of Technology, which is the ACT's TAFE (Technical and Further Education) school. CIT offers a 450 programs of technical and vocational education, and has 600 enrolled international students from more than 50 countries.

SHOPPING

The suburbs have an extensive collection of malls at the major town centers, typically the suburban Westfield type. The best of these is the Westfield in Belconnen, which is north of Lake Burley Griffin. In Civic, the primary shopping area is Bunda Street, where the Canberra Center is located, and smaller shops and restaurants are found along City Walk.

The arts and crafts market is held in Kingston on Sunday and is a good source for ethnic food treats. Civic is also home to a crafts market on Saturday.

Getting Around

PUBLIC TRANSPORTATION

Canberra has a citywide bus service known as ACTION, which is used by about 5 percent of the population, while another 5 percent typically walk to work and the shops. The main bus interchanges are in Civic, Belconnen, Woden, and Tuggeranong. ACTION buses are distinctively orange, blue, and white, and primarily run routes from the suburbs to Civic or the Parliamentary Triangle. Fares are $3 per ride, with reduced fares for commuters buying weekly or monthly passes, off-peak, or pensioners. During peak hours, Xpresso buses offer faster, limited-stop service to the suburbs.

Periodically, there is talk of a high-speed rail link between Canberra and Sydney, or Canberra and Melbourne, but it usually dies down after the budget numbers come in.

HIGHWAYS

There's good news and bad news when it comes to driving around Canberra. The good news: There is hardly any urban traffic congestion. The bad news: Canberra's curvy street pattern takes some getting used to. Buy a Gregory's map and keep it handy in the car.

The main thoroughfares are called parkways and generally allow swift travel between the various suburban districts at 50–60 kph. There are speed cameras on the roads, so beware. They will snap your license plate's picture if you speed, and you will be mailed a hefty speeding fine that can cost you more than $200, and after a second offense you may well find your license taken away. But the speed cams are easy to spot, and there's really no need to speed given the pace of traffic.

The main road to Sydney is the M31, the Hume Highway, and it is a three-hour journey if there's no traffic, but the Hume can really stack up in the outlying suburbs.

Surrounding the city are ring roads, which can be used by residents in outlying areas to cut down on travel time. Canberra Airport is near the Eastern Ring Road.

CANBERRA AIRPORT

Canberra International Airport is east of the city in Pialligo, about 10 minutes by car from Civic outside of peak periods, and it's a snap to use. Only four airlines serve Canberra, offering nonstop service to Adelaide, Brisbane, Perth, Melbourne, Sydney, Newcastle, and Albury. The airlines are Qantas, Brindabella, Virgin Blue, and Tiger Airways. You may wonder why Canberra styles itself as an international airport when there is only direct service, and why the nation's capital does not have nonstop service to Tasmania: They are two of Australia's enduring mysteries.

A number of office buildings have sprung up in the airport grounds, leading to some extra traffic during peak commuting periods.

PRIME LIVING LOCATIONS

THE GREAT DIVIDING RANGE

The Great Dividing Range refers to the spine of mountains that runs from the Snowy Mountains along the New South Wales–Victoria border, through the Blue Mountains west of Sydney, and north into the Tablelands of northern New South Wales. They are storied in history, for much of Australia's pioneer literature and "bush ballad" poetry comes from this region, including the bush ballad "Man from Snowy River." Until the past 20 years, however, the region was more heard of than seen, because of a lack of infrastructure and commercial opportunity. But with population pressure combining with increased highway and commercial infrastructure, more and more people are giving the towns near the Great Dividing Range a close look for retirement, second homes, or for short-term and long-term career assignments in the heart of the bush, on the edge of the Outback, or at locations such as the south coast of New South Wales, where country lifestyles exist in towns right up to and along the coast.

© TOURISM NEW SOUTH WALES

THE BRIEF STORY OF THE GREAT DIVIDING RANGE

The original colonists of New South Wales, settled in Sydney from 1788 and reaching the edge of the mountains before the end of the 18th century, found the Blue Mountains an impassable boundary for many years. It wasn't until 1813 that William Charles Wentworth, Lt. William Lawson, and Gregory Blaxland made the most celebrated early crossing (aside from informal crossings made by escaping convicts) and sighted the fertile plains to the west.

The first major settlement beyond the mountains, Bathurst, was founded in 1823 and remains the major New South Wales country center today, a frequent stop for immigrants courtesy of postings at Charles Sturt University, named for another explorer from pioneer days.

Further exploration discovered easier passages to the rangelands beyond the mountains, westward from Newcastle and Goulburn in the 1820s, and these remain major thoroughfares to the west.

In 1835, Europeans made first contact with the Snowy Mountains in the south. The high point in the Australian Alps, and the highest point in Australia, Mount Kosciuszko, was achieved in 1840 by Count Pavel Edmund Strzelecki, who named the mountain for Polish patriot and American Revolutionary War general Tadeusz Kosciuszko.

In the early days of the region, squatters raising cattle and sheep were the dominant economic and cultural force, but gold was discovered near Bathurst in 1851, and the subsequent discoveries to the south, near Melbourne, and in Grenfell in New South Wales, transformed the entire region, bringing population and gold fever.

Following the end of the gold rush era in the 1860s, the era of the bush balladeers brought a glimpse of bush culture to the now-prosperous cities of Sydney and Melbourne. Lawyers and journalists such as Henry Lawson and Andrew "Banjo" Paterson, who divided their time between Sydney and the bush, provided the Australians with their first sense of a national mythology and culture in "The Man from Snowy River," "Waltzing Matilda," "Clancy of the Overflow," "Past Carin'," and "Up the Country."

Following World War II, the ambitious Snowy River Scheme began to tap the hydroelectric and irrigation potential of the mountain watershed, and over 25 years more than 100,000 workers built an extensive array of seven power plants and 16 dams that reverse the flow of the Snowy River from the Pacific to the dry interior, which continues to provide nearly 4 percent of Australia's electric power today. It also provides the water assurance for 40 percent of Australia's agricultural output.

The Snowies and the Blue Mountains became popular as second-home

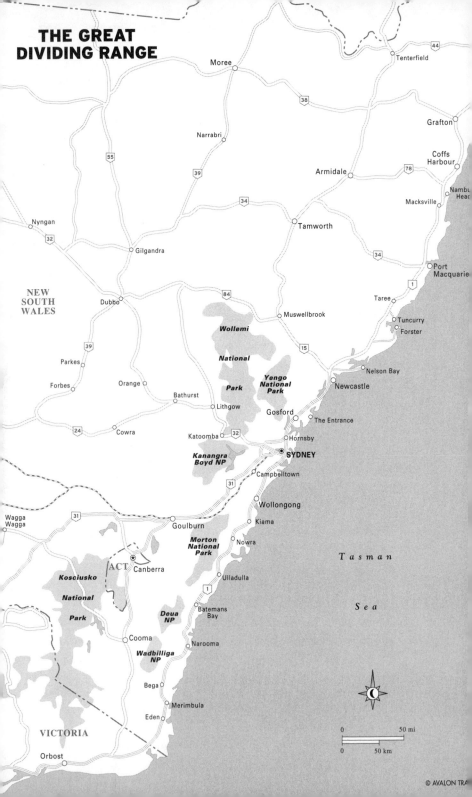

THE GREAT
DIVIDING RANGE

Moree

Tenterfield

44

38

Narrabri

Grafton

55

Coffs
Harbour

Armidale

78

39

34

Macksville

Nambu
Head

Nyngan

Tamworth

32

Gilgandra

34

Port
Macquarie

84

Dubbo

Muswellbrook

Taree

NEW
SOUTH
WALES

Wollemi

Tuncurry
Forster

15

39

National

Nelson Bay

Parkes

*Yengo
National
Park*

Newcastle

Forbes

Orange

Park

Bathurst

Lithgow

Gosford

24

Cowra

Katoomba

32

The Entrance

Hornsby

SYDNEY

*Kanangra
Boyd NP*

31

Campbelltown

Wollongong

Wagga
Wagga

31

Kiama

Goulburn

*Morton
National
Park*

Nowra

ACT

Canberra

Kosciusko

T a s m a n

Ulladulla

1

National

*Deua
NP*

Batemans
Bay

S e a

Park

Cooma

Narooma

*Wadbilliga
NP*

Bega

Merimbula

VICTORIA

Eden

0   50 mi

0   50 km

Orbost

© AVALON TRA

panoramic view of the Snowy Mountains

destinations commencing in the 1960s, and the Northern Tablelands have begun to increase in popularity as a result of the spread of the wine industry in northern New South Wales, among other high-ticket farming pursuits. Horse-breeding, B&B operations, and hobby farming continue to attract immigrants directly or in many cases after a short period in Sydney or Melbourne.

The Lay of the Land

The Great Dividing Range is actually a series of interconnected small ranges, such as the Snowy Mountains and Northern Tablelands. These are mixed with highly eroded high tablelands, such as the Blue Mountains, that present sharp cliff escarpments, waterfalls, and other natural wonders that are a result of erosion or the microclimates that have flourished in the carved-out valleys.

Major cities in the region are Perisher and Thredbo in the midst of the Snowies, the epicenter of the Australian ski industry; Cooma in the southwest, which continues to support the Snowy Mountain Scheme infrastructure; Katoomba, Lithgow, Bathurst, and Orange, the main towns of the Blue Mountains, where many second homes are maintained and tourism holds sway; and Scone, Tamworth, Toowoomba, and Armidale in the north, where agriculture and some tourism form the economic backbone. East of the Southern Tablelands, an extensive series of small towns from Bateman's Bay to Kiama provide retirement options, small-town entrepreneurial opportunities, and second homes for Sydneysiders.

BATHURST AVERAGE TEMPERATURES AND RAINFALL

	Rainfall (mm)	Daily High (°C)	Daily Low (°C)
January	69	28	13
February	58	27	13
March	49	25	11
April	42	20	7
May	42	16	4
June	44	12	2
July	49	11	1
August	49	13	1
September	46	16	3
October	61	20	6
November	61	23	9
December	63	26	12

Source: Australian Bureau of Meteorology

CLIMATE

The eastern slopes are some of the wettest areas in the temperate zones of the country. More than half of all eucalyptus tree species are found only in this region, and temperate rainforests are found at Barrington Tops, with an astonishing collection of birds and tropical foliage. Meanwhile, the western side of the mountains in the edge of Australia's dry interior, suitable for cattle and sheep raising except where river irrigation has made agriculture possible. Generally, the mountain areas are cool in the summers, cold in the winters, and dry throughout the year except on the eastern slopes where heavy rainforest-level rainfall will occur. The coastal areas are generally mild in the winter and warm and humid in the summer.

Where to Live

SNOWY MOUNTAINS

The gateway city to the Snowies is Cooma, which is where the engineers who run the Snowy River Scheme generally live and work. Cooma operates a thriving tourism industry. The town dates back to the 1820s and is located at 800 meters above sea level, which keeps it cool and dry. The town has the only high school in the region, and children from outlying towns such as Jindabyne are bused in. Ironically for its role in the Snowy River Scheme, Cooma takes its water from the Murimbidgee River, which dried up completely in the 2006 drought, and the town is frequently on severe water restrictions as low as 26 gallons per person per day.

Up in the mountains, Perisher Valley, Smiggin Holes, Guthega, and Blue Cow are the main towns of the Perisher ski area, while Thredbo offers a complete village experience and a permanent population of 300, which swells to thousands in the high summer and winter seasons, with tourists and seasonal workers both in evidence. The ski resorts are notoriously expensive in both daily life and real estate, due to the excess demand for alpine skiing and limited supply.

Median home prices are $205,000 for houses, $190,000 for units, and rentals average $150 per week.

BLUE MOUNTAINS

The towns of the Blue Mountains are Katoomba, Lithgow, Bathurst, and Orange, with Katoomba offering a classic mountain experience with plenty of spectacular homes and weekender retreats for Sydneysiders, as well as a profusion of B&Bs and small hotels catering to the Sydney trade. With a population of 9,000, it offers low-rise, four-season, artsy lifestyles with art deco–era construction almost always at hand. Nearby Laura and Wentworth Falls are about half the size of Katoomba and offer the same scenic and lifestyle pleasures without the amenities and crowds that tourism brings to Katoomba.

© TOURISM NEW SOUTH WALES

Blue Mountains historic house, now a local inn

Farther west, the coal town of Lithgow and the mining and agricultural centers of Orange and Bathurst beckon. They provide the services for the outlying areas. Orange and Bathurst each have a population of around 40,000 and cater to tourists as well as providing educational resources. They have historic house districts that feature early 20th century Australian country style, with flat, broad roofs providing broad, shaded porches.

Median home prices for Katoomba are $300,000 for houses, $235,000 for units, and rentals average $200 per week.

NORTHERN TABLELANDS

The main towns of the New England (Northern Tablelands) region are Armidale and Tamworth, which provide services to the agricultural industry that surround them, as well as a full-on taste of Australian country style and culture. The main employer in Armidale is the University of New England, which brings cosmopolitan culture into the country through its diverse range of courses. Tamworth is the self-styled "country music capital of Australia," including a 40-foot-tall Golden Guitar. It offers a more typical country experience built around the cattle and sheep industries. Tamworth's newest suburbs are on the south side of the Peel River, while the CBD is on the north side.

Median home prices for Tamworth are $237,000 for houses, $217,000 for units, and rentals average $170 per week.

SOUTH COAST

The main towns of the south coast are Bateman's Bay, Kiama, and Nowra, although the Mollymook/Ulladulla area has been well-known as a second-home and tourist destination for decades. Boaters tend to head for Bateman's, which is a tad industrial for some tastes but has the closest proximity to Canberra and excellent sport-fishing resources and marinas. Kiama and Berry cater primarily to tourism, including some art tourists who head for artists' offerings at Jamberoo. There are some excellent entrepreneurial opportunities for wineries around Berry, which has a favorable microclimate. All the towns of the south coast offer opportunities for small-business development, owing to the steady influx of weekenders and second-home owners from Sydney and Canberra. Retirees tend to head for Shoalhaven towns such as Bawley Point and Kiola for complete retreat, or Jervis Bay or Sussex Inlet for a closer-to-civilization experience.

Median home prices for Bateman's Bay are $315,000 for houses, $228,000 for units, and rentals average $180 per week.

CENTRAL AND NORTH COAST

The central and northern coast area generally is selected by retirees and by small-business entrepreneurs who are attracted by the small town, coastal lifestyle as well as the opportunities presented by a growing population. Gosford is the gateway city to the central coast, and the coastal towns of Terrigal and Wamberal offer incredible beach lifestyle—those who can afford it will find no better place on earth. Newcastle, with its population of 200,000, interrupts the beachside splendor with its rugged industrial might built around steel, coal, power, and shipping. Northwest of Newcastle, the Hunter Valley is filled with small hobby wine-producing or wine job options in Australia's best-known wine district outside of South Australia's Barossa Valley.

North of the Hunter Balley, lifestyle options at Forster, Coffs Harbour, Kempsey, and on to Taree range from oyster farming to hobby farming, as well as small tourism-related work such as B&B operation or resort work. The small-town Aussie country atmosphere isn't more authentic anywhere in the country. "Coffs" has used its "gateway to the tropics" location on the coast to position itself as a "banana republic" built on the banana plantations, tourism, surfing, and diving. The Great Dividing Range touches the coast at Coffs. The Akubra hat company, which produces Australia's internationally famed headgear, is based in Kempsey, while Taree is built around oysters, services to the surrounding agricultural district, and coastal tourism.

Median home prices for Gosford are $385,000 for houses, $252,000 for units, and rentals average $200 per week.

Daily Life

MEDIA RESOURCES

Most cities along the Great Dividing Range are served by a weekly or daily newspaper, with the Rural Press company (www.ruralpresssales.com.au) publishing more than 80 weekly community newspapers serving the various communities. Among the best known is the *Western Advocate,* published daily in Bathurst for more than 100 years. The *Central Western* is published daily in Orange, the *Lithgow Mercury* three times a week, the *Cooma-Monaro Express* twice a week, the *Tamworth Times* weekly, and the *Armidale Express* three times a week. Rural Press Limited (www.ruralpress.com) publishes a series of city guides, car guides, job guides, and property guides for all the major cities.

All sectors of Australia have access to Foxtel satellite and the ABC national television service, with commercial station service typically available via satellite. ABC Radio provides six national stations that are available in most areas, except for small pockets in valleys with difficult radio access. Main cities such as Bathurst, Orange, Tamworth, Armidale, and Bateman's Bay have up to four commercial radio stations, typically offering popular music on most channels, with one community affairs station. More than half of the stations are now on the FM dial. Towns close to Newcastle in the north have free-to-air television service on the Seven, Nine, and Ten Networks.

RADIO STATIONS IN THE GREAT DIVIDING RANGE

ARMIDALE
FM

- 101.1 MHz Triple J ABC
- 101.9 MHz ABC New England ABC
- 103.5 MHz ABC Classic FM ABC
- 104.3 MHz 2KY Sky Channel Racing/Sport
- 106.9 MHz TUNE! FM University of New England

AM

- 720 kHz Radio National ABC

BATHURST
FM

- 88.9 MHz SBS Radio Special Broadcasting Service Multicultural
- 95.9 MHz Triple J ABC
- 96.7 MHz Radio National ABC
- 97.5 MHz ABC Classic FM ABC

- 100.9 MHz 2KY Sky Channel Racing/Sport Narrowcast

BEGA
FM

- 93.7 MHz 2BAR
- 99.3 MHz ABC Classic FM ABC
- 100.1 MHz Triple J ABC
- 100.9 MHz Radio National ABC
- 104.3 MHz POWERFM NSW South Coast
- 105.9 MHz East Coast Radio 2EC

AM

- 765 kHz East Coast Radio 2EC
- 810 kHz Radio National ABC

COOMA
FM

- 90.5 MHz Monaro FM Community Radio
- 95.3 MHz Radio National ABC

HEALTH CARE

Primarily, the cities of the Great Dividing Range are in New South Wales and are covered by the New South Wales Health System.

There are four basic health regions under the state government's health scheme for rural New South Wales: Greater Southern, Greater Western, North Coast, and Hunter New England. All of the south coast cities fall into the former, as well as the Snowy Mountains; the Blue Mountains fall into the Greater Western, while the northern cities such as Scone, Tamworth, Toowoomba, and Armidale fall into the Hunter New England region.

Most of the best known hospitals are relatively near the main cities, but New South Wales offers an Isolated Patients Travel and Accommodation Assistance Scheme (IPTAAS) for people who need to access specialist medical or oral surgical treatment not available locally and who live more then 100 kilometers from the nearest specialist. Bathurst, Orange, Tamworth, and Armidale all are referring hospitals offering multidisciplinary care.

- 96.9 MHz 2KY Racing/Sport
- 97.7 MHz Snow FM

AM

- 918 kHz 2XL
- 1602 kHz ABC South East ABC

JINDABYNE

FM

- 95.5 MHz ABC Riverina ABC
- 97.1 MHz Radio National ABC
- 102.7 MHz 2KY Racing Radio
- 104.3 MHz SBS Radio SBS

KATOOMBA
FM

- 87.6 MHz Noise FM
- 89.1 MHz 2Blu FM Community Radio
- 96.1 MHz The Edge 96.1 Australian Radio Network

PERISHER
FM

- 98.7 MHz 2XL Capital Radio Network
- 101.9 MHz Snow FM Capital Radio Network

TAMWORTH
FM

- 87.6 and 87.8 MHz Heartland FM Country Music
- 89.7 MHz Rhema FM Christian
- 90.5 MHz 2KY Racing Radio
- 93.9 MHz Radio National ABC
- 94.7 MHz Triple J ABC
- 103.1 MHz ABC Classic FM ABC

AM

- 648 kHz ABC New England ABC

SCHOOLS

The school year runs from January to December and has four terms, with holiday breaks for Easter, winter, spring, and summer. Private schools generally have 15–20 fewer school days.

As in all of New South Wales, children are required to attend school between ages 6 and 15. Primary school is years 1–6, and high school is years 7–12.

Generally, students in the Great Dividing Range area attend public schools; private schools are far fewer in number owing to the sparse population. For private schools, day school and boarding options are still the norm in the countryside, whereas boarding schools have all but died out in Sydney. However, The Armidale School is a member of the prestigious, Sydney-based Greater Public Schools association, and it offers a boarding program for students from outlying towns; Blue Mountain Grammar School serves the eastern slope of the Blue Mountains and is based in Wentworth Falls. Oxley College and Chevalier College, in Bowral, along with St. Stanislaus,

DIMBOOLA

There just isn't any better way to understand the Australian country culture than by attending – and participating in – the classic Australian comedy *Dimboola*. This is the play that inspired the long-running American classic *Tony n' Tina's Wedding*. In both cases, the audience becomes a part of the performance. Jack Hibberd wrote the play, back in the early 1970s, and it has been seen by more Australians, and been performed more times, than any other Aussie production. It is also a wickedly funny send up of the loutish side of Australian country culture, the kind that gave birth to the phrase "the Australian cultural cringe." Dimboola is an actual town in rural Victoria, but the rest is all fiction as Morrie and Reen get married in the presence of their increasingly drunken, terribly dysfunctional families.

As Morrie's Protestant family clashes with Reen's Catholic family, insults turn to punches as chaos breaks out, with wickedly funny scenes. "No worries!" shout the participants, but there are worries aplenty in what Hibberd called "the testing of strengths of the newly conjugated tribes." The play, set at a wedding breakfast, features drunken "yobbos" (louts), a pregnant bride, a befuddled groomsman confused by drink, and classic Australian characters named Mavis, Mutton, and Knocka, and a perfectly obnoxious flower girl, Astrid, with serious intestinal issues.

All Saints, and Scots School in Bathurst, provide the best of the private school experiences.

For girls, Frensham School provides a prestigious boarding and day school environment in Mittagong in the southern highlands. Tamworth Anglican is a girls' day/boarding school in Tamworth, while PLC Armidale and New England Girls are based in Armidale and offer day/boarding options.

Charles Sturt University is a multicampus university serving the Great Dividing Range region. It has excelled in fields such as agriculture and education. The University of New England is based in Armidale and offers a broad selection of coursework as well as extensive international student programs.

SHOPPING

In rural life, mall shopping is the exception rather than the rule. Shopping centers tend to be smaller, featuring supermarkets and local services rather than full-blown shopping experiences. Most people in the country areas make occasional trips to Sydney or Melbourne for specialized shopping needs. Bathurst, Orange, Tamworth, and Armidale are the most self-contained for shopping; in smaller towns, residents will make trips to Sydney or to regional towns even for some regular necessities, either for cost reasons or availability.

Getting Around

PUBLIC TRANSPORTATION

Regional cities such as Bathurst, Orange, and Armidale have local bus service, but in these spread-out locales, residents depend on cars and trains for the majority of transport needs, as well as regional airlines. The Rail Corporation of New South Wales (www.countrylink.info) will provide rail service schedules and up-to-the-minute fares. There are four country rail services, serving the south coast cities; the Blue Mountains towns such as Bathurst and Orange; the Northern Tablelands towns such as Tamworth and Armindale, and the Northern coast cities such as Taree, with continuing service to Brisbane. On-line booking is available from www.countrylink.info.

HIGHWAYS

The lifelines of the Great Dividing Range are the Hume Highway, the Princes Highway, the Great Western Highway, and the Pacific Highway. The Princes connects Sydney to the south coastal areas from Kiama to Bateman's Bay and beyond. The Hume Highway connects Sydney and Canberra, with most of the Southern Tablelands towns accessed via exits onto regional roads. The Great Western Highway connects Sydney with the Blue Mountains and inner-western towns of Katoomba, Lithgow, Bathurst, and Orange, and continues to Bourke and Broken Hill in the Outback. The Pacific Highway connects Sydney with Brisbane, adding access to Armidale and Tamworth via connecting regional roads and passing directly through the central and northern coastal towns.

REGIONAL AIRPORTS

Tamworth, Armidale, Bathurst, and Orange are served by regional air service, while south coast residents head for Canberra or Sydney airport by car. Bathurst is served by Air Link and Rex, flying turboprop aircraft with primary service to and from Sydney. Qantas Link provides service from Sydney to Tamworth via Boeing 717s. Rex connects Sydney with both Bathurst and Cooma (serving the Snowy Mountains and ski areas) on turboprops. Virgin Blue is starting up Embraer regional jet service but has not yet announced service into the Great Dividing Range area.

SOUTHWESTERN AUSTRALIA

According to parochial Sydneysiders and Melburnians, beyond their metropolitan fringes is the bush. Beyond the bush, they will tell you, is the Outback. Beyond the Outback is a place no one ever goes, called the Back of Beyond or the Never-Never, spoken of in hushed tones, remembering all the explorers who perished in search of it. Beyond that, which is to say off the edge of the world, are Adelaide and Perth and the great industries and gardenlike cities of southwestern Australia.

Eastern Australians know that, somewhere in the west, if you follow the setting sun, you will find the states of South Australia and Western Australia. Fans of Australian Rules football, cricket, and basketball will recall occasionally spotting teams from the far west in various national competitions. Wine aficionados are known to praise the vintages issued from the Barossa Valley in South Australia, which is Australia's Napa Valley.

© TOURISM WESTERN AUSTRALIA

But by and large the western states and cities are unknown places to many Australians, and precious few people from outside the country see these states except as tourists, or if the automotive, mining, or wine industry brings them there.

It's a pity, for Adelaide and Perth are two of the most attractive cities in the country, and two of the most highly urbanized. Perth is Australia's fourth largest city, and more than 70 percent of the population of Western Australia lives in the Perth metro area. The same ratio holds for Adelaide and the state of South Australia. By contrast, 60 percent of the population of New South Wales lives in Sydney, and around 40 percent of Queensland's population lives in Brisbane.

It's true, Perth is remote, but Adelaide and Melbourne are, at 480 kilometers apart, the two closest state capitals by land. The isolation of the southwest is rooted more in their economic self-sufficiency and distinctiveness than in distance.

The primary reason to move to Adelaide and Perth is for industry, which is to say the wine industry in South Australia or the mining industry in Western Australia. Both are world class. South Australia is also the primary home of the Australian automotive industry, and expats may find themselves southwest-bound on that account. Teachers and students also will occasionally make their base in the southwest, although the universities in this region have not yet assembled the international reputation of, say, the University of Sydney or Monash.

However, relocatees to either of the two western capitals will find that these youngest of Australian cities—and in particular this applies to Perth—have the most modern and well-considered city designs along with simply delightful urban and suburban environments. The call of the Outback is not at all far away.

Adelaide

Adelaide, the fifth largest city in the country with a population of 1.1 million, is situated along the Gulf of St. Vincent on the edge of what is now known as the Great Southern Ocean, and has spread along a roughly north–south axis since its founding in 1836 as a free settlement along the Torrens River.

The city possesses the most Mediterranean climate of all the Australian capital cities, away from the subtropical summers in Sydney and Brisbane and the chillier winters of Melbourne and Canberra. It sports a wet season in the winter months and dry and warm conditions in the summer.

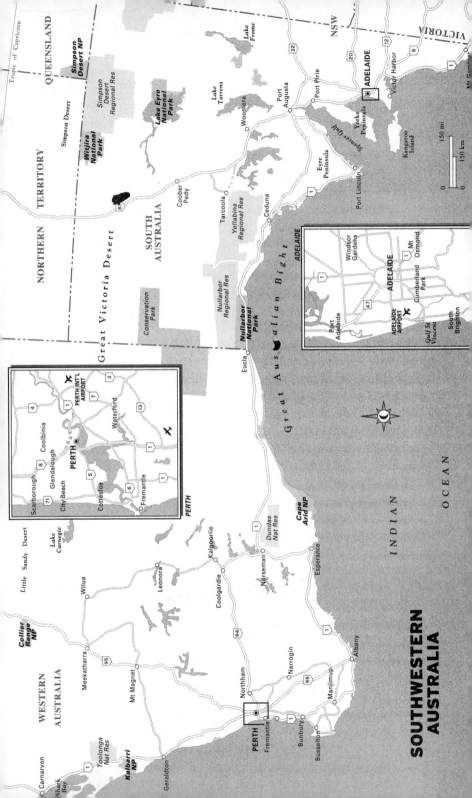

© SOUTH AUSTRALIA TOURISM

city skyline and Adelaide Oval, home of the state cricket team, the South Australian Redbacks

For almost all of its history, Adelaide's wide boulevards and highways had been more than adequate for transportation, so the public transit, Adelaide Metro, is not up to the level of Sydney's or Melbourne's, and traffic snarls have been increasing in recent years due to the city's growth. The city's population has been slowing in growth in recent years, making it possible for road development to catch up in the next few years.

Adelaide is the "garden city" of Australia for its sparkling city plan based upon tree-lined squares throughout the original section of the city, which is surrounded by large parklands. But the city has become known as the most culturally alive of the smaller capital cities, and although it shares nothing in terms of climate with an American city like Boston, in cultural terms it is comparable, for it has a distinctive commitment to arts and culture that cannot rival Sydney or Melbourne for sheer "culture quantity" but frequently matches them or bests them for "culture quality" in its arts festivals.

Most expats learn about Adelaide and the state of South Australia by tasting it, for its unique soils have been home for generations to Australia's finest wine-growing region in the neighboring Barossa Valley. Penfold's Grange Hermitage is just one of the truly world-class wines that are produced here, and locals take quiet but unmistakable pride in their role in producing the country's greatest wines. Australia has one of the highest wine consumption rates in the world, and table wines are typically served at home, and even on occasion to school-age children, so it is not unimportant to the city's image to play such a central role in wine-making.

South Australians are considered to be a sensible people, disdaining what they might term the smugness of Melbourne and the brashness of Sydney. The city has always maintained an ambience somewhere in between the two major cities, perhaps more substantial than light-but-vibrant Sydney, yet less ponderous than grave-but-erudite Melbourne. But, as the original home of News Corporation and the global Murdoch newspaper and television empire, it has occasionally contributed not only to a more spicy Australian scene but has spiced up international media as well.

The Brief Story of Adelaide

The area surrounding Adelaide was the ancestral home of the Kaurna tribe of Indigenous Australians, who were nearly wiped out by smallpox epidemics that spread from the eastern cities even before the first British settlements in 1836. The Kaurna were responsible for some of the clearing of the original bushland that surrounded the swampy coastal areas, owing to their controlled bushfires that created grasslands suitable for attracting and hunting emus and kangaroos.

The British arrived in 1836, urged on by colonial promoter Edward Gibbon Wakefield (who later promoted the initial settlement of New Zealand). From its foundation Adelaide was intended to be a contrast to, and improvement upon, the convict settlements along the east coast. A free settlement, South Australia also disavowed the free land grants that pleased poor settlers but led to labor shortages in the capitals. Rather, poor emigrants from Britain were given free passage financed by land sales to wealthier emigrant investors, and the poor emigrants formed the labor pool for the new colony. The capital city, named for Queen Adelaide, was provided from the outset with wide principal boulevards, broad surrounding parklands, and access to a steady water supply, in contrast to the eastern convict settlements.

Wool and silver mining were the backbone of early industry, and the colony was connected to the east in 1853 with the navigation of the Murray River. The colony became self-governing in 1856 and expanded rapidly until crop failures and a global economic depression ended a period of rapid expansion. Fortunately for Adelaide, a series of copper discoveries at Broken Hill, to the north, shielded the city from a stronger downturn that affected the major cities. By the time of federation in 1901, Adelaide was firmly established as Australia's third most populous and important city.

The boom-and-bust primary industry cycle continued to produce a boom in the 1910s and a severe depression in the 1930s, but the state capitalized on military industrial development during World War II to establish the center

© SOUTH AUSTRALIA TOURISM

Glenelg, on the South Australian coast east of central Adelaide

of the national auto industry in the state. Rapid increase in job creation rates led to the introduction of subsidized immigration in the 1940s, and more than 200,000 Southern and Eastern Europeans emigrated to South Australia between the 1940s and the 1970s, giving the state a much broader cultural base. Arts development dates from the 1970s and continues strongly today.

A major setback occurred in 1992 when the State Bank of South Australia, a state-owned bank that had gone on an acquisitions binge in the 1980s, suddenly collapsed as the result of a string of bad loans. This left the state mired in billions of dollars in debt. The scandal caused a financial crisis that was finally resolved near the turn of the millennium with a privatization of the bank's assets. The state has finally put the bank collapse firmly in its past, but during the past 20 years Adelaide has fallen to fifth in population and in importance among the major Australian cities, losing out to fast-growing Brisbane and Perth.

THE LAY OF THE LAND

Adelaide is 480 kilometers northeast of Melbourne and straddles the St. Vincent Gulf. Laid out in a series of city squares and surrounded by wide belts of greenery, Adelaide is easily the most sensibly organized of all Australian cities and arguably the most "green."

The city is centered around Torrens River, which forms the northern border of the central business district, or CBD. The area north of the river is, not surprisingly, called North Adelaide.

ADELAIDE AVERAGE TEMPERATURES AND RAINFALL

	Rainfall (mm)	Daily High (°C)	Daily Low (°C)
January	19	29	17
February	14	29	17
March	26	26	15
April	39	22	12
May	63	19	10
June	83	16	8
July	78	15	7
August	68	17	8
September	64	19	10
October	49	22	11
November	30	25	14
December	27	27	16

Source: Australian Bureau of Meteorology

CLIMATE

Adelaide is comparable in temperature range to the eastern cities, roughly equivalent to Sydney's climate in range, but the city has wet winters and dry summers, in contrast to the wet summer/dry winter pattern in more tropical cities. Snow is unknown, as is a hard frost; the major adjustment is understanding that excellent summer weather is balanced by a comparatively rainy winter, although overall rainfall is comparatively light at around 70 centimeters annually. Approximately 60 percent of total rainfall comes between May and September.

WHERE TO LIVE
City of Adelaide

The CBD sits on the south side of the Torrens River, while the predominantly residential North Adelaide occupies the river's north shore. The two areas were originally surveyed in the 1830s and form the historic part of the city. They are surrounded (like a doughnut) by the city's fabled ring of parklands. A ring road roughly follows the inside edge of the parklands around the city and makes it relatively convenient to get around.

North Adelaide primarily features single-family homes and is generally considered to be the best place to live in town. Homes over $1 million are the rule rather than the exception. North Adelaide is also the location of the famed Adelaide Oval, home of the South Australia Redbacks, the state cricket team, as well as many international cricket matches. North Adelaide is divided into an upper and lower section, with Upper North Adelaide set on a hill that is home to the lively O'Connell Street commercial area, and some of the better views of the city. Lower North Adelaide is a quieter area but has a number of historic buildings and pubs.

The CBD is the only part of the city not subject to severe building height restrictions, so there are a lot more flats in high-rise buildings available. A lot of buildings feature short-term accommodations and are within walking distance of the city center. A particularly nice location is near the Central Markets, on Gouger Street, which has an excellent collection of restaurants and cafés as well as small shops that sell every kind of fresh food imaginable.

DESIGNING ADELAIDE

When it comes to the street plan, Sydney is just a jumble and a mess, relying for its beauty on a splendid setting along Sydney Harbour. Adelaide, by contrast, never had the same physical assets, but its founder gave it a design, based on the design of Philadelphia, Pennsylvania, that continues to make it one of the most attractive, parklike cities in the country.

Colonel William Light was given the post of surveyor-general of South Australia in the earliest days of the colony's settlement. He designed Adelaide on a grid of streets featuring wide boulevards and large public squares, and surrounding the city with a ringed system of five parklands, so that Adelaide would always have fresh, clean air. It was one of the last great city designs, and his setting of the city next to the Torrens River, at the point of maximum rainfall from the mountains to maximize crop yields, is generally considered a master stroke. He separated the commercial center of Adelaide from the residential center of North Adelaide, so that the parklands form an "8" around the two enclaves.

But it is the Adelaide Parklands he is most remembered for, with individual parklands numbered 1 through 29, commencing in the north near the Adelaide Golf Links and continuing clockwise around the city. The parklands are home to some of the state's most important cultural buildings, including the Adelaide Festival Centre, the Art Gallery of South Australia, the Adelaide Aquatic Centre, Government House, the South Australian Museum, and the Adelaide Zoo. Victoria Park contains a racecourse that has been proposed as a home for the Adelaide 500, a move opposed by residents.

It is ironic that, given Light's insistence on accurate surveying, his monument on Motefiore Hill is in the wrong location. Situated in North Adelaide, it is said to be on the spot where Light first envisioned Adelaide. Recent scholarship has located the scene well to the south, but Light continues to gaze southward over the city he envisioned, which remains one of the most beautiful residential cities in the world.

Median home prices for the Adelaide CBD are $411,000 for houses, $330,000 for units, and rentals average $270 per week.

North Adelaide

Beyond the ring of parkland, a series of suburbs has sprung up since World War II, of which Salisbury and Elizabeth are among the most prominent. The northern ring of suburbs has an iffy reputation among locals, especially Elizabeth and Angle Park. Salisbury Heights is situated on a hill and offers some views and some good homes at affordable prices, but generally this part of town is the least attractive, as it is the heart of the industrial part of the city.

Median home prices for Salisbury Heights are $290,000 for houses, $225,000 for units, and rentals average $185 per week.

Eastern Suburbs

The eastern suburbs, which start on the inside of the parkland area, are growing area for new arrivals. They are especially popular with Asian immigrants. The attractions are affordable homes—many less than $500,000 that are quite attractive and spacious—as well as convenience to the CBD for commuters. The traffic is quite easy to negotiate in this part of town. Like all outlying Adelaide areas, it primarily consists of small blocks of flats and single-family homes. The Adelaide Hills area, centered on Mount Baker, is one of the fastest-growing parts of the city. The farther up in the hills, the cooler in the summer, and it has a countryside feel but is within commuting distance of the CBD. St. Peter's College, generally considered the finest in Adelaide, is in the suburb of St. Peter's on the inner east side, and is quite attractive.

Western Suburbs and Beaches

Aside from the tony gardens of North Adelaide, the most popular area in Adelaide is the beach suburbs of the western suburbs. The top end at the beach is Glenelg, while nearby beach suburbs such as Grange and Henley Beach offer affordability and a feeling of being far away from the hubbub of the city. Glenelg has high-rises and is heavy with tourists, with the resulting crowds in high season and extra amenities year-round, including The Beachhouse, a major entertainment center for the city. Seacliff and Hallett Cove have more of a community feel and are less beset by high-rises and tourism.

Closer to the city, suburbs like Mansfield Park are generally to be avoided, but the homes are far more affordable (30 percent less than on the coast, or more), and the shopping in Marion and Oakland Park is excellent. Three-bedroom homes in the $400,000 range are quite common, even in the nicer areas, although the top beachside suburbs have numerous homes over $1 million.

Median home prices for Grange are $489,000 for houses, $241,000 for units, and rentals average $200 per week.

Southern Suburbs

If there is a growing suburban sprawl in Adelaide, this is where it is, as the city has been stretching south for some time. On the inner south, Unley Park is one of the more expensive areas in the city, while suburbs such as Blackwood, Eden Hills, Bellevue Heights, and Bel Air are within 20 minutes commuting time to the CBD and quite attractive. Farther out are better values and younger families, in suburbs such as Aberfoyle Park. The commute becomes fairly tough to the far south, and Hackham and surrounds in the far south is a sector to avoid. In the southeast, Blackwood is a transport hub; it has very good schools and a near-rural look and feel that is popular with middle-class families.

LIVING TRULY DOWN UNDER

Somewhere beyond the Outback, between the Never Never and the Back of Beyond, are the most unusual permanent homes in Australia, the dugout cave homes of Coober Pedy, 800 kilometers north of Adelaide, situated on the Sturt Highway. The town bills itself as the "opal capital of the world," and it has been extensively used as a set for filmmakers, usually as a stand-in for the end of the world. Films such as *Mad Max Beyond Thunderdome* and *Until the End of the World* have given Coober an international fame as one of the least attractive spots on earth.

In Coober's case, glory comes from holes in the desert where immigrants have been pulling opals out of the desert since 1915, when the first strikes were made, and increasingly since the Charles Sturt Highway that passes by was paved in 1987.

Owing to a shortage of wood, searing Outback heat, and the absence of electricity for air conditioning, the residents of Coober have been digging homes straight down into the ground for generations. A typical dugout home will have as many as three bedrooms carved out of the rock, with living room, kitchen, and bathrooms. The houses do not require air-conditioning as they maintain a constant temperature.

Almost all of the town's residents are active in the opal trade (Australia produces nearly 97 percent of the world's opals), and more than half of them live underground in dugout houses. The residents, however, maintain one equally distinguished amenity aboveground: the Coober Pedy Golf Course, which is entirely tree-less and turf-less. Golfers carry pieces of turf around the links with them to hit the ball off of. The course is the only one in the world with reciprocal playing rights at the Royal & Ancient Golf Club of St. Andrews, the ancestral home of golf.

Countless Europeans have tried their luck in Coober Pedy, and most move on after a few months or years. But in a 1996 study, 42 different nationalities were recognized among the residents, giving Coober Pedy the most diversified population in the country.

Just not the most visible.

Median home prices for Blackwood are $402,000 for houses, $252,000 for units, and rentals average $210 per week.

DAILY LIFE
Media Resources

Adelaide is the historic home of News Corporation, the Murdoch media empire, and the papers in town are Murdoch papers. *The Advertiser* is racier, while the national newspaper *The Australian* is more conservative in style. There is a wide selection of community newspapers, known as the *Messenger* papers, while the alternative weekly in town is *The Independent*. *The Advertiser* sports a lively website, Adelaide Now, at www.news.com.au/adelaidenow, which is a popular city guide as well as a source for free news and gossip.

As in all Australian cities, the three main television networks (Seven, Nine, and Ten) are available, along with the two government channels (ABC and SBS) and satellite service from Foxtel. There are reportedly 23 radio stations in Adelaide, but about a dozen offer more than special interest or government fare. Big Pond serves up cable and Internet service, among a number of providers.

Health Care

The South Australian health system is similar to that of the rest of Australia, including a network of hospitals, community health centers, home and disability care, a health screening system, and a dental system.

Medical care is free in South Australia for those who choose to go through the public health system, but expect long wait times, especially for non-urgent items, where the wait for surgery can run into a number of years.

The teaching hospital in Adelaide is Royal Adelaide, while the other majors are the Women and Children's, the Queen Elizabeth, and the Flinders Medical Center (associated with Flinders University), all in the 300–700 bed range and excellent. The Royal Adelaide is scheduled for replacement by an ultramodern 800-bed center.

Schools

The Adelaide school year runs from January to December and has four terms, with holiday breaks for Easter, winter, spring, and summer.

As of 2009, school attendance will be compulsory from ages 6 until 17, and students may take a Leaving Certificate after year 10. However, most students stay on for years 11 and 12, to complete the SACE (South Australian Certificate of Education), which is generally a prerequisite for university studies. Adelaide has numerous schools offering the International Baccalaureate

(IB) as an alternative to the SACE, and it has the highest concentration of IB certificate holders in the country. Adelaide has a number of "special interest" high schools, where students follow concentrated studies in the arts, music, or sport.

There are more than 100 public schools in Adelaide and dozens of private secondary schools, with more than half of the private schools religious in nature. Pembroke School, St. John's, St. Peters College, and Saint Ignatius College are among the schools generally considered at the top rank among private schools, while Glenunga International High School, which offers the IB program, is generally considered the top public school.

The three top universities in Adelaide are the University of Adelaide, the University of South Australia (UOSA), and Flinders University. Flinders is the newest, UOSA is the successor to the former South Australia Institute of Technology, and the University of Adelaide is the "prestige" university. There are also five TAFE colleges around the city, offering numerous programs for technical and vocational education, often in conjunction with work/study programs in the trades.

Shopping

The suburbs have an extensive collection of malls at the major town centers, primarily on the east side of the city, and typically of the suburban, anchor-tenant, Westfield type. The primary fresh food shopping is at the Central Markets in the CBD. Rundle Street in the CBD is the home of Rundle Mall, the main CBD shopping area, and stretching east along Rundle Street is a sprightly assortment of cafés, restaurants, and boutiques. Many of the cultural landmarks in this culturally focused city, including the botanical gardens and the wine center, are on the "East End" out this way, including numerous landmark buildings along North Terrace.

GETTING AROUND
Public Transportation

The good news about Adelaide public transport is that the Adelaide Metro exists and offers bus, rail, and tram services. The bad news is that Adelaide Metro is a pale shadow of the service offered in other cities. Bus service was privatized a few years back, but all buses receive priority via dedicated bus lanes, including the "O-Bahn." The rail system is not used by many people, although there are six lines serving all sections of the city and feeding into the CBD. A popular tram service links Glenelg on the coast with the CBD and runs down from Victoria Square and through King William Street to the Morphett Street Bridge.

Highways

Most commuters have historically preferred to commute by car, but traffic problems have been multiplying, especially to the south where the development of the Southern Expressway and Port River Expressway have helped but not solved the rising congestion. Anyone who suggests you travel south along the South Road is either joking or should not be driving—the road is notoriously jammed with commuters heading toward the southern suburbs from the CBD.

A new freeway eastward toward the Adelaide Hills, the Southeastern, has proven more functional and popular, and has greatly eased the commute in a fast-growing area.

Adelaide and North Adelaide are divided by the Torrens River, so a series of bridges—the Morphett Street Bridge, the Adelaide, and the Torrens—are bottleneck points for crossings. The Torrens is remarkably narrow, so the bridges are short.

Overall, Adelaide's traffic problems are relatively minor compared to those of Sydney and Melbourne, except for congestion in the CBD, which parallels that in the major cities.

Adelaide International Airport

Adelaide International Airport was extensively remodeled and expanded in 2005, so it offers the best overall air terminal experience in the country. The airport is served by five international airlines, with direct service to Hong Kong, Kuala Lumpur, Singapore, and Auckland. Tiger, Virgin Blue, and Qantas offer domestic service to all capitals as well as some regional cities such as Alice Springs and Cairns. Free wireless Internet is available throughout the airport, which also offers a comprehensive shopping experience. In all, it's a true delight to visit, and an excellent asset for the city.

Perth

Perth, the third largest city in the country with a population of 1.5 million and the fastest growing, commands the far west coast of Australia at a point where the Swan River meets the Indian Ocean. The city, founded in 1829 as an agricultural venture of free settlers called the Swan River Colony, has become the center of the Australian resources industry and the heart of Australia's resources boom.

Though it is the least British of cities in its traditions and outlook—feeling more like an American oil town than a British industrial center—it has been hugely popular over the years with British expats and continues to attract a heavy influx from the United Kingdom. When asked, they point to the great beaches, the outdoor lifestyle, and the fantastic year-round weather. Not to mention that London's Economic Intelligence Unit named Perth one of the five best places to live on earth.

Perth is certainly one of the five most remote big cities, nearly 2,400 kilometers from the nearest town of more than 100,000 residents, but that hasn't stopped it from becoming the fastest-growing city in Oz, and to many tastes, the finest. Hugging the far southwestern shore, it combines a mild Mediterranean climate with a proximity to Australia's most important oil, gas, iron, bauxite, and uranium resources. Its main streets form the "Resources Quarter," and there is certainly no town on earth that thinks more about ore.

Typically, most expats first hear about Perth because of a job. Sydney and Melbourne tend to produce the most publicity, but Perth is a job magnet, with job growth over a 1.5 percent rate the past 10 years. The city is projected to have a population of two million by 2031.

If Australia is "The Lucky Country," Perth is "The Lucky City," with relatively inexpensive real estate affording most residents the opportunity to enjoy the western sunsets from well-manicured homes in what one report called "an English middle-class paradise." Perth has its challenges—a water shortage, rising real estate prices and traffic levels, and a undeserved reputation for being good "from the neck down," a reference to the general lack of a knowledgeable workforce in the city. But as long as energy prices continue to rise, Australia's natural resources center is sure to attract immense numbers of expats and immigrants from the eastern states and abroad.

downtown Perth, seen from the Swan River

PRIME LIVING LOCATIONS

The Brief Story of Perth

Perth was founded as the capital of a British colony of free settlers, who named their settlement the Swan River Colony. Having first been sighted by Dutch traders in the late 17th century, the place where the Swan River meets the Indian Ocean had been settled by indigenous Australian tribes for approximately 5,000 years before European contact. The Noongar people held sway over the area, using it for hunting lands and calling the location Boorloo.

The city was named for Perth, Scotland, which was the hometown of the serving British secretary of state for colonies, Sir George Murray, who also represented Perthshire in the British Parliament. Although the colony was established as a free settlement, the first permanent building was a prison, the Round House, built in 1830, which still stands today in Fremantle.

A series of battles between the Indigenous Australians and the European settlers resulted in the withdrawal of the natives from the immediate Swan River Colony area by 1843, and in 1850 the colony was opened to convicts in order to provide a cheap source of labor. The colony's importance increased steadily in the late 19th century when it became increasingly clear that the huge Western Australian region was home to vast reserves of resources such as gold, aluminum, diamonds, coal, and oil. Perth emerged as the trading and services center for a gigantic natural resources industry, and continues to grow rapidly for this reason even today.

The colony, which was renamed Western Australia, remained completely isolated from the rest of Australia, and Western Australia was the last of the six Australian colonies to pass a referendum in favor of federation, which it did in 1900. The colony was promised a transcontinental railroad as an incentive. Feeling ignored by the rest of Australia during the depths of the Great Depression, the state voted by a 2–1 margin to secede from the commonwealth in 1933, but the plan was never carried out.

After World War II, a natural resources boom ignited in the state, and Western Australia remains one of the most important sources of aluminum, iron, and coal for the whole of the Asia-Pacific region, as well as the most important source of precious metals and diamonds in Australia. Perth has grown from the smallest of the Australian capitals in population to the fourth largest, after Sydney, Melbourne, and Brisbane. At its current 10 percent annual growth rate, the city will shortly pass Brisbane to become the third most populated in the country. Western Australia provided its first prime minister to the nation in 1983 when Bob Hawke became the national leader.

THE LAY OF THE LAND

The magnificent city of Perth occupies the mouth of the Swan River as it meets the Indian Ocean, and the metropolitan area stretches well to the north and south of the Swan, keeping most of the suburbs close to the moderating sea breezes and the attractive beaches. As with most Australian cities, the historic city of Perth is quite small, and covers the CBD, while the surrounding suburbs are organized into a series of municipal governments. The best-known area outside of the CBD is Fremantle, the main port area, to the south of the CBD. The CBD occupies the north side of the Swan.

The city is generally flat and is built around the Swan and Serpentine river systems, with the Serpentine draining into the Indian Ocean south of the city near the booming city of Mandurah.

The city is oriented to the river, and the main street, St. Georges Terrace, runs parallel to the Swan, where it experiences the prevailing warm westerly trade winds that create a wind tunnel effect more days than not, between the canyon of tall buildings that are home to the major resources corporations.

There are 17 local government areas and 11 outlying shires that make up the Perth metropolitan area. The top locations to live generally are along the beaches or near the CBD, while the major growth in recent years has been to the south. Commuters live generally no farther south than Mandurah, about an hour south of the CBD, while those who can avoid commuting have made

cyclist along the Swan River

AVERAGE TEMPERATURES AND RAINFALL

	Rainfall (mm)	Daily High (°C)	Daily Low (°C)
January	9	30	18
February	13	30	18
March	19	28	17
April	46	25	14
May	123	21	12
June	182	18	10
July	173	17	9
August	135	18	9
September	80	20	10
October	55	21	12
November	22	25	14
December	14	27	16

Source: Australian Bureau of Meteorology

small regional cities such as Bunbury (190 kilometers south of Perth) among the fastest-growing cities in the country.

CLIMATE

The city is extremely dry in the summer, and warm, with wet and cool winters. In the summer, most afternoons bring a strong southwesterly, "the Fremantle Doctor," which can drop the temperature by up to 15°C in as little as a half hour, making evenings cool and pleasant.

WHERE TO LIVE
North of the River (NOR)

The tony part of the city comprises homes that have river views or are located in the beach suburbs. Top places to consider for those on a big budget, or supported by corporate dollars, are inner suburbs such as Subiaco, Nedlands, Dalkeith, Mosman Park, Peppermint Grove, and Cottesloe Beach. Cottesloe is particularly prized for those that like a fun beachside environment with plenty of shops and restaurants, but be warned about the small waves: Perth is home to very poor surf. The big mansions are to be found in the Dalkeith and Peppermint Grove areas, and Peppermint Grove is in particular an "old money" suburb. Mosman is, just like its Sydney counterpart, very upmarket, although it's pronounced "Mozzman," which only the true Sydney old-timers use on the other side of the country.

Median home prices for Subiaco are $770,000 for houses, $475,000 for units, and rentals average $370 per week.

Fremantle and South Perth

Along the Canning Highway out of the CBD are attractive, low-density suburbs sporting mostly single-family homes, continuing from Applecross to Fremantle. The Canning is increasingly beset with traffic, so there's a trade-off in commuting hassle against cooling summer afternoon breezes the farther toward the water one chooses.

Just to the south of this single-family belt is the young urban professional corridor of South Perth, which has a number of attractive high-rises to choose from for a more urban environment that's still accessible to the river by foot, with Mends Street the yuppie capital of restaurants and cafés.

Fremantle is a lot of fun, though it is a historic port town with plenty of heavy industry around the port areas. The newer beachside homes on the south side are in Rockingham, adjacent to Fremantle. Some commuters go as far south as Mandurah, the fastest-growing area in Australia, around an hour to the south of the CBD. It has a very attractive lifestyle along the water, including a number of marinas that cater to the boat people who have been maintaining holiday homes here for years. There's a rail line to Perth, highly recommended for commuters who make the Mandurah choice.

Median home prices for Fremantle are $652,500 for houses, $359,000 for units, and rentals average $280 per week.

North and Eastern Suburbs

The eastern suburbs begin with attractive Victoria Park, which is low-key and a bit older with a wide selection of older houses and apartments that are relatively easy on the budget yet close to the CBD. East Perth is even closer, and is jammed with apartments, including a wave of townhouse construction. The farther you head east, the younger the resident group, with Ellenbrook about 24 kilometers east of the CBD anchoring the far east. The eastern suburbs are generally more affordable and experiencing less spectacular new construction, so the traffic congestion is less apt to increase over time. The northern suburbs are a good place to head to buy lots for new construction, but the developments can be fairly stark in the early years while the trees grow in, and traffic is increasing along the Kwinana Freeway. Joondalup is home to a large number of new arrivals from overseas, mostly Brits, who form almost 20 percent of the population.

Median home prices for the CBD are $575,000 for houses, $343,000 for units, and rentals average $270 per week.

DAILY LIFE
Media Resources

Perth has one major newspaper, the tabloid-style *West Australian* (known universally as "the West"), although there is a tabloid Sunday newspaper, the *Sunday Times,* published by the Murdoch empire. Although most suburbs are served by a weekly community newspaper from Community Newspaper Group (17 papers in total), no alternative weekly has yet gained traction in town. The most comprehensive online guide to city life is www.thewest.com.au.

For television, the three main television networks (Seven, Nine, and Ten) are available, along with the two government channels, ABC and SBS. Foxtel provides the main satellite service. More than 10 radio stations offer programming

---

SOUTHWESTERN AUSTRALIA RADIO STATIONS

ADELAIDE

AM

- 729 kHz ABC Radio National ABC
- 891 kHz 891 ABC Adelaide ABC
- 972 kHz NewsRadio ABC

FM

- 92.7 MHz Fresh FM Dance Top 40
- 93.7 MHz Three D Radio
- 99.9 MHz 5MBS (Classical)
- 101.5 MHz Radio Adelaide Radio Adelaide
- 102.3 MHz MIX 102.3 FM ARN
- 103.9 MHz ABC Classic FM
- 104.7 MHz Triple M FM
- 105.5 MHz Triple J
- 106.3 MHz SBS Radio
- 107.9 MHz Life FM

PERTH

AM

- 585 kHz 6PB ABC
- 720 kHz 720 ABC Perth ABC
- 810 kHz 6RN ABC
- 882 kHz 6PR Fairfax Media
- 1080 kHz 6IX Capital Radio Network

FM

- 92.9 MHz 92.9
- 93.7 MHz Nova 93.7
- 94.5 MHz Mix 94.5
- 96.1 MHz 96FM Fairfax Media
- 97.7 MHz ABC Classic FM ABC
- 99.3 MHz Triple J ABC

in most formats, with six government stations offering alternative music to straight news. Newsradio 585 offers the typical drive-time fare of traffic, sports, and news.

Health Care

Perth has an extensive array of private and public hospitals providing top-level care to the metropolitan area, as well as a network of community health centers. St. John of God in Joondalup is the largest private hospital in Australia. The primary children's hospital is Princess Margaret, a public hospital in Subiaco.

Schools

The Perth school year runs from January to December and has four terms, with holiday breaks for Easter, winter, spring, and summer.

In Western Australia, children are required to attend school between ages 5 and 17, and are required to complete year 12, but they may attend a TAFE (Technical and Further Education) College for the final two years and take vocational or trade courses. Preschool is completed at age 5, followed by seven years of primary school and five years of secondary school (years 8–12).

Roughly 40 percent of Western Australian students attend a private school, with roughly half of those attending Catholic schools and the others in non-denominational or Protestant schools. Top traditional private schools have included Guilford Grammar, Scotch College, Hale, Wesley College, and Methodist Ladies College (MLC).

The University of Western Australia, one of the elite group of eight Australian unis, is considered the top university in the state. Murdoch University is the second-oldest, while Curtin University of Technology, with 40,000 students, is the largest in the state. A dozen TAFE colleges in Western Australia serve more than 100,000 students per year.

Shopping

The Perth Markets are the best known area, along King Edwards Street, a cornucopia of options. They're open generally the first Saturday of the month for the farmers market and at least one additional day for art, food, and garden markets. The main pedestrian mall in the CBD is High Street, while the St. Johns center offers the large-scale downtown shopping mall environment featuring top anchor stores. Boutique-style shopping is found primarily in the well-to-do suburbs along the river and toward the beach, such as in Subiaco.

GETTING AROUND
Public Transportation

Public transit is provided by Transperth, which operates river, bus, and rail service to all suburban areas. Buses in the CBD are free. Rail service has been repeatedly improved and extended to try and keep up with Perth's increasing sprawl, particularly to the north, where a new line to Joondalup debuted a few years back. The trains are electric and run from 5:30 A.M. until midnight. A new line to Mandurah to the south has expanded the range of service dramatically. Buses generally run every 15–30 minutes, with heavier service during commuter hours, and either feed to railway hubs or go directly to the CBD. For intersuburban service, stick to rail or car. Transperth operates a trans-Swan ferry service between Barrack Street in the CBD and a jetty in South Perth, which is popular with young, urban professionals who occupy the South Perth high-rises.

Highways

In Perth, the car is king, but the highways are struggling under the rate of growth, and traffic can be tough, although rarely on the monumentally jammed scale as in Sydney or Melbourne.

Three freeways and nine highways make up the main offering, with the Mitchell Freeway dominating the northern corridor, the Graham Farmer taking commuters out west toward the beaches, and the Kwinana Freeway heading south toward Mandurah. All are a tough drive during commuting hours, but there is hope that the new Mandurah rail line will ease the pressure on the Kwinana in the near term.

Perth International Airport

Perth International Airport is 18 kilometers east of the CBD in Redcliffe. It is a popular gateway to Asia and has the only direct service among Australian airports to Africa. Twelve international airlines offer service to Jakarta, Singapore, Bangkok, Kuala Lumpur, Mauritius, Hong Kong, Johannesburg, and Auckland, with connecting service to the United Arab Emirates. Tiger, Virgin Blue, JetStar, and Qantas offer domestic service to all capitals and Canberra, as well as to popular regional cities such as Cairns. Ten regional airlines offer service to small cities.

RESOURCES

Embassies and Consulates

AUSTRALIAN CONSULATE-GENERAL, ATLANTA
Atlanta Financial Center
Suite 1140
3353 Peachtree Road NE
Atlanta, GA 30326
United States
tel. 404/760-3400
fax 404/760-3401
Office hours: 8:30 A.M.–5 P.M. Monday–Friday

AUSTRALIAN CONSULATE-GENERAL, CHICAGO
123 North Wacker Drive, Suite 1330
Chicago, IL 60606
United States
tel. 312/419-1480
fax 312/419-1499
Office hours: 8:40 A.M.–4 P.M. Monday–Friday

AUSTRALIAN CONSULATE-GENERAL, HONOLULU
1000 Bishop Street, Penthouse
Honolulu, HI 96813
United States
tel. 808/529-8100
fax 808/529-8142
Office hours: 8 A.M.–4 P.M. Monday–Friday

AUSTRALIAN CONSULATE-GENERAL, NEW YORK
150 East 42nd Street
34th Floor
New York, NY 10017
United States
tel. 212/351-6500
fax 212/351-6501
Office hours: 9 A.M.–5 P.M. Monday–Friday

U.S. CONSULATE-GENERAL, MELBOURNE
553 St. Kilda Road
Melbourne, VIC 3004
tel. 03/9526-5900
fax 03/9510-4646
http://melbourne.usconsulate.gov
Office hours: 9 A.M.–4 P.M. Monday–Friday

U.S. CONSULATE-GENERAL, PERTH
4th Floor
16 St. George's Terrace
Perth, WA 6000
tel. 08/9202-1224
tel. 08/9476-0081 (after hours)
fax 08-9231-9444
http://perth.usconsulate.gov
Office hours: 8:30 A.M.–4:30 P.M. Monday–Friday

U.S. CONSULATE-GENERAL, SYDNEY
MLC Centre, Level 59
19-29 Martin Place
Sydney, NSW 2000
tel. 02/9373-9200
tel. 02/4422-2201 (after hours)
fax 02/9373-9184
http://sydney.usconsulate.gov
Office hours: 8 A.M.–5 P.M. Monday–Friday

U.S. EMBASSY
Moonah Place
Yarralumla, ACT 2600
tel. 02/6214-5600
fax 02/6214-5970
http://canberra.usembassy.gov
Office hours: 8 A.M.–5 P.M. Monday–Friday

Planning Your Fact-Finding Trip

GUIDED TOURS

AUSTRALIA BIKE TOURS
www.mountainbiketours.com.au

AUSTRALIA WALKING TOURS
www.auswalk.com.au

GLOBUS
www.globusjourneys.com

INFOHUB TOUR
www.infohub.com

NATURE BOUND AUSTRALIA
www.natureboundaustralia.com

SHORT-TERM RENTALS

RENT AUSTRALIA
www.rentaustralia.com

SHORT STAYS
www.shortstays.net

Making the Move

VISAS AND IMMIGRATION

AUSTRALIAN DEPARTMENT OF IMMIGRATION
www.immi.gov.au

AUSTRALIA MIGRATION
www.australia-migration.com

MIGRATION EXPERT
www.migrationexpert.com

AUSTRALIAN EXPATRIATE INFORMATION

AUSTRALIA EXPAT FORUM
www.expatforum.com

EXFIN: THE AUSTRALIAN EXPATRIATE GATEWAY
www.exfin.com

EXPATRIATECONNECT
www.expatsaustralia.com

INTERNATIONAL MOVING COMPANIES

AUSMOVE
www.ausmove.co.nz

INTERNATIONAL MOVERS
www.intlmovers.com

WALKERS MOVING AND STORAGE
www.walkmove.com.au

Housing Considerations

REAL ESTATE AGENCIES

HOMEHOUND
www.homehound.com.au

LJ HOOKER
www.ljhooker.com.au

REALESTATE.COM.AU
www.realestate.com.au

Education

UNIVERSITIES

AUSTRALIAN EDUCATION NETWORK
www.australian-universities.com
A general guide to Australia's universities.

THE AUSTRALIAN NATIONAL UNIVERSITY
Canberra, ACT 0200
tel. 02/6125-5111
www.anu.edu.au

DEAKIN UNIVERSITY
Burwood Highway
Burwood, VIC 3125
tel. 03/9244-6100
www.deakin.edu.au

GRIFFITH UNIVERSITY
QLD 4222
tel. 07/3735-7700
www.griffith.edu.au

LA TROBE UNIVERSITY
VIC 3086
tel. 03/9479-1111
www.latrobe.edu.au

MACQUARIE UNIVERSITY
NSW 2109
tel. 02/9850-7111
www.mq.edu.au

MONASH UNIVERSITY
VIC 3800
tel. 03/9902-6000
www.monash.edu.au

UNIVERSITIES AUSTRALIA
www.universitiesaustralia.edu.au

UNIVERSITY OF MELBOURNE
VIC 3010
tel. 03/8344-4000
www.unimelb.edu.au

UNIVERSITY OF NEW SOUTH WALES
Sydney, NSW 2052
tel. 02/9385-1000
www.unsw.edu.au

THE UNIVERSITY OF QUEENSLAND
Brisbane, QLD 4072
tel. 07/3365-1111
www.uq.edu.au

UNIVERSITY OF SOUTH AUSTRALIA
G.P.O. Box 2471
Adelaide, SA 5001
tel. 08/8302-6611
www.unisa.edu.au

UNIVERSITY OF SYDNEY
Sydney, NSW 2006
tel. 02/9351-2222
www.usyd.edu.au

UNIVERSITY OF TECHNOLOGY, SYDNEY
15 Broadway
Ultimo, NSW 2007
tel. 02/9514-2000

ASSOCIATION OF INDEPENDENT SCHOOLS

THE ASSOCIATION OF INDEPENDENT SCHOOLS OF THE AUSTRALIAN CAPITAL TERRITORY
www.ais.act.edu.au

THE ASSOCIATION OF INDEPENDENT SCHOOLS OF NEW SOUTH WALES
www.aisnsw.edu.au

THE ASSOCIATION OF INDEPENDENT SCHOOLS OF THE NORTHERN TERRITORY
www.aisnt.asn.au

THE ASSOCIATION OF INDEPENDENT SCHOOLS OF QUEENSLAND
www.aisq.qld.edu.au

THE ASSOCIATION OF INDEPENDENT SCHOOLS OF SOUTH AUSTRALIA
www.ais.sa.edu.au

THE ASSOCIATION OF INDEPENDENT SCHOOLS OF TASMANIA
www.aist.tas.edu.au

THE ASSOCIATION OF INDEPENDENT SCHOOLS OF VICTORIA
www.ais.vic.edu.au

THE ASSOCIATION OF INDEPENDENT SCHOOLS OF WESTERN AUSTRALIA
www.ais.wa.edu.au

DEPARTMENT OF EDUCATION

ACT DEPARTMENT OF EDUCATION
www.det.act.gov.au

NEW SOUTH WALES DEPARTMENT OF EDUCATION
www.det.nsw.edu.au

NORTHERN TERRITORY DEPARTMENT OF EDUCATION
www.deet.nt.gov.au

QUEENSLAND DEPARTMENT OF EDUCATION
www.education.qld.gov.au

SOUTH AUSTRALIA DEPARTMENT OF EDUCATION
www.decs.sa.gov.au

TASMANIA DEPARTMENT OF EDUCATION
www.education.tas.gov.au

VICTORIA DEPARTMENT OF EDUCATION
www.education.vic.gov.au

WESTERN AUSTRALIA DEPARTMENT OF EDUCATION
www.det.wa.edu.au

Employment

JOB HUNTING

AUSTRALIAN JOB SEARCH
https://jobsearch.gov.au

JOBS AUSTRALIA
www.ja.com.au

RECRUIT.NET
http://australia.recruit.net

SEEK.COM
www.seek.com.au

WORKING IN AUSTRALIA
www.workingin-australia.com

Finance

BANKS

ADELAIDE BANK
www.adelaidebank.com.au

ADVANCE BANK
www.advance.com.au

AUSTRALIA & NEW ZEALAND BANKING GROUP LIMITED (ANZ)
www.anz.com.au

BANKERS TRUST INVESTMENT BANK
www.btal.com.au

BANK OF SOUTH AUSTRALIA
www.banksa.com.au

BANKWEST
www.bankwest.com.au

CITYBANK AUSTRALIA
www.citibank.com.au

**COMMONWEALTH
BANK OF AUSTRALIA**
www.commbank.com.au

HERITAGE BUILDING SOCIETY
www.heritageonline.com.au

ST. GEORGE BANK
www.stgeorge.com.au

Communications

TELEPHONE PROVIDERS

OPTUS
www.optus.com.au

PRIMUS TELECOM
www.primus.com.au

TELSTRA
www.telstra.com

MOBILE PHONE COMPANIES

THREE
www.three.com.au

VIRGIN MOBILE
www.virginmobile.com.au

VODAFONE AUSTRALIA
www.vodafone.com.au

INTERNET PROVIDERS

BIG POND
www.bigpond.com

POSTAL AND EXPRESS MAIL SERVICES

AUSTRALIA POST
www.auspost.com.au

DHL AUSTRALIA
www.dhl.com.au

NEWSPAPERS AND ONLINE MEDIA

General
THE AUSTRALIAN
www.theaustralian.news.com.au

FINANCIAL REVIEW
www.afr.com

RURAL PRESS
www.ruralpress.com.au

Sydney
SYDNEY DAILY TELEGRAPH
www.news.com.au/dailytelegraph

SYDNEY MORNING HERALD
www.smh.com.au

Melbourne
THE AGE
www.theage.com.au

HERALD SUN
www.news.com.au/heraldsun

Brisbane and the Queensland Coast
BRISBANE COURIER MAIL
www.news.com.au/couriermail

Canberra
CANBERRA TIMES
www.canberra.yourguide.com.au

Southwestern Australia
*ADELAIDE ADVERTISER/
ADELAIDE NOW*
www.news.com.au/adelaidenow

SUNDAY TIMES/PERTH NOW
www.news.com.au/perthnow

CABLE AND SATELLITE TELEVISION

FOXTEL
www.foxtel.com.au

Travel and Transportation

COMMUTING

ADELAIDE METRO
www.adelaidemetro.com.au

BRISBANE TRANSLINK
www.translink.com.au

METLINK MELBOURNE
www.metlinkmelbourne.com.au

SYDNEY BUSES
www.sydneybuses.info

SYDNEY FERRIES
www.sydneyferries.info

SYDNEY CITY RAIL
www.cityrail.info

TRANSPERTH
www.transperth.wa.gov.au

AIR TRAVEL

EXPEDIA AUSTRALIA
www.expedia.com.au

QANTAS
www.qantas.com.au

VIRGIN BLUE
www.virginblue.com.au

LONG DISTANCE RAIL

RAIL AUSTRALIA
www.railaustralia.com.au

Prime Living Locations

SYDNEY

State Government

NEW SOUTH WALES GOVERNMENT
www.nsw.gov.au

Health

NSW HEALTH
73 Miller St.
North Sydney, NSW 2060
tel. 02/9391-9000
www.health.nsw.gov.au

Organizations

AMERICAN AUSTRALIAN ASSOCIATION
19 Martin Place
Sydney, NSW 2000
tel. 02/9338-6988
www.americanaustralian.org.au
infosydney@aaanyc.org

AMERICAN CHAMBER OF COMMERCE IN AUSTRALIA
88 Cumberland St., Suite 4
Sydney, NSW 2000

tel. 02/9241-1907
fax 02/9251-5220
www.amcham.com.au

AMERICAN CITIZENS ABROAD
49 Abbotsford Road
Homebush, NSW 2140
tel. 02/9746-6827
merced@fl.net.au

AMERICAN CLUB
131 Macquarie St., 15th Floor
Sydney, NSW 2000
tel. 02/9241-2015
www.amclub.com.au

AMERICAN LEGION
60 Gurney Road
Chester Hill, NSW 2163
tel. 02/9644-6854
austraymond@one.net.au

THE AMERICAN SOCIETY
G.P.O. Box 602
Sydney, NSW 2001
tel. 04/2524-8892
www.americansociety.com.au
info@americansociety.com.au

RESOURCES

MELBOURNE
State Government
VICTORIA ONLINE
www.vic.gov.au

Health
VICTORIAN GOVERNMENT HEALTH INFORMATION
tel. 03/9096-0000
www.health.vic.gov.au

Organizations
AMERICAN CHAMBER OF COMMERCE (VICTORIA)
500 Collins Street, Level 21
Melbourne, VIC 3000
tel. 03/9614-7744
vic@amcham.com.au

AMERICAN CLUB OF VICTORIA
340 Nicholson Street
Yarraville, VIC 3013
tel. 03/9687-4109
mbaldiac@alphalink.com.au

AUSTRALIAN AMERICAN ASSOCIATION OF VICTORIA
P.O. Box 13286
Melbourne Law Courts, VIC 8010
www.australianamerican.org
info@australianamerican.org

BRISBANE AND THE QUEENSLAND COAST
State Government
QUEENSLAND GOVERNMENT
www.qld.gov.au

Health
QUEENSLAND HEALTH
Queensland Health Building
147-163 Charlotte St.
Brisbane, Queensland 4000
tel. 07/3234-0111
www.health.qld.gov.au

Organizations
AUSTRALIAN AMERICAN ASSOCIATION, BRISBANE CHAPTER
G.P.O. Box 2175
Brisbane, QLD 4001
tel. 07/3278-6366
www.americancommunityaustralia.com
aaa@americancommunityaustralia.com

AMERICAN CHAMBER OF COMMERCE IN AUSTRALIA
www.amcham.com.au

CANBERRA
State Government
ACT GOVERNMENT
www.act.gov.au

Health
ACT HEALTH
02/6207-7777
www.health.act.gov.au

Organizations
AUSTRALIAN AMERICAN ASSOCIATION
P.O. Box 1268
Woden, ACT 2607
www.aaafed.asn.au

THE GREAT DIVIDING RANGE
State Government
NEW SOUTH WALES GOVERNMENT
www.nsw.gov.au

Health
NSW HEALTH
73 Miller St.
North Sydney, NSW 2060
tel. 02/9391-9000
www.health.nsw.gov.au

SOUTHWESTERN AUSTRALIA

State Government

GOVERNMENT OF WESTERN AUSTRALIA
www.wa.gov.au

SOUTH AUSTRALIA CENTRAL
www.sa.gov.au

Health

GOVERNMENT OF WESTERN AUSTRALIA DEPARTMENT OF HEALTH
P.O. Box 8172
Perth Business Centre, WA 6849
tel. 1-800/022-222
www.health.wa.gov.au

SOUTH AUSTRALIA CENTRAL DEPARTMENT OF HEALTH
Citi Centre Building
11 Hindmarsh Square
Adelaide SA 5000
tel. 8/8226-6000
www.health.sa.gov.au

Organizations

AMERICAN CHAMBER OF COMMERCE (SOUTH AUSTRALIA AND NORTHERN TERRITORY)
231 Adelaide Terrace
Perth, WA 6000
tel. 08/9325-9540
wa@amcham.com.au

AMERICAN WOMEN'S ASSOCIATION
tel. 04/0529-8780
americans@bigpond.com

AMERICAN WOMEN'S CLUB OF PERTH
G.P.O. Box T1669
Perth, WA 6001
www.awcperth.org
Welcome@awcperth.org

AUSTRALIAN AMERICAN ASSOCIATION, SOUTH AUSTRALIA CHAPTER
P.O. Box 6714
Halifax Street
Adelaide, SA 5000
tel. 04/0029-5853
www.australianamericaninsa.org.au
enquiries@australianamericaninsa.org.au

AUSTRALIAN AMERICAN ASSOCIATION, WESTERN AUSTRALIA CHAPTER
P.O. Box 926
Subiaco, WA 6904
www.aaawa.com.au

Glossary

arcade small shopping area, usually in the CBD

arvo afternoon

Aussie (pronounced "Ozzie"): Australian

Back o'Bourke, Back of Beyond, Beyond the Black Stump a long way away

barbie barbecue

barrack to cheer

barrister trial lawyer

battler someone who struggles valiantly, typically financially

beaut, beauty fantastic

bingle accident

bloke guy

bloody very

bludger lazy person

bonza great

booze bus police vehicle used for catching drunk drivers

bottle shop liquor store

building society savings and loan bank

bum fanny (fanny is a vulgarity in Australia; do not use)

bunging it on over-selling

bush anywhere beyond the city

BYO bring your own (e.g., beer)

CBD central business district; downtown

chemist pharmacist

chook a chicken

Clayton's fake, alternative

conveyance due diligence or inspection period

cooee literally, within hearing distance; figuratively, far away (he's not within cooee of Sydney)

courgette zucchini

cozzie swimsuit

crook sick (you "feel crook")

cuppa cup of tea

dag nerd

daks trousers

dead set true

dear expensive

dill a foolish person

dinky-die the real thing, genuine

dobber informer

dobbing/dobbing someone in informing, tattling

drongo a foolish person

esky ice chest, drinks container

fair dinkum genuine

fair go a fair chance

Fremantle Doctor the cooling afternoon breeze in Perth

galah a foolish person

g'day hello

gobsmacked astonished

good on ya well done

greengrocer fruit and vegetable store or department

Green P class 1 provisional driver's license

grog liquor

I reckon Yes, I agree.

John Dory local white fish

L-plate learner's driving permit

Maccas McDonald's

mateship loyalty

mate's rate discount for a friend

middy small beer glass in New South Wales

milk bar takeaway food shop

mince ground beef

Never Never the Outback

ocker an Australian who speaks Strine

Outback the hot, dry interior

Oz Australia

petrol gasoline

pom, pommy an Englishman

pot small beer glass in Queensland and Victoria

pozzy position (get a good pozzy at the football stadium)

prawn shrimp

prezzy present, gift

Rack off! Get lost!

Red P class 2 provisional driver's license

rego vehicle registration

return round-trip (a return ticket)

ridgy-didge true, real

rissole sausage-filled pastry

rort fraud

roundabout traffic circle

rubbish (verb): to criticize

schooner large beer glass

seppos Yank; American

serviette napkin

settlement real estate closing
sister registered nurse
snag sausage
solicitor commercial lawyer
Southerly Buster the cooling after-noon breeze in Sydney
spill battle, often used with respect to political leadership contests
spit the dummy get upset
sprung caught
sticking plaster Band-Aid
strata a condominium association
strides trousers
Strine Australian dialect
sunnies sunglasses
surgery doctor's office
ta thank you
tall poppies/cutting the tall poppies very important people (often sarcastic)

tea dinner
tosser a foolish person
tram Melbourne streetcar
Tresca Sprite
tucker food
unis universities (pronounced "YOU-knees")
unit apartment
ute utility vehicle, pickup truck
veggies vegetables
whinge complain
wog illness
wuss coward
yakka work
yewy u-turn
yobbo a foolish person
yonks ages

Australian Measurements

CLOTHING AND SHOES

Dress Sizes
U.S. 2—Australia 4
U.S. 4—Australia 6
U.S. 6—Australia 8
U.S. 8—Australia 10
U.S. 10—Australia 12
U.S. 12—Australia 14

Shoe Sizes
In Australia, shoe sizes are a half size smaller than in the United States. To convert shoe sizes, subtract one-half the U.S. shoe size to obtain the correct Australian size; for example, a size 8½ shoe in the United States is a size 8 in Australia.

Suggested Reading

GENERAL

Bryson, Bill. *In a Sunburned Country.* Sydney: Broadway, 2001. This fact-filled, anecdote-filled cornucopia of Australiana is from perhaps the best-known travel humorist.

Horne, Donald. *The Lucky Country.* Sydney: Penguin, 1967. This brilliant explo-ration of Australian culture was written in the 1960s but is applicable today.

Hughes, Robert. *The Fatal Shore: The Epic of Australia's Founding.* Sydney: Penguin, 1967. An acclaimed art critic turns his eye to the convict story. His vivid writing resulted in a book considered a masterpiece on early Aussie history.

FICTION

Anderson, Jessica. *Tirra Lirra by the River.* Sydney: Picador Australia, 2007. An old woman looks back on an extraordinary life in Queensland and London.

Carey, Peter. *Oscar and Lucinda.* New York: Vintage, 1997. A Booker Prize winner in 1988, this is one of the most acclaimed Aussie novels ever. A love story, and much more.

Franklin, Miles *My Brilliant Career.* Sydney: Bibliobazaar, 2007. The acclaimed turn-of-the-20th-century classic, made into a landmark film in 1979 by Bruce Beresford.

White, Patrick. *Voss.* New York: Viking, 1957. In the generally accepted masterpiece of Australia's only Nobel Prize winner, romance between an explorer and a young woman turns into dark obsession.

Winton, Tim. *Cloudstreet.* Sydney: Picador Australia, 2002. This is Australia's most admired work of fiction, according to www.bookworm.com.au. Two rural families begin again in the big city.

LANGUAGE

Lauder, Afferback. *Let Stalk Strine.* Sydney: Australia in Print, 1989. This is a classic and hilarious study of the Australian dialect. Followups include *Nose Tone Unturned, Fraffly Well Spoken,* and *Fraffly Suite.*

O'Grady, John. *They're a Weird Mob.* Sydney: Ure Smith, 1965. This 1957 classic is about an Italian journalist who takes a job as a bricklayer to learn about Australians and speaking Strine. Hilarious.

CHILDREN'S BOOKS

Lindsay, Norman. *The Magic Pudding.* Sydney: Dover, 2006. This classic children's tale features Bunyip Bluegum, an itinerant Aussie koala traveling at the turn of the 20th century in Australia.

Pedley, Ethel. *Dot and the Kangaroo.* Sydney: Echo Library, 2008. This classic children's tale was made into a film in the 1970s. A little girl becomes lost in the Outback.

Thiele, Colin. *Storm Boy.* Sydney: New Holland, 2004. Classic young adult fiction about a boy, his pelican, his father, and an Indigenous Australian man.

TRAVEL GUIDES

Dragicevich, Peter, and Jolyon Attwooll. *Lonely Planet Sydney.* Sydney: Lonely Planet, 2008. This is the definitive travel guide focused on Sydney.

Fodor's Australia 2008. New York: Fodor's, 2005. Fodor's guide is updated every year. It's packed with information and written by locals.

Johnson, Marael, and Andrew Hempstead. *Moon Australia.* Berkeley: Avalon Travel, 2005. Many consider this guide, now in its third edition, to be the standout best on Australia as a whole.

Suggested Films

The Castle. Directed by Rob Sitch. 98 minutes. Village Roadshow, 1997. A classic Aussie cult film, virtually unknown outside of Oz but beloved at home, this is the story of a family whose home in the suburbs is threatened by an airport expansion. The father refuses to move, setting off a series of comic incidents in a send-up of Australian culture (or lack thereof).

Crocodile Dundee. Directed by Peter Faiman. 98 minutes. Paramount, 1986. This comedy classic introduced famed Aussie comic Paul Hogan to the world. He plays a crocodile hunter, naturally, who gets in any number of comic and romantic entanglements.

Mad Max. Directed by George Miller. 99 minutes. Village Roadshow, 1979. In this vaguely futuristic film about biker gangs and the lone policeman who takes revenge on them, Mel Gibson's voice was dubbed for the American market because producers thought his thick Aussie accent would not be understood. Amazing car chases and stunts. The sequels, *The Road Warrior* and *Mad Max Beyond Thunderdome,* were even more popular.

Muriel's Wedding. Directed by P. J. Hogan. 106 minutes. Miramax, 1995. Toni Collette's breakthrough film is a classic comedy about an ugly duckling who leaves behind a small town to explore life in the city.

My Brilliant Career. Directed by Gillian Armstrong. 100 minutes. Blue Underground, 1979. This is a coming-of-age film about a spirited young woman, expertly played by newcomer Judy Davis. It was Davis's breakthrough film, as well as Gillian Armstrong's, who went on to helm *Little Women* and *Oscar and Lucinda.*

Picnic at Hanging Rock. Directed by Peter Weir. 115 minutes. Atlantic, 1975. Peter Weir's atmospheric mystery is about a picnic at a girl's school that results in the disappearance of three girls. It's widely considered one of the breakthrough films that propelled the renaissance of Aussie films in the 1970s.

Sunday Too Far Away. Directed by Peter Faiman. 98 minutes. South Australian Film, 1975. Jack Thompson stars in the story of an Australian sheep station in the 1950s as bonuses disappear and non-union laborers show up. Shearers' wives used to say of their husbands, "Friday night too tired; Saturday night too drunk; Sunday, too far away," which gave the movie its title.

The Year of Living Dangerously. Directed by Peter Weir. 115 minutes. MGM, 1983. This moody romantic thriller made an international star out of Mel Gibson and showed that Sigourney Weaver could do more than fight off an alien. A Sydney journalist is sent to Jakarta as the 1965 coup unfolds, and discovers his capacity for love and betrayal (both good and bad) through his encounters with a diminutive man named Billy Kwan (played by Linda Hunt), fellow journalists, the government, the communist conspirators, and a beautiful British intelligence agent.

Index

Acknowledgments

A book of this size and scope requires some grateful acknowledgment to a number of people who have worked behind the scenes to bring this book to you or kept the author happy and alive during the research and writing. Thanks to: Mitchell Chesher and Flavia Marples Lane for some great photography; the staffs at all the state tourism commissions for an assist in photo research; Alex, Amy, and Will Shaw, and Isabel Lane for being the wonderful people they always have been; Matthew Strassberg, Dan Butler, Francois Kunc and Grant Lamond for their mateship; the Byron Bay Beach Club and The Archives for many good times; Nancy Lane who went through it, always smiling and always there; and Jim and Louise Lane for their hospitality, love and support.

Thanks to Elizabeth Jang, for sensitive photo editing; Brice Ticen, for wrangling a great set of maps; Grace Fujimoto, for her great support of the project; and to Elizabeth Hansen, a model of grace, patience and inspiration and an exemplary editor. This book is dedicated to Flavia with love.

Photo Credits

www.moon.com

For helpful advice on planning a trip, visit www.moon.com for the **TRAVEL PLANNER** and get access to useful travel strategies and valuable information about great places to visit. When you travel with Moon, expect an experience that is uncommon and truly unique.

MAP SYMBOLS

▭ Expressway	○ City/Town	✕ Airfield	▱ Archaeological Site
═══ Primary Road	◉ State Capital	✈ Airport	⚱ Church
▭ Secondary Road			⛽ Gas Station
┄┄ Unpaved Road	⊛ National Capital	▲ Mountain	〰 Mangrove
⋯⋯ Ferry	★ Point of Interest	▲▲ Park	Reef
━━ Railroad	■ Other Location	🎿 Skiing Area	Swamp

CONVERSION TABLES

°C = (°F – 32) / 1.8
°F = (°C x 1.8) + 32
1 inch = 2.54 centimeters (cm)
1 foot = 0.304 meters (m)
1 yard = 0.914 meters
1 mile = 1.6093 kilometers (km)
1 km = 0.6214 miles
1 fathom = 1.8288 m
1 chain = 20.1168 m
1 furlong = 201.168 m
1 acre = 0.4047 hectares
1 sq km = 100 hectares
1 sq mile = 2.59 square km
1 ounce = 28.35 grams
1 pound = 0.4536 kilograms
1 short ton = 0.90718 metric ton
1 short ton = 2,000 pounds
1 long ton = 1.016 metric tons
1 long ton = 2,240 pounds
1 metric ton = 1,000 kilograms
1 quart = 0.94635 liters
1 US gallon = 3.7854 liters
1 Imperial gallon = 4.5459 liters
1 nautical mile = 1.852 km

°FAHRENHEIT	°CELSIUS
230	110
220	
210	100 WATER BOILS
200	
190	90
180	80
170	
160	70
150	
140	60
130	50
120	
110	40
100	
90	30
80	
70	20
60	
50	10
40	
30	0 WATER FREEZES
20	-10
10	
0	-20
-10	
-20	-30
-30	
-40	-40

INCH 0 1 2 3 4

CM 0 1 2 3 4 5 6 7 8 9 10

**MOON LIVING ABROAD
IN AUSTRALIA**

Avalon Travel
a member of the Perseus Books Group
1700 Fourth Street
Berkeley, CA 94710, USA
www.moon.com

Editor and Series Manager: Elizabeth Hansen
Copy Editor: Deana Shields
Graphics and Production Coordinator:
    Elizabeth Jang
Cover Designer: Elizabeth Jang
Cartography Director: Mike Morgenfeld
Map Editor: Brice Ticen
Cartographers: Kat Bennett, Suzanne Service
Indexer: Judy Hunt

ISBN-10: 1-59880-139-2
ISBN-13: 978-1-59880-139-2
ISSN: 1943-3778

Printing History
1st Edition — November 2008
5 4 3 2 1

KEEPING CURRENT

Although we strive to produce the most up-to-date guidebook that we possibly can, change
is unavoidable. Between the time this book goes to print and the time you read it, the
cost of goods and services may have increased, and a handful of the businesses noted
in these pages will undoubtedly move, alter their prices, or close their doors forever.
Exchange rates fluctuate—sometimes dramatically—on a daily basis. Federal and local
legal requirements and restrictions are also subject to change, so be sure to check with
the appropriate authorities before making the move. If you see anything in this book that
needs updating, clarification, or correction, please drop us a line. Send your comments via
email to feedback@moon.com, or use the address above.